JUDITH

WISDOM COMMENTARY

Volume 16

Judith

Jennifer L. Koosed
Robert Paul Seesengood

Amy-Jill Levine
Volume Editor

Barbara E. Reid, OP
General Editor

A Michael Glazier Book

LITURGICAL PRESS
Collegeville, Minnesota

www.litpress.org

A Michael Glazier Book published by Liturgical Press

1 2 3 4 5 6 7 8 9

Library of Congress Cataloging-in-Publication Data

Names: Koosed, Jennifer L., author. | Seesengood, Robert Paul, author. | Levine, Amy-Jill, 1956– editor. | Reid, Barbara E., editor.

Title: Judith / Jennifer L. Koosed, Robert Paul Seesengood ; Amy-Jill Levine, volume editor, Barbara E. Reid, OP, general editor.

Description: Collegeville, Minnesota : Liturgical Press, 2022. | Series: Wisdom commentary ; volume 16 | "A Michael Glazier Book." | Includes bibliographical references and index. | Summary: "This commentary investigates the book of Judith through a feminist lens, informed by critical masculinity studies, queer theory, and reception criticism"— Provided by publisher.

Identifiers: LCCN 2022009224 (print) | LCCN 2022009225 (ebook) | ISBN 9780814681152 (hardcover) | ISBN 9780814681404 (epub) | ISBN 9780814681404 (pdf)

Subjects: LCSH: Bible. Judith—Feminist criticism. | BISAC: RELIGION / Biblical Commentary / Old Testament / Historical Books | RELIGION / Biblical Studies / Old Testament / Historical Books

Classification: LCC BS1735.52 .K66 2022 (print) | LCC BS1735.52 (ebook) | DDC 229/.24—dc23/eng/20220606

LC record available at https://lccn.loc.gov/2022009224

LC ebook record available at https://lccn.loc.gov/2022009225

Contents

Acknowledgments

We like Judith. It has been a joy to have her as a companion for these past few years, to read her book, view paintings that take her as their subject, and think about all the different ways she has been understood over the centuries. We have enjoyed speaking about her with other people and learning about her more from our Contributing Voices, many of whom have also given us the pleasure of actual, not just scholarly, conversation and friendship.

We would like to thank the editors of the Wisdom Commentary series. Seung Ai Yang shepherded us through the process from the beginning. Her encouraging messages kept us on track. Amy-Jill Levine stepped in at the end to read the manuscript. Her insightful comments and astute suggestions pushed us to think more deeply and write more clearly about our intriguing heroine. Barbara Reid has overseen it all with great attention to every detail. Our editors have made this a much better book.

The sabbaticals granted to us by Albright College were invaluable; Rob took one during the spring of 2017, and Jennifer followed with one during the spring of 2018. In both cases, funding not only supported time but also facilitated access to critical scholarly resources, venues, and books (and took some of the load from the endlessly patient interlibrary loan librarians of Albright's Gingrich Library). Thank you to our campus and department colleagues for your support.

Parts of this manuscript had early hearings by local congregations. Thanks to the people of Kesher Zion Synagogue; Calvary United Church of Christ; Friendship Circle of the Jewish Federation of Reading; and

First Presbyterian Church in Pottstown. Jennifer also gave the presidential address of the Mid-Atlantic Society of Biblical Literature in 2018 on Judith in the #MeToo Era. Thank you, everyone, for your insightful questions, keen interest, and enthusiastic support; this is also a better book because of you.

Continuing to draw the circles of community, we want to thank our family. Poor Simon has had to tolerate serially distracted parents, grumbling intermittently about proofreading, scholarly arguments, or obscure Greek. Abigail, at least, has had the small conciliation of Judith as a middle name, shared with her paternal grandmother whom she never got to meet but has learned to love nevertheless. Along with the rest of our family, they have given us their patience, encouragement, and, above all, love. Their love creates a space apart from our work, where the energy and confidence necessary for it are cultivated.

Abbreviations

AB	Anchor Bible
ANE	Ancient Near East
AYBRL	Anchor Yale Bible Reference Library
BCE	Before the Common Era
BibInt	Biblical Interpretation Series
BibInt	*Biblical Interpretation*
BR	*Biblical Research*
BTB	*Biblical Theology Bulletin*
CE	Common Era
CEJL	Commentaries on Early Jewish Literature
EJL	Early Judaism and Its Literature
FCB	Feminist Companion to the Bible
GBS	Guides to Biblical Scholarship
IFT	Introductions in Feminist Theology
JBL	*Journal of Biblical Literature*
JFSR	*Journal of Feminist Studies in Religion*
JPS	Jewish Publication Society
JSOT	*Journal for the Study of the Old Testament*

JSOTSup	Journal for the Study of the Old Testament Supplement series
LHBOTS	The Library of Hebrew Bible/Old Testament Studies
LXX	Septuagint
NABRE	New American Bible Revised Edition
NIV	New International Version
NJB	New Jerusalem Bible
NRSV	New Revised Standard Version
OBT	Overtures to Biblical Theology
OTE	*Old Testament Essays*
PL	Patrologia Latina
SBL	Society of Biblical Literature
SBLSymS	Society of Biblical Literature Symposium Series
SJOT	*Scandinavian Journal of the Old Testament*
ZAW	*Zeitschrift für die alttestamentliche Wissenschaft*

Contributors

Dr. Robin Gallaher Branch received her PhD in Hebrew studies from the University of Texas at Austin in 2000. She was a Fulbright Scholar in 2002 and 2003 at North-West University in Potchefstroom, South Africa, and continues to serve there as a research associate. She is an adjunct professor in the Department of Religion and Philosophy at Christian Brothers University and publishes in diverse media on biblical subjects.

Dr. Steed Vernyl Davidson is professor of Hebrew Bible and dean of the faculty at McCormick Theological Seminary. He teaches from the perspective of postcolonial biblical criticism in order to draw attention to the legacies and continuation of European colonialism and their implications for biblical interpretation.

Dr. Rhiannon Graybill is associate professor of religious studies at Rhodes College in Memphis, Tennessee. She researches gender, sexuality, and sexual violence in and around the Hebrew Bible.

Ms. Jessica Jernigan graduated from Bryn Mawr College with a degree in religion. She is a writer and an editor. Her work has appeared in *Women's Review of Books*, *Bitch*, and *Electric Literature*.

Dr. Linda Learman teaches in the Women's and Gender Studies program and the English Department at Adrian College. Her work focuses on writing studies and pedagogy as well as feminist studies.

Rev. Barbara K. Peronteau is ordained in the United Church of Christ and is the interim pastor at St. James Lutheran Church (ELCA) in San Leandro, California. She earned her MDiv from Union Theological Seminary;

completed CPE at Reading Hospital, Reading, Pennsylvania; and received two certificates for intentional interim ministry from the Art of Transitional Ministry. She is one of only a handful of fabulous trans women clergy serving the Church in the pulpit.

Dr. Caryn Tamber-Rosenau is instructional assistant professor of Jewish studies and religious studies at the University of Houston. She is the author of *Women in Drag: Gender and Performance in the Hebrew Bible and Early Jewish Literature* (Gorgias, 2018).

Dr. Melissa C. Stewart is a professor of religion in the Department of Philosophy, Religion, and Leadership at Adrian College in Michigan and director of the Institute of Study Abroad. Her research focuses on Protestant views of Mary, the Mother of Jesus, and on interdisciplinary team teaching.

Foreword

"Tell It on the Mountain"—or, "And You Shall Tell Your Daughter [as Well]"

Athalya Brenner-Idan

Universiteit van Amsterdam/Tel Aviv University

What can Wisdom Commentary do to help, and for whom?

The commentary genre has always been privileged in biblical studies. Traditionally acclaimed commentary series, such as the International Critical Commentary, Old Testament and New Testament Library, Hermeneia, Anchor Bible, Eerdmans, and Word—to name but several—enjoy nearly automatic prestige, and the number of women authors who participate in those is relatively small by comparison to their growing number in the scholarly guild. There certainly are some volumes written by women in them, especially in recent decades. At this time, however, this does not reflect the situation on the ground. Further, size matters. In that sense, the sheer size of the Wisdom Commentary is essential. This also represents a considerable investment and the possibility of reaching a wider audience than those already "converted."

Expecting women scholars to deal especially or only with what are considered strictly "female" matters seems unwarranted. According to Audre Lorde, "The master's tools will never dismantle the master's house."[1] But this maxim is not relevant to our case. The point of this commentary is not to destroy but to attain greater participation in the interpretive dialogue about biblical texts. Women scholars may bring additional questions to the readerly agenda as well as fresh angles to existing issues. To assume that their questions are designed only to topple a certain male hegemony is not convincing.

At first I did ask myself: is this commentary series an addition to calm raw nerves, an embellishment to make upholding the old hierarchy palatable? Or is it indeed about becoming the Master? On second and third thoughts, however, I understood that becoming the Master is not what this is about. Knowledge is power. Since Foucault at the very least, this cannot be in dispute. Writing commentaries for biblical texts by feminist women and men for women and for men, of confessional as well as non-confessional convictions, will sabotage (hopefully) the established hierarchy but will not topple it. This is about an attempt to integrate more fully, to introduce another viewpoint, to become. What excites me about the Wisdom Commentary is that it is not offered as just an alternative supplanting or substituting for the dominant discourse.

These commentaries on biblical books will retain nonauthoritative, pluralistic viewpoints. And yes, once again, the weight of a dedicated series, to distinguish from collections of stand-alone volumes, will prove weightier.

That such an approach is especially important in the case of the Hebrew Bible/Old Testament is beyond doubt. Women of Judaism, Christianity, and also Islam have struggled to make it their own for centuries, even more than they have fought for the New Testament and the Qur'an. Every Hebrew Bible/Old Testament volume in this project is evidence that the day has arrived: it is now possible to read *all* the Jewish canonical books as a collection, for a collection they are, with guidance conceived of with the needs of women readers (not only men) as an integral inspiration and part thereof.

In my Jewish tradition, the main motivation for reciting the Haggadah, the ritual text recited yearly on Passover, the festival of liberation from

1. Audre Lorde, "The Master's Tools Will Never Dismantle the Master's House," in *Sister Outsider: Essays and Speeches* (Berkeley, CA: Crossing Press, 1984, 2007), 110–14. First delivered in the Second Sex Conference in New York, 1979.

bondage, is given as "And you shall tell your son" (from Exod 13:8). The knowledge and experience of past generations is thus transferred to the next, for constructing the present and the future. The ancient maxim is, literally, limited to a male audience. This series remolds the maxim into a new inclusive shape, which is of the utmost consequence: "And you shall tell your son" is extended to "And you shall tell your daughter [as well as your son]." Or, if you want, "Tell it on the mountain," for all to hear.

This is what it's all about.

Editor's Introduction to Wisdom Commentary

"She Is a Breath of the Power of God" (Wis 7:25)

Barbara E. Reid, OP

General Editor

Wisdom Commentary is the first series to offer detailed feminist interpretation of every book of the Bible. The fruit of collaborative work by an ecumenical and interreligious team of scholars, the volumes provide serious, scholarly engagement with the whole biblical text, not only those texts that explicitly mention women. The series is intended for clergy, teachers, ministers, and all serious students of the Bible. Designed to be both accessible and informed by the various approaches of biblical scholarship, it pays particular attention to the world in front of the text, that is, how the text is heard and appropriated. At the same time, this series aims to be faithful to the ancient text and its earliest audiences; thus the volumes also explicate the worlds behind the text and within it. While issues of gender are primary in this project, the volumes also address the intersecting issues of power, authority, ethnicity, race, class, and religious belief and practice. The fifty-eight volumes include the books regarded as canonical by Jews (i.e., the Tanakh); Protestants (the "Hebrew Bible" and the New Testament); and Roman Catholic, Anglican, and Eastern

Orthodox Communions (i.e., Tobit, Judith, 1 and 2 Maccabees, Wisdom of Solomon, Sirach/Ecclesiasticus, Baruch, including the Letter of Jeremiah, the additions to Esther, and Susanna and Bel and the Dragon in Daniel).

A Symphony of Diverse Voices

Included in the Wisdom Commentary series are voices from scholars of many different religious traditions, of diverse ages, differing sexual identities, and varying cultural, racial, ethnic, and social contexts. Some have been pioneers in feminist biblical interpretation; others are newer contributors from a younger generation. A further distinctive feature of this series is that each volume incorporates voices other than that of the lead author(s). These voices appear alongside the commentary of the lead author(s), in the grayscale inserts. At times, a contributor may offer an alternative interpretation or a critique of the position taken by the lead author(s). At other times, they may offer a complementary interpretation from a different cultural context or subject position. Occasionally, portions of previously published material bring in other views. The diverse voices are not intended to be contestants in a debate or a cacophony of discordant notes. The multiple voices reflect that there is no single definitive feminist interpretation of a text. In addition, they show the importance of subject position in the process of interpretation. In this regard, the Wisdom Commentary series takes inspiration from the Talmud and from *The Torah: A Women's Commentary* (ed. Tamara Cohn Eskenazi and Andrea L. Weiss; New York: URJ Press and Women of Reform Judaism, The Federation of Temple Sisterhoods, 2008), in which many voices, even conflicting ones, are included and not harmonized.

Contributors include biblical scholars, theologians, and readers of Scripture from outside the scholarly and religious guilds. At times, their comments pertain to a particular text. In some instances they address a theme or topic that arises from the text.

Another feature that highlights the collaborative nature of feminist biblical interpretation is that a number of the volumes have two lead authors who have worked in tandem from the inception of the project and whose voices interweave throughout the commentary.

Woman Wisdom

The title, Wisdom Commentary, reflects both the importance to feminists of the figure of Woman Wisdom in the Scriptures and the distinct wisdom that feminist women and men bring to the interpretive process. In the Scriptures, Woman Wisdom appears as "a breath of the power of God, and a pure emanation of the glory of the Almighty" (Wis 7:25), who was present and active in fashioning all that exists (Prov 8:22-31; Wis 8:6). She is a spirit who pervades and penetrates all things (Wis 7:22-23), and she provides guidance and nourishment at her all-inclusive table (Prov 9:1-5). In both postexilic biblical and nonbiblical Jewish sources, Woman Wisdom is often equated with Torah, e.g., Sirach 24:23-34; Baruch 3:9–4:4; 38:2; 46:4-5; 2 Baruch 48:33, 36; 4 Ezra 5:9-10; 13:55; 14:40; 1 Enoch 42.

The New Testament frequently portrays Jesus as Wisdom incarnate. He invites his followers, "take my yoke upon you and learn from me" (Matt 11:29), just as Ben Sira advises, "put your neck under her [Wisdom's] yoke and let your souls receive instruction" (Sir 51:26). Just as Wisdom experiences rejection (Prov 1:23-25; Sir 15:7-8; Wis 10:3; Bar 3:12), so too does Jesus (Mark 8:31; John 1:10-11). Only some accept his invitation to his all-inclusive banquet (Matt 22:1-14; Luke 14:15-24; compare Prov 1:20-21; 9:3-5). Yet, "wisdom is vindicated by her deeds" (Matt 11:19, speaking of Jesus and John the Baptist; in the Lukan parallel at 7:35 they are called "wisdom's children"). There are numerous parallels between what is said of Wisdom and of the *Logos* in the Prologue of the Fourth Gospel (John 1:1-18). These are only a few of many examples. This female embodiment of divine presence and power is an apt image to guide the work of this series.

Feminism

There are many different understandings of the term "feminism." The various meanings, aims, and methods have developed exponentially in recent decades. Feminism is a perspective and a movement that springs from a recognition of inequities toward women, and it advocates for changes in whatever structures prevent full flourishing of human beings and all creation. Three waves of feminism in the United States are commonly recognized. The first, arising in the mid-nineteenth century and lasting into the early twentieth, was sparked by women's efforts to be involved in the public sphere and to win the right to vote. In the 1960s and 1970s, the second wave focused on civil rights and equality for women. With the third wave, from the 1980s forward, came global feminism and the emphasis on the contextual nature of interpretation. Now a fourth wave may be emerging, with a stronger emphasis on the intersectionality of women's concerns with those of other marginalized groups and the increased use of the internet as a platform for discussion and activism.[1] As feminism has matured, it has recognized that inequities based on gender are interwoven with power imbalances based on race, class, ethnicity, religion, sexual identity, physical ability, and a host of other social markers.

Feminist Women and Men

Men as well as nonbinary people who choose to identify with and partner with feminist women in the work of deconstructing systems of domination and building structures of equality are rightly regarded as feminists. Some men readily identify with experiences of women who are discriminated against on the basis of sex/gender, having themselves had comparable experiences; others who may not have faced direct discrimination or stereotyping recognize that inequity and problematic characterization still occur, and they seek correction. This series is pleased to include feminist men both as lead authors and as contributing voices.

Feminist Biblical Interpretation

Women interpreting the Bible from the lenses of their own experience is nothing new. Throughout the ages women have recounted the biblical stories, teaching them to their children and others, all the while interpreting them afresh for their time and circumstances.[2] Following is a very brief sketch of select foremothers who laid the groundwork for contemporary feminist biblical interpretation.

One of the earliest known Christian women who challenged patriarchal interpretations of Scripture was a consecrated virgin named Helie, who lived in the second century CE. When she refused to marry, her

1. See Martha Rampton, "Four Waves of Feminism" (October 25, 2015), at https://www.pacificu.edu/magazine/four-waves-feminism; and Ealasaid Munro, "Feminism: A Fourth Wave?," *Political Insight* (September 2013), https://journals.sagepub.com/doi/pdf/10.1111/2041-9066.12021.

2. For fuller treatments of this history, see chap. 7, "One Thousand Years of Feminist Bible Criticism," in Gerda Lerner, *Creation of Feminist Consciousness: From the Middle Ages to Eighteen-Seventy* (New York: Oxford University Press, 1993), 138–66; Susanne Scholz, "From the 'Woman's Bible' to the 'Women's Bible,' The History of Feminist Approaches to the Hebrew Bible," in *Introducing the Women's Hebrew Bible*, IFT 13 (New York: T&T Clark, 2007), 12–32; Marion Ann Taylor and Agnes Choi, eds., *Handbook of Women Biblical Interpreters: A Historical and Biographical Guide* (Grand Rapids: Baker Academic, 2012).

parents brought her before a judge, who quoted to her Paul's admonition, "It is better to marry than to be aflame with passion" (1 Cor 7:9). In response, Helie first acknowledges that this is what Scripture says, but then she retorts, "but not for everyone, that is, not for holy virgins."[3] She is one of the first to question the notion that a text has one meaning that is applicable in all situations.

A Jewish woman who also lived in the second century CE, Beruriah, is said to have had "profound knowledge of biblical exegesis and outstanding intelligence."[4] One story preserved in the Talmud (b. Ber. 10a) tells of how she challenged her husband, Rabbi Meir, when he prayed for the destruction of a sinner. Proffering an alternate interpretation, she argued that Psalm 104:35 advocated praying for the destruction of sin, not the sinner.

In medieval times the first written commentaries on Scripture from a critical feminist point of view emerge. While others may have been produced and passed on orally, they are for the most part lost to us now. Among the earliest preserved feminist writings are those of Hildegard of Bingen (1098–1179), German writer, mystic, and abbess of a Benedictine monastery. She reinterpreted the Genesis narratives in a way that presented women and men as complementary and interdependent. She frequently wrote about the Divine as feminine.[5] Along with other women mystics of the time, such as Julian of Norwich (1342–ca. 1416), she spoke authoritatively from her personal experiences of God's revelation in prayer.

In this era, women were also among the scribes who copied biblical manuscripts. Notable among them is Paula Dei Mansi of Verona, from a distinguished family of Jewish scribes. In 1288, she translated from Hebrew into Italian a collection of Bible commentaries written by her father and added her own explanations.[6]

Another pioneer, Christine de Pizan (1365–ca. 1430), was a French court writer and prolific poet. She used allegory and common sense

3. Madrid, Escorial MS, a II 9, f. 90 v., as cited in Lerner, *Feminist Consciousness*, 140.

4. See Judith R. Baskin, "Women and Post-Biblical Commentary," in *The Torah: A Women's Commentary*, ed. Tamara Cohn Eskenazi and Andrea L. Weiss (New York: URJ Press and Women of Reform Judaism, The Federation of Temple Sisterhoods, 2008), xlix–lv, at lii.

5. Hildegard of Bingen, *De Operatione Dei*, 1.4.100; PL 197:885bc, as cited in Lerner, *Feminist Consciousness*, 142–43. See also Barbara Newman, *Sister of Wisdom: St. Hildegard's Theology of the Feminine* (Berkeley: University of California Press, 1987).

6. Emily Taitz, Sondra Henry, Cheryl Tallan, eds., *JPS Guide to Jewish Women 600 B.C.E.–1900 C.E.* (Philadelphia: JPS, 2003), 110–11.

to subvert misogynist readings of Scripture and celebrated the accomplishments of female biblical figures to argue for women's active roles in building society.[7]

By the seventeenth century, there were women who asserted that the biblical text needs to be understood and interpreted in its historical context. For example, Rachel Speght (1597–ca. 1630), a Calvinist English poet, elaborates on the historical situation in first-century Corinth that prompted Paul to say, "It is well for a man not to touch a woman" (1 Cor 7:1). Her aim was to show that the biblical texts should not be applied in a literal fashion to all times and circumstances. Similarly, Margaret Fell (1614–1702), one of the founders of the Religious Society of Friends (Quakers) in Britain, addressed the Pauline prohibitions against women speaking in church by insisting that they do not have universal validity. Rather, they need to be understood in their historical context, as addressed to a local church in particular time-bound circumstances.[8]

Along with analyzing the historical context of the biblical writings, women in the eighteenth and nineteenth centuries began to attend to misogynistic interpretations based on faulty translations. One of the first to do so was British feminist Mary Astell (1666–1731).[9] In the United States, the Grimké sisters, Sarah (1792–1873) and Angelina (1805–1879), Quaker women from a slaveholding family in South Carolina, learned biblical Greek and Hebrew so that they could interpret the Bible for themselves. They were prompted to do so after men sought to silence them from speaking out against slavery and for women's rights by claiming that the Bible (e.g., 1 Cor 14:34) prevented women from speaking in public.[10] Another prominent abolitionist, Isabella Baumfree, was a former slave who adopted the name Sojourner Truth (ca. 1797–1883); she quoted the Bible liberally in her speeches[11] and in so doing challenged cultural assumptions and biblical interpretations that undergird gender inequities.

7. See further Taylor and Choi, *Handbook of Women Biblical Interpreters*, 127–32.

8. Her major work, *Women's Speaking Justified, Proved and Allowed by the Scriptures*, published in London in 1667, gave a systematic feminist reading of all biblical texts pertaining to women.

9. Mary Astell, *Some Reflections upon Marriage* (New York: Source Book Press, 1970, reprint of the 1730 edition; earliest edition of this work is 1700), 103–4.

10. See further Sarah Grimké, *Letters on the Equality of the Sexes and the Condition of Woman* (Boston: Isaac Knapp, 1838).

11. See, for example, her most famous speech, "Ain't I a Woman?," delivered in 1851 at the Ohio Women's Rights Convention in Akron, OH; Modern History Sourcebook, https://sourcebooks.fordham.edu/mod/sojtruth-woman.asp.

Another monumental work that emerged in nineteenth-century England was that of Jewish theologian Grace Aguilar (1816–1847), *The Women of Israel*,[12] published in 1845. Aguilar's approach was to make connections between the biblical women and contemporary Jewish women's concerns. She aimed to counter the widespread notion that women were degraded in Jewish law and that only in Christianity were women's dignity and value upheld. Her intent was to help Jewish women find strength and encouragement by seeing the evidence of God's compassionate love in the history of every woman in the Bible. While not a full commentary on the Bible, Aguilar's work stands out for its comprehensive treatment of every female biblical character, including even the most obscure references.[13]

The first person to produce a full-blown feminist commentary on the Bible was Elizabeth Cady Stanton (1815–1902). A leading proponent in the United States for women's right to vote, she found that whenever women tried to make inroads into politics, education, or the work world, the Bible was quoted against them. Along with a team of like-minded women, she produced her own commentary on every text of the Bible that concerned women. Her pioneering two-volume project, *The Woman's Bible*, published in 1895 and 1898, urges women to recognize that texts that degrade women come from the men who wrote the texts, not from God, and to use their common sense to rethink what has been presented to them as sacred.

Nearly a century later, *The Women's Bible Commentary*, edited by Carol A. Newsom and Sharon H. Ringe (Louisville: Westminster John Knox, 1992), appeared. This one-volume commentary features North American feminist scholarship on each book of the Protestant canon. Like Cady Stanton's commentary, it does not contain comments on every section of the biblical text but only on those passages deemed relevant to women. It was revised and expanded in 1998 to include the Apocrypha/Deuterocanonical books, and the contributors to this new volume reflect the global face of contemporary feminist scholarship. The revisions made in the third edition, which appeared in 2012, represent the profound advances in feminist biblical scholarship and include newer voices (with Jacqueline E. Lapsley as an additional editor). In both the second and third editions, *The* has been dropped from the title.

12. The full title is *The Women of Israel or Characters and Sketches from the Holy Scriptures and Jewish History Illustrative of the Past History, Present Duty, and Future Destiny of the Hebrew Females, as Based on the Word of God.*

13. See further Eskenazi and Weiss, *The Torah: A Women's Commentary*, xxxviii; Taylor and Choi, *Handbook of Women Biblical Interpreters*, 31–37.

Also appearing at the centennial of Cady Stanton's *The Woman's Bible* were two volumes edited by Elisabeth Schüssler Fiorenza with the assistance of Shelly Matthews. The first, *Searching the Scriptures: A Feminist Introduction* (New York: Crossroad, 1993), charts a comprehensive approach to feminist interpretation from ecumenical, interreligious, and multicultural perspectives. The second volume, published in 1994, provides critical feminist commentary on each book of the New Testament as well as on three books of Jewish Pseudepigrapha and eleven other early Christian writings.

In Europe, similar endeavors have been undertaken, such as the one-volume *Kompendium Feministische Bibelauslegung*, edited by Luise Schottroff and Marie-Theres Wacker (Gütersloh: Gütersloher Verlagshaus, 2007), featuring German feminist biblical interpretation of each book of the Bible, along with Deuterocanonical apocryphal books, and several extrabiblical writings. This work, now in its third edition, was translated into English.[14] A multivolume project, The Bible and Women: An Encyclopaedia of Exegesis and Cultural History, edited by Mary Ann Beavis, Irmtraud Fischer, Mercedes Navarro Puerto, and Adriana Valerio, is currently in production. This project presents a history of the reception of the Bible as embedded in Western cultural history and focuses particularly on gender-relevant biblical themes, biblical female characters, and women recipients of the Bible. The volumes are published in English, Spanish, Italian, and German.[15]

14. *Feminist Biblical Interpretation: A Compendium of Critical Commentary on the Books of the Bible and Related Literature*, trans. Lisa E. Dahill, Everett R. Kalin, Nancy Lukens, Linda M. Maloney, Barbara Rumscheidt, Martin Rumscheidt, and Tina Steiner (Grand Rapids: Eerdmans, 2012). Another notable collection is the three volumes edited by Susanne Scholz, *Feminist Interpretation of the Hebrew Bible in Retrospect*, Recent Research in Biblical Studies 7, 8, 9 (Sheffield: Sheffield Phoenix, 2013, 2014, 2016).

15. The first volume, on the Torah, appeared in Spanish in 2009, in German and Italian in 2010, and in English in 2011 (Atlanta: SBL). The other available volumes are as follows: *Feminist Biblical Studies in the Twentieth Century*, ed. Elisabeth Schüssler Fiorenza (2014); *The Writings and Later Wisdom Books*, ed. Christl M. Maier and Nuria Calduch-Benages (2014); *Gospels: Narrative and History*, ed. Mercedes Navarro Puerto and Marinella Perroni; Amy-Jill Levine, English ed. (2015); *The High Middle Ages*, ed. Kari Elisabeth Børresen and Adriana Valerio (2015); *Early Jewish Writings*, ed. Eileen Schuller and Marie-Theres Wacker (2017); *Faith and Feminism in Nineteenth-Century Religious Communities*, ed. Michaela Sohn-Kronthaler and Ruth Albrecht (2019); *The Early Middle Ages*, ed. Franca Ela Consolino and Judith Herrin (2020); *Prophecy and Gender in the Hebrew Bible*, ed. L. Juliana Claassens and Irmtraud Fischer (2021); and *Rabbinic Literature*, ed. Tal Ilan, Lorena Miralles-Maciá, and Ronit Nikolsky (2022). For further information, see https://www.bibleandwomen.org.

Another groundbreaking work is the collection The Feminist Companion to the Bible Series, edited by Athalya Brenner (Sheffield: Sheffield Academic, 1993–2015), which comprises twenty volumes of commentaries on the Old Testament. The parallel series, Feminist Companion to the New Testament and Early Christian Writings, edited by Amy-Jill Levine with Marianne Blickenstaff and Maria Mayo Robbins (Sheffield: Sheffield Academic, 2001–2010), contains thirteen volumes. These two series are not full commentaries on the biblical books but comprise collected essays on discrete biblical texts.

Works by individual feminist biblical scholars in all parts of the world abound, and they are now too numerous to list in this introduction. Feminist biblical interpretation has reached a level of maturity that now makes possible a commentary series on every book of the Bible. In recent decades, women have had greater access to formal theological education, have been able to learn critical analytical tools, have put their own interpretations into writing, and have developed new methods of biblical interpretation. Until recent decades the work of feminist biblical interpreters was largely unknown, both to other women and to their brothers in the synagogue, church, and academy. Feminists now have taken their place in the professional world of biblical scholars, where they build on the work of their foremothers and connect with one another across the globe in ways not previously possible. In a few short decades, feminist biblical criticism has become an integral part of the academy.

Methodologies

Feminist biblical scholars use a variety of methods and often employ a number of them together.[16] In the Wisdom Commentary series, the authors will explain their understanding of feminism and the feminist reading strategies used in their commentary. Each volume treats the biblical text in blocks of material, not an analysis verse by verse. The entire text is considered, not only those passages that feature female characters or that speak specifically about women. When women are not apparent in the narrative, feminist lenses are used to analyze the dynamics in the text between male characters, the models of power, binary ways of thinking, and the dynamics of imperialism. Attention is given to how the whole text functions and how it was and is heard, both in its original context

16. See the seventeen essays in Caroline Vander Stichele and Todd Penner, eds., *Her Master's Tools? Feminist and Postcolonial Engagements of Historical-Critical Discourse* (Atlanta: SBL, 2005), which show the complementarity of various approaches.

and today. Issues of particular concern to women—e.g., poverty, food, health, the environment, water—come to the fore.

One of the approaches used by early feminists and still popular today is to lift up the overlooked and forgotten stories of women in the Bible. Studies of women in each of the Testaments have been done, and there are also studies on women in particular biblical books.[17] Feminists recognize that the examples of biblical characters can be both empowering and problematic. The point of the feminist enterprise is not to serve as an apologetic for women; it is rather, in part, to recover women's history and literary roles in all their complexity and to learn from that recovery.

Retrieving the submerged history of biblical women is a crucial step for constructing the story of the past so as to lead to liberative possibilities for the present and future. There are, however, some pitfalls to this approach. Sometimes depictions of biblical women have been naïve and romantic. Some commentators exalt the virtues of both biblical and contemporary women and paint women as superior to men. Such reverse discrimination inhibits movement toward equality for all. In addition, some feminists challenge the idea that one can "pluck positive images out of an admittedly androcentric text, separating literary characterizations from the androcentric interests they were created to serve."[18] Still other feminists find these images to have enormous value.

One other danger with seeking the submerged history of women is the tendency for Christian feminists to paint Jesus and even Paul as liberators of women in a way that demonizes Judaism.[19] Wisdom Commentary

17. See, e.g., Alice Bach, ed., *Women in the Hebrew Bible: A Reader* (New York: Routledge, 1999); Tikva Frymer-Kensky, *Reading the Women of the Bible* (New York: Schocken Books, 2002); Carol Meyers, Toni Craven, and Ross Shepard Kraemer, eds., *Women in Scripture* (Grand Rapids: Eerdmans, 2001); Irene Nowell, *Women in the Old Testament* (Collegeville, MN: Liturgical Press, 1997); Katharine Doob Sakenfeld, *Just Wives? Stories of Power and Survival in the Old Testament and Today* (Louisville: Westminster John Knox, 2003); Mary Ann Getty-Sullivan, *Women in the New Testament* (Collegeville, MN: Liturgical Press, 2001); Bonnie Thurston, *Women in the New Testament: Questions and Commentary*, Companions to the New Testament (New York: Crossroad, 1998).

18. J. Cheryl Exum, "Second Thoughts about Secondary Characters: Women in Exodus 1.8–2.10," in *A Feminist Companion to Exodus to Deuteronomy*, FCB 6, ed. Athalya Brenner (Sheffield: Sheffield Academic, 1994), 75–97, at 76.

19. See Judith Plaskow, "Anti-Judaism in Feminist Christian Interpretation," in *Searching the Scriptures: A Feminist Introduction*, vol. 1, ed. Elisabeth Schüssler Fiorenza with Shelly Matthews (New York: Crossroad, 1993), 117–29; Amy-Jill Levine, "The

aims to enhance understanding of Jesus as well as Paul as Jews of their day and to forge solidarity among Jewish and Christian feminists.

Feminist scholars who use historical-critical methods analyze the world behind the text; they seek to understand the historical context from which the text emerged and the circumstances of the communities to whom it was addressed. In bringing feminist lenses to this approach, the aim is not to impose modern expectations on ancient cultures but to unmask the ways that ideologically problematic mind-sets that produced the ancient texts are still promulgated through the text. Feminist biblical scholars aim not only to deconstruct but also to reclaim and reconstruct biblical history as women's history, in which women were central and active agents in creating religious heritage.[20] A further step is to construct meaning for contemporary women and men in a liberative movement toward transformation of social, political, economic, and religious structures.[21] In recent years, some feminists have embraced new historicism, which accents the creative role of the interpreter in any construction of history and exposes the power struggles to which the text witnesses.[22]

Literary critics analyze the world of the text: its form, language patterns, and rhetorical function.[23] They do not attempt to separate layers

---

New Testament and Anti-Judaism," in *The Misunderstood Jew: The Church and the Scandal of the Jewish Jesus* (San Francisco: HarperSanFrancisco, 2006), 87–117.

20. See, for example, Phyllis A. Bird, *Missing Persons and Mistaken Identities: Women and Gender in Ancient Israel* (Minneapolis: Fortress, 1997); Elisabeth Schüssler Fiorenza, *In Memory of Her: A Feminist Theological Reconstruction of Christian Origins* (New York: Crossroad, 1994); Ross Shepard Kraemer and Mary Rose D'Angelo, eds., *Women and Christian Origins* (New York: Oxford University Press, 1999).

21. See, e.g., Sandra M. Schneiders, *The Revelatory Text: Interpreting the New Testament as Sacred Scripture*, rev. ed. (Collegeville, MN: Liturgical Press, 1999), whose aim is to engage in biblical interpretation not only for intellectual enlightenment but, even more important, for personal and communal transformation. Elisabeth Schüssler Fiorenza (*Wisdom Ways: Introducing Feminist Biblical Interpretation* [Maryknoll, NY: Orbis Books, 2001]) envisions the work of feminist biblical interpretation as a dance of Wisdom that consists of seven steps that interweave in spiral movements toward liberation, the final one being transformative action for change.

22. See Gina Hens-Piazza, *The New Historicism*, GBS, Old Testament Series (Minneapolis: Fortress, 2002).

23. Phyllis Trible was among the first to employ this method with texts from Genesis and Ruth in her groundbreaking book *God and the Rhetoric of Sexuality*, OBT (Philadelphia: Fortress, 1978). Another pioneer in feminist literary criticism is Mieke Bal (*Lethal Love: Feminist Literary Readings of Biblical Love Stories* [Bloomington: Indiana University

of tradition and redaction but focus on the text holistically, as it is in its present form. They examine how meaning is created in the interaction between the text and its reader in multiple contexts. Within the arena of literary approaches are reader-oriented approaches, narrative, rhetorical, structuralist, post-structuralist, deconstructive, ideological, autobiographical, and performance criticism.[24] Narrative critics study the interrelation among author, text, and audience through investigation of settings, both spatial and temporal; characters; plot; and narrative techniques (e.g., irony, parody, intertextual allusions). Reader-response critics attend to the impact that the text has on the reader or hearer. They recognize that when a text is detrimental toward women there is the choice either to affirm the text or to read against the grain toward a liberative end. Rhetorical criticism analyzes the style of argumentation and attends to how the author is attempting to shape the thinking or actions of the hearer. Structuralist critics analyze the complex patterns of binary oppositions in the text to derive its meaning.[25] Post-structuralist approaches challenge the notion that there are fixed meanings to any biblical text or that there is one universal truth. They engage in close readings of the text and often engage in intertextual analysis.[26] Within this approach is deconstructionist criticism, which views the text as a site of conflict, with competing narratives. The interpreter aims to expose the fault lines and overturn and reconfigure binaries by elevating the underling of a pair and foregrounding it.[27] Feminists also use other post-

---

Press, 1987]). For surveys of recent developments in literary methods, see Terry Eagleton, *Literary Theory: An Introduction*, 3rd ed. (Minneapolis: University of Minnesota Press, 2008); Janice Capel Anderson and Stephen D. Moore, eds., *Mark and Method: New Approaches in Biblical Studies*, 2nd ed. (Minneapolis: Fortress, 2008); Michal Beth Dinkler, *Literary Theory and the New Testament*, AYBRL (New Haven: Yale University Press, 2019).

24. See, e.g., J. Cheryl Exum and David J. A. Clines, eds., *The New Literary Criticism and the Hebrew Bible* (Valley Forge, PA: Trinity Press International, 1993); Edgar V. McKnight and Elizabeth Struthers Malbon, eds., *The New Literary Criticism and the New Testament* (Valley Forge, PA: Trinity Press International, 1994).

25. See, e.g., David Jobling, *The Sense of Biblical Narrative: Three Structural Analyses in the Old Testament*, JSOTSup 7 (Sheffield: University of Sheffield Press, 1978).

26. See, e.g., Stephen D. Moore, *Poststructuralism and the New Testament: Derrida and Foucault at the Foot of the Cross* (Minneapolis: Fortress, 1994); *The Bible in Theory: Critical and Postcritical Essays* (Atlanta: SBL, 2010); Yvonne Sherwood, *A Biblical Text and Its Afterlives: The Survival of Jonah in Western Culture* (Cambridge: Cambridge University Press, 2000).

27. David Penchansky, "Deconstruction," in *The Oxford Encyclopedia of Biblical Interpretation*, ed. Steven McKenzie (New York: Oxford University Press, 2013), 196–205. See, for example, Danna Nolan Fewell and David M. Gunn, *Gender, Power, and Promise:*

modern approaches, such as ideological and autobiographical criticism. The former analyzes the system of ideas that underlies the power and values concealed in the text as well as that of the interpreter.[28] The latter involves deliberate self-disclosure while reading the text as a critical exegete.[29] Performance criticism attends to how the text was passed on orally, usually in communal settings, and to the verbal and nonverbal interactions between the performer and the audience.[30]

From the beginning, feminists have understood that interpreting the Bible is an act of power. In recent decades, feminist biblical scholars have developed hermeneutical theories of the ethics and politics of biblical interpretation to challenge the claims to value neutrality of most academic biblical scholarship. Feminist biblical scholars have also turned their attention to how some biblical writings were shaped by the power of empire and how this still shapes readers' self-understandings today. They have developed hermeneutical approaches that reveal, critique, and evaluate the interactions depicted in the text against the context of empire, and they consider implications for contemporary contexts.[31] Feminists also analyze the dynamics of colonization and the mentalities of colonized peoples in the exercise of biblical interpretation. As Kwok Pui-lan explains, "A postcolonial feminist interpretation of the Bible needs to investigate the deployment of gender in the narration of identity, the negotiation of power differentials between the colonizers and the colonized, and the reinforcement of patriarchal control over spheres

The Subject of the Bible's First Story (Nashville: Abingdon, 1993); David Rutledge, *Reading Marginally: Feminism, Deconstruction and the Bible*, BibInt 21 (Leiden: Brill, 1996).

28. See David Jobling and Tina Pippin, eds., *Semeia* 59: *Ideological Criticism of Biblical Texts* (Atlanta: Scholars Press, 1992); Terry Eagleton, *Ideology: An Introduction* (London: Verso, 2007).

29. See, e.g., Ingrid Rosa Kitzberger, ed., *Autobiographical Biblical Interpretation: Between Text and Self* (Leiden: Deo, 2002); P. J. W. Schutte, "When *They*, *We*, and the Passive Become *I*—Introducing Autobiographical Biblical Criticism," *HTS Teologiese Studies / Theological Studies* 61 (2005): 401–16.

30. See, e.g., Holly E. Hearon and Philip Ruge-Jones, eds., *The Bible in Ancient and Modern Media: Story and Performance* (Eugene, OR: Cascade Books, 2009).

31. E.g., Gale Yee, ed., *Judges and Method: New Approaches in Biblical Studies* (Minneapolis: Fortress, 1995); Warren Carter, *The Gospel of Matthew in Its Roman Imperial Context* (London: T&T Clark, 2005); *The Roman Empire and the New Testament: An Essential Guide* (Nashville: Abingdon, 2006); Elisabeth Schüssler Fiorenza, *The Power of the Word: Scripture and the Rhetoric of Empire* (Minneapolis: Fortress, 2007); Judith E. McKinlay, *Reframing Her: Biblical Women in Postcolonial Focus* (Sheffield: Sheffield Phoenix, 2004).

where these elites could exercise control."[32] Methods and models from sociology and cultural anthropology are used by feminists to investigate women's everyday lives, their experiences of marriage, childrearing, labor, money, illness, etc.[33]

As feminists have examined the construction of gender from varying cultural perspectives, they have become ever more cognizant that the way gender roles are defined within differing cultures varies radically. As Mary Ann Tolbert observes, "Attempts to isolate some universal role that cross-culturally defines 'woman' have run into contradictory evidence at every turn."[34] Some women have coined new terms to highlight the particularities of their socio-cultural context. Many African American feminists, for example, call themselves *womanists* to draw attention to the double oppression of racism and sexism they experience.[35] Similarly, many US Hispanic feminists speak of themselves as *mujeristas* (*mujer* is Spanish for "woman").[36] Others prefer to be called "Latina feminists."[37] As a gender-neutral or nonbinary alternative, many today use Latinx or Latine. *Mujeristas*, Latina and Latine feminists emphasize that the context

32. Kwok Pui-lan, *Postcolonial Imagination and Feminist Theology* (Louisville: Westminster John Knox, 2005), 9. See also Musa W. Dube, ed., *Postcolonial Feminist Interpretation of the Bible* (St. Louis: Chalice, 2000); Cristl M. Maier and Carolyn J. Sharp, *Prophecy and Power: Jeremiah in Feminist and Postcolonial Perspective* (London: Bloomsbury, 2013); L. Juliana Claassens and Carolyn J. Sharp, eds., *Feminist Frameworks and the Bible: Power, Ambiguity, and Intersectionality*, LHBOTS 630 (London: Bloomsbury T&T Clark, 2017).

33. See, for example, Carol Meyers, *Discovering Eve: Ancient Israelite Women in Context* (New York: Oxford University Press, 1991); Luise Schottroff, *Lydia's Impatient Sisters: A Feminist Social History of Early Christianity*, trans. Barbara and Martin Rumscheidt (Louisville: Westminster John Knox, 1995); Susan Niditch, *"My Brother Esau Is a Hairy Man": Hair and Identity in Ancient Israel* (Oxford: Oxford University Press, 2008).

34. Mary Ann Tolbert, "Social, Sociological, and Anthropological Methods," in *Searching the Scriptures*, 1:255–71, at 265.

35. Alice Walker coined the term (*In Search of Our Mothers' Gardens: Womanist Prose* [New York: Harcourt Brace Jovanovich, 1967, 1983]). See also Katie G. Cannon, "The Emergence of Black Feminist Consciousness," in *Feminist Interpretation of the Bible*, ed. Letty M. Russell (Philadelphia: Westminster, 1985), 30–40; Renita J. Weems, *Just a Sister Away: A Womanist Vision of Women's Relationships in the Bible* (San Diego: Lura Media, 1988); Nyasha Junior, *An Introduction to Womanist Biblical Interpretation* (Louisville: Westminster John Knox, 2015).

36. Ada María Isasi-Díaz (*Mujerista Theology: A Theology for the Twenty-First Century* [Maryknoll, NY: Orbis Books, 1996]) is credited with coining the term.

37. E.g., María Pilar Aquino, Daisy L. Machado, and Jeanette Rodríguez, eds., *A Reader in Latina Feminist Theology* (Austin: University of Texas Press, 2002).

for their theologizing is *mestizaje* and *mulatez* (racial and cultural mixture), done *en conjunto* (in community), with *lo cotidiano* (everyday lived experience) of Latina women as starting points for theological reflection and the encounter with the divine. Intercultural analysis has become an indispensable tool for working toward justice for women at the global level.[38]

Some feminists are among those who have developed lesbian, gay, bisexual, and transgender (LGBT+) interpretation. This approach focuses on issues of sexual identity and uses various reading strategies. Some point out the ways in which categories that emerged in recent centuries are applied anachronistically to biblical texts to make modern-day judgments. Others show how the Bible is silent on contemporary issues about sexual identity. Still others examine same-sex relationships in the Bible by figures such as Ruth and Naomi or David and Jonathan. In recent years, queer theory has emerged; it emphasizes the blurriness of boundaries not just of sexual identity but also of gender roles. Queer critics often focus on texts in which figures transgress what is traditionally considered proper gender behavior.[39]

Feminists have also been engaged in studying the reception history of the text[40] and have engaged in studies in the emerging fields of disability theory and of children in the Bible.

38. See, e.g., María Pilar Aquino and María José Rosado-Nunes, eds., *Feminist Intercultural Theology: Latina Explorations for a Just World*, Studies in Latino/a Catholicism (Maryknoll, NY: Orbis Books, 2007). See also Michelle A. Gonzalez, "Latina Feminist Theology: Past, Present, and Future," *JFSR* 25 (2009): 150–55. See also Elisabeth Schüssler Fiorenza, ed., *Feminist Biblical Studies in the Twentieth Century: Scholarship and Movement*, The Bible and Women 9.1 (Atlanta: SBL, 2014), who charts feminist studies around the globe as well as emerging feminist methodologies.

39. See, e.g., Bernadette J. Brooten, *Love Between Women: Early Christian Responses to Female Homoeroticism* (Chicago: University of Chicago Press, 1996); Mary Rose D'Angelo, "Women Partners in the New Testament," *JFSR* 6 (1990): 65–86; Deirdre J. Good, "Reading Strategies for Biblical Passages on Same-Sex Relations," *Theology and Sexuality* 7 (1997): 70–82; Deryn Guest, *When Deborah Met Jael: Lesbian Feminist Hermeneutics* (London: SCM, 2005); Teresa Hornsby and Ken Stone, eds., *Bible Trouble: Queer Readings at the Boundaries of Biblical Scholarship* (Atlanta: SBL, 2011); Joseph A. Marchal, "Queer Studies and Critical Masculinity Studies in Feminist Biblical Studies," in *Feminist Biblical Studies in the Twentieth Century*, ed. Schüssler Fiorenza, 261–80.

40. See Sharon H. Ringe, "When Women Interpret the Bible," in *Women's Bible Commentary*, ed. Carol A. Newsom, Sharon H. Ringe, and Jacqueline E. Lapsley, 3rd ed. (Louisville: Westminster John Knox, 2012), 5; Taylor and Choi, *Handbook of Women Biblical Interpreters;* Yvonne Sherwood, "Introduction," in *The Bible and Feminism: Remapping the Field* (New York: Oxford University Press, 2017).

Feminists also recognize that the struggle for women's equality and dignity is intimately connected with the struggle for respect for Earth and for the whole of the cosmos. Ecofeminists interpret Scripture in ways that highlight the link between human domination of nature and male subjugation of women. They show how anthropocentric ways of interpreting the Bible have overlooked or dismissed Earth and Earth community. They invite readers to identify not only with human characters in the biblical narrative but also with other Earth creatures and domains of nature, especially those that are the object of injustice. Some use creative imagination to retrieve the interests of Earth implicit in the narrative and enable Earth to speak.[41]

Biblical Authority

By the late nineteenth century, some feminists, such as Elizabeth Cady Stanton, began to question openly whether the Bible could continue to be regarded as authoritative for women. They viewed the Bible itself as the source of women's oppression, and some rejected its sacred origin and saving claims. Some decided that the Bible and the religious traditions that enshrine it are too thoroughly saturated with androcentrism and patriarchy to be redeemable.[42]

In the Wisdom Commentary series, questions such as these may be raised, but the aim of this series is not to lead readers to reject the authority of the biblical text. Rather, the aim is to promote better understanding of the contexts from which the text arose and of the rhetorical effects it has on people in contemporary contexts. Such understanding can lead to a deepening of faith, with the Bible serving as an aid to bring flourishing of life.

Language for God

Because of the ways in which the term "God" has been used to symbolize the divine in predominantly male, patriarchal, and monarchical modes, feminists have designed new ways of speaking of the divine. Some have called attention to the inadequacy of the term *God* by trying

41. E.g., Norman C. Habel and Peter Trudinger, *Exploring Ecological Hermeneutics*, SBLSymS 46 (Atlanta: SBL, 2008); Mary Judith Ress, *Ecofeminism in Latin America*, Women from the Margins (Maryknoll, NY: Orbis Books, 2006).

42. E.g., Mary Daly, *Beyond God the Father: A Philosophy of Women's Liberation* (Boston: Beacon, 1985).

to visually destabilize our ways of thinking and speaking of the divine. Rosemary Radford Ruether proposed *God/ess*, as an unpronounceable term pointing to the unnameable understanding of the divine that transcends patriarchal limitations.[43] Some have followed traditional Jewish practice, writing *G-d*. Elisabeth Schüssler Fiorenza has adopted *G*d*.[44] Others draw on the biblical tradition to mine female and non-gender-specific metaphors and symbols.[45] In Wisdom Commentary, there is not one standard way of expressing the divine; each author will use her or his preferred ways. The one exception is that when the tetragrammaton, YHWH, the name revealed to Moses in Exodus 3:14, is used, it will be without vowels, respecting the Jewish custom of avoiding pronouncing the divine name out of reverence.

Nomenclature for the Two Testaments

In recent decades, some biblical scholars have begun to call the two Testaments of the Bible by names other than the traditional nomenclature: Old and New Testament. Some regard "Old" as derogatory, implying that it is no longer relevant or that it has been superseded. Consequently, terms like Hebrew Bible, First Testament, and Jewish Scriptures and, correspondingly, Christian Scriptures or Second Testament have come into use. There are a number of difficulties with these designations. The term "Hebrew Bible" does not take into account that parts of the Old Testament are written not in Hebrew but in Aramaic.[46] Moreover, for Roman Catholics and Eastern Orthodox believers, the Old Testament includes books written in Greek—the Deuterocanonical books, considered Apocrypha by Protestants.[47] The term "Jewish Scriptures" is inadequate because these

43. Rosemary Radford Ruether, *Sexism and God-Talk: Toward a Feminist Theology* (Boston: Beacon, 1993).

44. Elisabeth Schüssler Fiorenza, *Jesus: Miriam's Child, Sophia's Prophet; Critical Issues in Feminist Christology* (New York: Continuum, 1994), 191n3.

45. E.g., Sallie McFague, *Models of God: Theology for an Ecological, Nuclear Age* (Philadelphia: Fortress, 1987); Catherine Mowry LaCugna, *God for Us: The Trinity and Christian Life* (San Francisco: HarperCollins, 1991); Elizabeth A. Johnson, *She Who Is: The Mystery of God in Feminist Theological Discourse* (New York: Crossroad, 1992). See further Elizabeth A. Johnson, "God," in *Dictionary of Feminist Theologies*, ed. Letty M. Russell and J. Shannon Clarkson (Louisville: Westminster John Knox, 1996), 128–30.

46. Gen 31:47; Jer 10:11; Ezra 4:7–6:18; 7:12-26; Dan 2:4–7:28.

47. Representing the *via media* between Catholic and reformed, Anglicans generally consider the Apocrypha to be profitable, if not canonical, and utilize select Wisdom texts liturgically.

books are also sacred to Christians. Conversely, "Christian Scriptures" is not an accurate designation for the New Testament, since the Old Testament is also part of the Christian Scriptures. Using "First and Second Testament" also has difficulties, in that it can imply a hierarchy and a value judgment.[48] Jews generally use the term Tanakh, an acronym for Torah (Pentateuch), Nevi'im (Prophets), and Ketuvim (Writings).

In Wisdom Commentary, if authors choose to use a designation other than Tanakh, Old Testament, and New Testament, they will explain how they mean the term.

Translation

Modern feminist scholars recognize the complexities connected with biblical translation, as they have delved into questions about philosophy of language, how meanings are produced, and how they are culturally situated. Today it is evident that simply translating into gender-neutral formulations cannot address all the challenges presented by androcentric texts. Efforts at feminist translation must also deal with issues around authority and canonicity.[49]

Because of these complexities, the editors of the Wisdom Commentary series have chosen to use an existing translation, the New Revised Standard Version (NRSV), which is provided for easy reference at the top of each page of commentary. The NRSV was produced by a team of ecumenical and interreligious scholars, is a fairly literal translation, and uses inclusive language for human beings. Brief discussions about problematic translations appear in the inserts labeled "Translation Matters." When more detailed discussions are available, these will be indicated in footnotes. In the commentary, wherever Hebrew or Greek words are used, English translation is provided. In cases where a wordplay is involved, transliteration is provided to enable understanding.

Art and Poetry

Artistic expression in poetry, music, sculpture, painting, and various other modes is very important to feminist interpretation. Where possible, art and poetry are included in the print volumes of the series. In

48. See Levine, *The Misunderstood Jew*, 193–99.

49. Elizabeth Castelli, "*Les Belles Infidèles*/Fidelity or Feminism? The Meanings of Feminist Biblical Translation," in *Searching the Scriptures*, 1:189–204, here 190.

a number of instances, these are original works created for this project. Regrettably, copyright and production costs prohibit the inclusion of color photographs and other artistic work.

Glossary

Because there are a number of excellent readily available resources that provide definitions and concise explanations of terms used in feminist theological and biblical studies, this series will not include a glossary. We refer you to works such as *Dictionary of Feminist Theologies*, edited by Letty M. Russell and J. Shannon Clarkson, and volume 1 of *Searching the Scriptures*, edited by Elisabeth Schüssler Fiorenza with the assistance of Shelly Matthews. Individual authors in the Wisdom Commentary series will define the way they are using terms that may be unfamiliar.

A Concluding Word

In just a few short decades, feminist biblical studies has grown exponentially, both in the methods that have been developed and in the number of scholars who have embraced it. We realize that this series is limited and will soon need to be revised and updated. It is our hope that Wisdom Commentary, by making the best of current feminist biblical scholarship available in an accessible format to ministers, preachers, teachers, scholars, and students, will aid all readers in their advancement toward God's vision of dignity, equality, and justice for all.

Acknowledgments

There are a great many people who have made this series possible: first, Peter Dwyer, retired director of Liturgical Press, and Hans Christoffersen, editorial director of Liturgical Press, who have believed in this project and have shepherded it since it was conceived in 2008. Editorial consultants Athalya Brenner-Idan and Elisabeth Schüssler Fiorenza have not only been an inspiration with their pioneering work but have encouraged us all along the way with their personal involvement. Volume editors Mary Ann Beavis, Carol J. Dempsey, Gina Hens-Piazza, Amy-Jill Levine, Linda M. Maloney, Song-Mi Suzie Park, Ahida Pilarski, Sarah Tanzer, and Lauress Wilkins Lawrence have lent their extraordinary wisdom to the shaping of the series, have used their extensive networks of relationships to secure authors and contributors, and have worked tirelessly to guide their work to completion. Four others who have contributed greatly to the shaping of the project are Linda M. Day, Mignon Jacobs, Seung Ai Yang, and Barbara E. Bowe of blessed memory (d. 2010). Editorial and research assistant Susan M. Hickman provided invaluable support with administrative details and arrangements at the outset of the project. I am grateful to Brian Eisenschenk and Christine Henderson who assisted Susan Hickman with the Wiki. I am especially thankful to Lauren L. Murphy and Justin Howell for their work in copyediting; and to the staff at Liturgical Press, especially Colleen Stiller, production manager; Stephanie Lancour, production editor; Julie Surma, desktop publisher; Angie Steffens, production coordinator; and Tara Durheim, marketing director.

Authors' Introduction

Judith: the beautiful woman who infiltrates the enemy's camp as a secret agent, charms the general to get close to him, avoids his attempts at seduction and instead incapacitates him with wine (the ancient soporific), takes his own sword, and cuts off his head while he lies drunk on his bed. In Carey Moore's words, Judith is "the saint who murdered for her people."[1] The stuff of legend. The fantasy of the abused. The revenge of the oppressed. The story of Judith still intrigues with its steely heroine who manages the grisliest of actions with the most elegant poise.

Through the ages, Judith has fired the imagination, even as she has been at the center of questions and controversies. Judith is a part of the Septuagint (LXX)—the Greek version of the Jewish Scriptures that began to circulate in Greek-speaking Jewish communities starting in the second century BCE. Although written by and circulated among Jews, popular and perhaps considered Sacred Scripture in at least some Jewish communities, the book was not a part of the Jewish canon that came into its final form in the first or second century CE. Because the Christian canon built on the Greek versions of Jewish texts, Judith was a part of the Christian canon; thus, Christian copyists preserved this Jewish text. Yet, as Christianity split into denominations in the sixteenth century, its canonical status in Christianity changed. Retained in the Catholic and Eastern Orthodox canon, albeit as deuterocanonical (second canon), Protestants cut it out

1. Carey A. Moore, *Judith*, AB 40 (Garden City, NY: Doubleday, 1985), 31, 261. This favorite appellation appears throughout Moore's commentary.

altogether. Although Martin Luther considered Judith "a fine, good, holy, useful book, well worth reading,"[2] he was so flummoxed by its historical errors he could not recommend it for the canon, relegating it to apocryphal status. In particular, he could not get the historical information in Judith to align either with books that were undoubtedly Sacred Scripture (like Jeremiah and Ezra) or with important biblical commentators like the first-century Jewish philosopher Philo. In response, Catholics and Eastern Orthodox Christians both reaffirmed the canonical status of Judith in the Council of Trent (1546) and the Synod of Jerusalem (1672). Even without canonical imprimatur, many rabbis and Protestant leaders still knew and read Judith, and it was influential in Jewish and Protestant communities especially in the Middle Ages and early Reformation period.

Judith's fluctuating canonical status reflects the theological, ethical, and historical debates to which she has been subjected, debates sometimes steeped in sexism. Judith's moral character became a subject of debate as part of the Power of Women *topos* that circulated and grew popular right around the time that Luther drops Judith from the Protestant canon. In this late medieval representational theme, a woman inverts normative gender hierarchies by using her wit, cunning, beauty, and/or sex appeal to dominate a man. Writers on the theme often disparaged these women and encouraged men to assert and maintain patriarchal control.[3] Susan Smith argues, however, that at the time the theme was not always negatively coded and was sometimes used to celebrate powerful women. Instead of being unequivocally sexist or celebratory, the Power of Women *topos* became a "site of contest through which conflicting ideas about gender roles could be expressed."[4] Judith's detractors emphasize her duplicitousness, her sexual provocations, and her violence as acts of "moral turpitude."[5] Maybe (male) commentators are worried that they too will lose their heads to a woman as beautiful as she is deadly. As one of the few biblical books that is named after its female protagonist (she joins here the ranks of Ruth, Esther, and Susanna), she has also come to the attention of feminist interpreters, who also are divided on their assessment. She challenges the very meanings of "masculinity" and "femininity," even as she conforms

2. *Luther's Works*, vol. 35: *Word and Sacrament I*, ed. E. Theodore Bachmann (Minneapolis: Fortress, 1960), 337.

3. Susan L. Smith, "Woman on Top," in *Women and Gender in Medieval Europe: An Encyclopedia*, ed. Margaret Schaus (London: Taylor & Francis, 2006), 844.

4. Ibid., 845.

5. Edwin Cone Bissell, *The Book of Judith*, The Apocrypha of the Old Testament (New York: Scribner's Sons, 1886), 163, as cited in Moore, *Judith*, 65.

to stereotypes of the femme fatale. Feminists have either decried Judith as the embodiment of this sexist stereotype or celebrated Judith's gender-bending power. Along with feminist biblical scholar Pamela Milne, many have asked, "What shall we do with Judith?"[6]

This commentary will investigate the book of Judith through a feminist lens, informed especially by masculinity studies, queer theory, and reception criticism.[7] These interrelated and interlocking albeit not identical approaches do not yield a uniform perspective; rather, they reveal a multifaceted figure in a multifaceted story. The book of Judith and the character continue to compel because neither is easily categorized or explained. We do not propose to solve any of the interpretive cruxes, especially the feminist question of whether or not Judith is subversive. Instead, we will highlight different aspects of the story, present analysis and options for interpretation from a feminist perspective, and thus allow readers to know Judith, the book and its protagonist, more intimately and so to make up their own minds.

Overview of the Book of Judith

The book of Judith tells the story of an Israelite woman named Judith who saves her city, Bethulia, from an invading army led by the Assyrian general Holofernes by cutting off the general's head with his own sword. Although named for the heroine, the book does not introduce Judith until roughly halfway through the story. The first half, chapters 1–7, concerns the powers and propaganda of ancient empires. The story opens with the emperor Nebuchadnezzar of Assyria waging war against King Arphaxad of the Medes. Nebuchadnezzar summons support from vassal states to the west, including the regions of Galilee, Samaria, and Judah. These states refuse to muster, "for they were not afraid of him" (1:11). Once Nebuchadnezzar defeats the Medes, he determines to seek revenge for the insult to his honor by sending a massive army of over 120,000 foot soldiers and over twelve thousand supporting cavalry led by

6. Pamela J. Milne, "What Shall We Do with Judith? A Feminist Assessment of a Biblical 'Heroine,'" in *A Feminist Companion to Tobit and Judith*, FCB 20, 2nd ser., ed. Athalya Brenner-Idan with Helen Efthimiadis-Keith (London: Bloomsbury T&T Clark, 2015), 117–36.

7. For the interconnections among masculinity studies, queer theory, and feminist interpretation, see Joseph A. Marchal, "Queer Studies and Critical Masculinity Studies in Feminist Biblical Studies," in *Feminist Biblical Studies in the Twentieth Century: Scholarship and Movement*, ed. Elisabeth Schüssler Fiorenza (Atlanta: SBL Press, 2014), 261–80. Deryn Guest's *Beyond Feminist Biblical Studies* (Sheffield: Sheffield Phoenix, 2012) explores the similarities and tensions between gender, masculinity, queer, and feminist theories.

Holofernes (2:5). The army advances west with transport animals, food animals, chariots, and "a mixed crowd like a swarm of locusts" (2:20) that leaves desolation in its wake. Nebuchadnezzar specifically commissions Holofernes to destroy all local sacred spaces so that everyone "should worship Nebuchadnezzar alone" (3:8).

Hearing of Holofernes's advance and the destruction he wrought, especially to temples and shrines, the people of Israel become terrified and prepare, both militarily and spiritually, for his approach. They gather in food, secure towns, and fortify hilltops and the mountain passes. The mountain roads are so narrow that the invading soldiers can only advance two abreast, and so the local strategy renders Holofernes's greatest asset—his superior numbers—less effective. The Israelites also pray and fast and put on sackcloth and ashes. Making his only appearance in the book, the God of Israel hears their prayers and has "regard for their distress" (4:13).

Learning of this mobilized resistance, Holofernes flies into a rage and demands to know everything about these recalcitrant people. Enter Achior, the leader of the Ammonites in service to Nebuchadnezzar. When he steps forward to inform Holofernes of the Israelites' sacred history from Abraham to the return from Babylonian exile, he gives voice to the book's theological perspective. His speech ends by warning the general that as long as the people remain without sin, their God will defend them and they will never be defeated. Therefore, he urges Holofernes to turn aside lest the Assyrians "become the laughingstock of the whole world" (5:21). Instead of responding with prudence, Holofernes responds with pride by first proclaiming Nebuchadnezzar the only "lord of the whole earth" (6:4) and then by expelling Achior from the camp. Achior is taken by Holofernes's slaves, bound, and left in the plain near the town of Bethulia (Hebrew: "Virgin-ville"[8]). The locals find him and bring him to the magistrates. To his Israelite interlocutors, Achior recounts what happened and how Holofernes vowed to destroy them all. The scene ends with the people even more terrified than they were before.

Holofernes begins his campaign against Bethulia. The geographical advantages—the high hills and the narrow mountain passes—now become liabilities; what geography gives, it also takes away. Bethulia, a walled city, received its water from only one source—an external spring. Instead of his typical blitzkrieg, Holofernes decides (on the advice of his commanders) to capture the spring and to use the hills to lay siege to the town—the people of Bethulia are to be defeated by hunger and thirst rather than by military strike.

8. See https://books.openedition.org/obp/1045?lang=en.

The population of Bethulia is increasingly desperate as their water supplies dwindle and then dry up. Hoping that the Assyrians will treat them less harshly, they approach their leader Uzziah and beg him to surrender. Uzziah quiets the crowd with a compromise: wait five more days and if the siege is not over, he will surrender the town. At this point, almost halfway through the book, Judith appears (8:1).

The second half, chapters 8–16, follows Judith and her actions. This beautiful, wealthy, and pious widow was not present at the meeting between Uzziah and the townspeople, but she soon hears of it. Using her community standing to summon Uzziah and the other leaders, she rebukes them with a speech that expresses more of the book's theological perspective: the people of Bethulia have not sinned; rather, God is testing them. Judith asserts that she and her slave will, with God's help, save the city before the five days have elapsed.

After the men leave, Judith prostrates herself and offers a passionate prayer to God in which she invokes her ancestor Simeon and his revenge of his sister Dinah's rape. Her prayer also invokes "the God of the lowly, helper of the oppressed, upholder of the weak, protector of the forsaken, savior of those without hope" (9:11). She then bathes (where she found water is not recounted), perfumes herself, and puts on her most beautiful clothing and jewelry. She takes a sack of food and dishes with her, bids goodbye to the town elders, and she and her slave exit Bethulia's gates.

Judith is soon found by the Assyrian patrol who are entranced by both her wise words and her beautiful face. They take her directly to Holofernes's tent. She flatters the general, explains that the Bethulians learned of Holofernes's strength from Achior, and tells him that Bethulia is a sinful town that has taken for their own food the tithes that belong to God. Therefore, God is about to hand them over to destruction. Like his soldiers, Holofernes too is smitten by both her words and her looks. Holofernes gives her what she requests: to eat her own food on her own dishes, to have a private tent, and to have permission to leave the camp in the evenings to pray. After four days, Holofernes arranges a private banquet for just himself, his personal attendants, and Judith. After all, he says, "If we do not seduce her, she will laugh at us" (12:12).

Now, the story comes to its climax. Judith attends the banquet with the general, who is so excited by the prospect of sex with this beautiful woman that he drinks more than he had ever drunk in his life. Late into the evening, Holofernes's attendants withdraw, leaving the general and the widow alone in his tent. Instead of making his move, the drunken Holofernes passes out, and Judith seizes her opportunity. After a quick prayer to God, Judith grabs Holofernes's own sword, pulls up his head by his hair, and cuts it off with two strikes to his neck. Her slave is waiting outside with the bag in which they had carried their food. Judith conceals the head in this bag and, with her slave, leaves the camp, as per her established routine. She returns to Bethulia triumphant with their enemy's severed head.

Judith continues to direct the action as she commands the head to be hung from the city walls, orders the able-bodied men to take up arms, and summons Achior. The Ammonite soldier sees the general's head and faints in alarm. When he is revived, Judith recounts her story; Achior praises her and the God of Israel, and by circumcision he joins the Israelite people.

As the morning dawns and the Assyrian army realizes that Holofernes is dead, they panic and retreat. The Israelites rally, then slaughter the retreating army. The Bethulians, who do not participate in the rout, take the Assyrian camp. The rest of the victorious Israelites soon join them, and all loot the camp for several days.

The celebration of Judith and her victory begins. The women take a prominent role in this celebration as they dance, wave wands, and crown themselves with olive wreaths. The men follow the women in a parade around the town. Judith leads them all in a victory song all the way to Jerusalem, where the celebration continues for another three months. In the end, Judith returns home with her slave. Although she has suitors, she never remarries. Venerated by her people, Judith dies at the auspicious age of 105. "No one ever again spread terror among the Israelites during the lifetime of Judith, or for a long time after her death" (16:25). In other words, they all lived happily ever after.

A Brief Character Analysis of Judith

The book of Judith's truly remarkable heroine is first described as a devout, shapely, beautiful, and wealthy widow (Jdt 8:4, 7).[8] As her story progresses, she exhibits additional characteristics showing her the equal of Israel's finest warriors, although in a different way. Indeed her beheading of Holofernes—in his own tent, with his own sword, and surrounded by his own heretofore victorious army, no

9. Material for this selection came from my earlier work on Judith in *Bible History Daily*. See Robin Gallaher Branch, "Judith: A Remarkable Heroine, Parts 1 and 2" (https://www.biblicalarchaeology.org/daily/people-cultures-in-the-bible/people-in-the-bible/judith-a-remarkable-heroine/ and https://www.biblicalarchaeology.org/daily/people-cultures-in-the-bible/people-in-the-bible/judith-a-remarkable-heroine-part-2/).

less!—marks her as a political savior in Israel on par with David.

Judith is introduced with a lineage virtually unparalleled in the biblical text (Jdt 8:1-2). A descendant of Simeon, her genealogy includes sixteen progenitors and doesn't even make it back to Simeon! The genealogy, a significant textual marker, establishes her as a formidable literary character. In an interesting psychological insight, her prayer for help with her plan to save Israel and to assassinate Holofernes begins with a remembrance of Dinah's shame (Gen 34:2; Jdt 9:2-4). Judith expresses determination to erase this early, but still remembered, defamation.

Her covenant heritage combines prayer and action. Judith ranks along with Deborah (Jdg 4–5), the wife of Manoa (Jdg 13:23), Hannah (1 Sam 2:1-10), Naomi (Ruth 1:20-21), and Abigail (1 Sam 23–31) as theologians in the Old Testament; they all comment on God's character and actions. Other women wordsmiths in the biblical text are Lady Wisdom (Prov 8–9) and the Beloved in Song of Songs. In terms of verbosity, however, Judith exceeds them all. Her monologues and prayers highlight her theology. She credits God for the victory over the Assyrians and the killing of Holofernes (Jdt 16:5-6). Her theology includes possession and shows her leadership. In her closing prayer, she sings of "*my* territory," "*my* young men," "*my* infants," "*my* children," and "*my* maidens" (16:4; italics added).

Judith knows her power over men. Throughout the book, it seems Judith merely smiles and men collapse (10:7, 14, 19, 23). Wisely appealing to their senses of sight and smell, she mesmerizes them. Her weapons of warfare are sensual and material.

Judith used her assets—her spiritual training as a member of the covenant and the gifts God gave to her at birth and throughout life—to save her people. I would argue as well that she used her gifts for God's glory. Few women are given the gift of being attractive to men in general. Judith initially downplayed that gift. Perhaps she did not know how to handle it. She chooses to wear sackcloth around her waist and dress in widow's clothing (8:5), perhaps reflecting an inability to handle the gift of being breathtakingly attractive. She chooses to fast and remain celibate. She hides her sexuality and her known ability to attract men. Yet, it is exactly the gift of lovely face and form that saves her people and the temple. At the end of the story she is even more devout, shapely, beautiful, and wealthy. She interacts with people; she lets them see her beauty and enjoy it; she joyfully celebrates for weeks with her grateful nation. She loves and is beloved in return.

Robin Gallaher Branch

Strange Histories

Judith is a vivid and gripping tale, but it is not a historical account. It has characters from history, and it describes some common experiences of warfare, but Judith blends empires and enemies to create a general soup of Jewish conquest and survival narrative. Problems begin with the first verse, "It was the twelfth year of the reign of Nebuchadnezzar, who ruled over the Assyrians in the great city of Nineveh. In those days Arphaxad ruled over the Medes in Ecbatana" (1:1).[10] Despite the bounty of names, dates, and places—Nebuchadnezzar, Arphaxad, Assyrians, Medes, Nineveh, Ecbatana, "the twelfth year"— the account is nonsensical. The names are (almost) all attested, but the relationships among them are (almost) all ahistorical. Nebuchadnezzar did reign from about 605 BCE to 562 BCE, but he reigned over the Neo-Babylonian Empire, not the Assyrian. The great city Nineveh, the royal seat of the Assyrians during the reign of Sennacherib, was destroyed by Nebuchadnezzar's father Nabopolassar in 612 BCE; the historical Nebuchadnezzar may have heard stories from his father about its ruin, but he never reigned from there. Arphaxad is otherwise unknown (although information about the Medes is incomplete), and the Median Empire allied itself with Babylon and so was not the enemy of Nebuchadnezzar. By the time we reach the end of the verse, it is with relief that we find a fact: Ecbatana was indeed the capital of the Median Empire, at least under the Median king Phraortes, who reigned from 675 BCE to 653 BCE. The bizarre mish-mash must have been as jarring to the text's early audiences as the statement "It happened at the time when George Washington reigned in Tenochtitlan and Winston Churchill ruled over the Chinese" would be to people today.

There are, however, points of contact with Israelite history. In the first verse, Assyria and Babylon, empires that conquered Israelite lands, are conflated. The Assyrians conquered the northern territories of Israel and took the capital, Samaria, in 721 BCE, effectively erasing ten of Israel's twelve tribes from history. Refugees from the north flooded the south, and a few years later the Assyrian army followed them by moving against the Southern Kingdom of Judah. The Assyrian armies laid waste to the countryside, and in 701 BCE Sennacherib besieged Jerusalem. Although the Assyrians ultimately failed to take the city, the

10. Unless otherwise noted, translations are from the New Revised Standard Version (NRSV).

siege lasted years and brought enormous suffering to the people. In the next wave of ancient Near Eastern power politics, the Babylonians under the leadership of Nebuchadnezzar conquered Judah, seized Jerusalem, and destroyed the temple in 586 BCE. The Babylonian army then forced tens of thousands of Judahites into exile into Babylon.[11] These traumatic events are all deftly signaled in the first few words of the book of Judith.

The Medes too affected Israel's life. Although Arphaxad is otherwise unknown, both Isaiah (Isa 13:17; 21:2) and Jeremiah (Jer 25:25; 51:11, 28) mention the Medes, and Media is one of the four kingdoms symbolized in Daniel 2:36-45 by the statue in Nebuchadnezzar's dream. The kingdom also is part of the interpretation of the "handwriting on the wall" in Daniel 5:25-28, and it is symbolized by the second beast at the beginning of Daniel's apocalyptic revelation (Dan 7:5). Although there is no historical evidence that the Medes engaged Israel in battle, they left a threatening impression on Israel's imagination. In addition, the Medes appear to be the forerunners of the Persians, and the Persians did play a pivotal role in Israel's history. The Persian Empire conquered the Babylonians at the end of the sixth century BCE, and then King Cyrus repatriated waves of conquered Jews to rebuild Jerusalem and the temple. The Jews lived under Persian rule from 538 to 333.

Both Holofernes (or Orophernes) and Bagoas the eunuch (his closest attendant), Persian names, appear in court records. The historian Diodorus of Sicily (90–30 BCE) mentions two men named Holofernes: the first was a Cappadocian aristocrat who participated in the Persian campaign against Egypt during the reign of Artaxerxes III Ochus in the fourth century BCE; the second, also a Cappadocian ruler, lived in the second century BCE and was known for his drunkenness and his penchant for destroying other peoples' temples.[12] A person named Bagoas plays a larger role in Diodorus's narrative. He is described as Artaxerxes's closest companion, "a wily and devious figure, a brave, powerful eunuch who eventually assassinates Artaxerxes and his son(s)."[13] Like the use of real people and places in Judith 1:1, the names Holofernes and Bagoas may be gesturing to known people and events to evoke memories of violence and intrigue.

11. See David M. Carr, *Holy Resilience: The Bible's Traumatic Origins* (New Haven: Yale University Press, 2014) on the effects of these national disasters on the biblical Scripture.

12. Deborah Levine Gera, *Judith*, CEJL (Berlin: de Gruyter, 2014), 35 and 139.

13. Ibid., 36.

Some commentators have attempted to explain the inaccuracies in Judith's history by positing that the author was misinformed or that a long and complicated history of composition confused the original wording. The salvation history the Ammonite Achior recounts in chapter 5 undercuts those justifications. Achior's summary is a faithful reproduction of the historical narrative of the Hebrew Bible (particularly as interpreted by the theology of Deuteronomy: when Jews avoid idolatry, they are unbeatable; when they do not, they are conquered). Achior even explains the Babylonian conquest of Jerusalem, the destruction of the temple, and the subsequent captivity under the real Nebuchadnezzar (albeit without mentioning the Babylonians by name; see 5:17-18). He ends with the return from their exile, resettlement in Jerusalem, and the restoration of the temple. These last events are recounted in such a way that they imply a quick succession, perhaps even collapsing the Babylonian assault with the Persian restoration, events that spanned at least a century. The time may be telescoped, and the empires' names left unsaid, but the narrative is not only convergent with biblical texts but also supported by material and inscriptional evidence. The author of Judith is not ignorant of either the biblical meta-story or Israel's history. Therefore, Judith's historical inaccuracies are deliberate, so much so that it seems the book intends to signal itself as fiction.

Judith's opening historical review contains echoes of the story of Xerxes's invasion of Greece in books 7–8 of Herodotus's *History* (430 BCE),[14] echoes that invite comparison and bring into sharper relief the ways the writer of Judith makes history strange. As we will argue, the historical inaccuracies are not just a wink at the audience, intimating the fictional nature of the story; the historical inaccuracies are part of a wider project that advances ideologies of national identity, ones that are inextricably bound to ideologies of gender.

Hailed as one of the first examples of a sustained narrative history in Western literature, the *History* narrates the invasion of the Greek islands and mainland by the Persian king Xerxes in the fifth century BCE. After establishing his rule, Xerxes determines to expand his glory and assembles an army unlike any seen before. This army advances east,

14. Herodotus, *The History*, trans. David Grene (Chicago: University of Chicago Press, 1987). Mark Stephen Caponigro argues that the similarities are so striking that the author of Judith must have known Herodotus's work. See "Judith, Holding the Tale of Herodotus," in *"No One Spoke Ill of Her": Essays on Judith*, ed. James C. VanderKam, EJL 2 (Atlanta: Scholars Press, 1992), 47–59.

ravaging the coastline of Turkey (and the northern edge of Galilee) to cross the Hellespont and invade Europe. Herodotus describes how the army struggles to advance southward along the Greek peninsula but finds itself restricted to the narrow coastline or fraught mountain passes.

It is at one of these mountain passes that the Greeks stage their first major resistance to Xerxes's army. Because of the treacherous terrain, Xerxes's army is forced to march one or two abreast. Greeks, more familiar with the geography, harass the Persians' progress from high points along the way. The Greeks' plan involved moving people residing in the central plains and Athenian region to safer zones in the southern peninsula while having their navy attempt to cut the supply lines behind the advancing Persian army. Though the terrain slowed Xerxes's advance, the Greeks needed more time. In a famous narrative, integral to Greek notions of national identity, three hundred Spartan soldiers under the command of Leonidas mounted a resistance at the small fortified Greek outpost at Thermophilae (Greek: "fire gate," so named for the volcanic and hot springs in the region).

The Spartans held off Xerxes's army for over three days. They were defeated when a Greek-speaking mercenary in Xerxes's army came forward and volunteered to show a commando team how to attack the Spartans from the rear. Betrayed, the entire detachment of Spartans was killed, but in their valiant defense they checked the advance of Xerxes's armies long enough to allow tens of thousands of Greek citizens to reach safety. The Greeks honored their sacrifice with songs, poems, and a permanent monument at the site. They were eventually able to halt the advance of Xerxes at Salamis (a major harbor city, not far from Athens) by a decisive naval battle. With his ships destroyed, Xerxes's massive army became his liability; unable to resupply and harassed by Greek land and sea forces, he retreated back into Turkey. The small but plucky Greek forces had repelled the western world's largest standing army.

A modern historian of warfare might not be quite as surprised by the Greeks' victory. The Greeks had several advantages. They had a rigorous and effective military including strong land and sea forces. They had a common language and sense of identity that facilitated collaboration among the city-states in an organized resistance. They knew the terrain well, and the landscape—a central plateau surrounded by rugged, steep, volcanic mountains—was not conducive to a large invasionary land force. The Greeks were fighting for field, family, and home. They did not have to take any territory, merely to hold it; they did not have to defeat Xerxes's entire army, merely to eliminate its supply lines.

Reading Herodotus, however, we get a very different explanation. Herodotus persistently valorizes the Greeks and argues that they defeated the greater numbers and weaponry of the Persians because the Greeks were more civilized. The Greek educational systems, Herodotus asserts, produced a literate and disciplined male citizenry. Greek democracy, Herodotus argues, also gave every man a stake in the outcome and produced a deep devotion to the polis, a devotion that led many to sacrifice their all for their homeland. The Persians, by contrast, were mercenaries hired in service of Xerxes's ego. They fought for no ideals or values. Herodotus portrays them as either slavish and craven or domineering and cruel. They lacked order and discipline and would break ranks in either anger or fear. They spoke an unspeakable language (the Greek word for foreigners, βαρβάροι, is roughly translated as "babblers"). In short, they lacked civilization; the lack was so acute that, again and again, Herodotus questions their manliness, equal in his mind to full humanity. In other moments, he suggests they are rude, unintelligent, untamed, and savage beasts. The Greeks won, Herodotus argued, in the same way that the human huntsmen can defeat savage animals.

There are several parallels between Herodotus and Judith. In overview, both narrate an advancing, numberless horde attacking noble and plucky peoples who seek shelter among their homeland's rugged hills. In each, a great Mesopotamian empire pushes eastward in order to assuage the ego of a tyrant. In each, this army is checked in the hill country by a small group in a fortified outpost. In each, the invading army is ultimately defeated by an ideology. For Herodotus, the Greek civilization itself secures victory. For Judith, it is Jewish fidelity to God.

Both Herodotus and Judith are stories that use "history" in the service of wider ideologies.[15] Despite Herodotus's title as "the father of history," his narratives also employ fiction and flash.[16] They are not histories in the

15. On Herodotus's ideologies, see John D. Mikalson, *Herodotus and Religion in the Persian Wars* (Chapel Hill: University of North Carolina Press, 2003); and François Hartog, *The Mirror of Herodotus: The Representation of the Other in the Writing of History* (Berkeley: University of California Press, 1988). Some of Hartog's thesis has recently been softened; for example, Michèle Rosellini and Suzanne Saïd, "Women's Customs among the 'Savages' in Herodotus," in *Herodotus*, vol. 2: *Herodotus and the World*, ed. Rosaria Vignolo Munson (Oxford: Oxford University Press, 2013), 213–44; and Rosalind Thomas, "Ethnicity, Genealogy, and Hellenism," in *Herodotus*, 2:340–42.

16. On Herodotus's mixture of fiction and history, see Detlev Fehling, "The Art of Herodotus on the Margins of the World," in *Travel Fact and Travel Fiction: Studies on Fiction, Literary Traditions, Scholarly Discovery and Observation in Travel Writing*, ed.

modern, academic sense of the word. In both, the narrative of invasion and resistance is a way of articulating a larger debate about identity and the clash of ideologies. Both stories use similar narratives and themes to argue for constructions of identity so powerful that they can subvert physical limitations and traditional constructions of "power." Right belief, the right adherence to ethnic ideals, is more powerful than military strength. It may be a hidden power, but it is, nevertheless, very real.

Gender is a key component of the right ideology advanced in both stories. In ancient Greek communities, gender difference manifested in power differentials that correlated to wealth and social status. Masculinity existed on a continuum with rich, upper-class, male citizens at the high end. Masculinity was the result of control, precision, and discipline; it was the essence of civilized behavior. Herodotus draws out differences between the "manly" Spartans and the "effeminate" barbarians. In Herodotus, barbarians *as an outcome of the very essence of being a barbarian* are less masculine, which in this case also means less human, than the Greeks. Herodotus is not just writing a history. He is arguing, implicitly, for a particular configuration of power and authority. What appears to be unstoppable strength (the Persians leading a massive army) is, in fact, stoppable by superior civilization and discipline, the true hallmarks of "real men."

Jewish tradition, especially in Jewish Greek-speaking communities, participated in Greek constructions of masculinity but with some notable variations influenced by Jewish theology. Masculinity, again, is equivalent to power, which includes the elaborate projection of honor and deference. In Judith, both Holofernes and Nebuchadnezzar act in support of their pursuit of male honor. Nebuchadnezzar is seeking revenge for having been spurned. Holofernes is angry that such a small band of resistors is thwarting his larger army; he is particularly enraged by the suggestion from Achior that he and his soldiers cannot prevail against the weak and numerically insignificant Israelites. In the end, the Assyrian defeat is even more radical in its comment on true power than the Persian defeat. Holofernes, and by implication Nebuchadnezzar, is defeated and thus emasculated by a single woman.

The book of Judith is not arguing that women are more masculine (and therefore more powerful) than men; it is arguing that the ultimate male power and honor is God's. Judith is the conduit of that power because of

Zweder von Martels, Brill Studies in Intellectual History 53 (Leiden: Brill, 1994), 1–15; and *Herodotus and His "Sources": Citation, Invention, and Narrative Art*, Arca Classical and Medieval Texts, Papers and Monographs 21 (Leeds: Francis Carrus, 1989), 53–54.

her confidence and her discipline, both of which arise as a result of her faith and her piety. Her female body and seductive words exacerbate the Assyrian humiliation and serve to bring God's power into even sharper relief. The narrative, like Herodotus's *History*, offers a particular appraisal of power and, by implication, masculinity. What appears to be an invincible force and the ultimate expression of (male) honor and power is undone by what appears to be an insignificant people (the Jews), by hill folk, by a single woman. What appears to be unstoppable strength is, in fact, stoppable by superior theology. In a move similar to Herodotus's assertions that Greek cultural superiority is really the source of significant strength and power, Judith argues that Jewish religious superiority can defeat the strongest army of the most dominant empire, even through the work of a woman. Judith, imitating Herodotus, is implicitly also arguing that Jewish biblical values and covenant fidelity are equivalent to Greek artistic, cultural, intellectual, and democratic values.

Both Herodotus and the author of Judith use historical narrative as a vehicle for a type of national aggrandizement linked to ideologies of gender. There are, however, significant differences in their projects. Elaborations, exaggerations, and fabrications aside, the clash between Persian and Greek forces actually happened; the battle between Assyria and the Israelites depicted in the book of Judith did not. Greece became a significant world power, and Herodotus was, in part, telling the history of this rise in political fortunes. Israel never was and never became a significant world power; instead, Israel was the nation conquered over and over again by Near Eastern and Mediterranean empires for millennia. As such, the temporal dissonances of Judith, the strange histories with their ideological agendas, ring in other registers.

We will show in our reading of Judith that the problems with history, so obvious in the first verse, continue throughout the narrative to the very last line (for example, when exactly did Judith free her slave?). These more subtle chronological glitches help produce a story that runs counter to the typical grand narratives of history (like the ones told by Herodotus), narratives that tell the stories of kings and generals, dramatic clashes on the battlefield, momentous world events. This grand narrative is unsettled by a widow from a small and insignificant people who, along with her slave, upends a world superpower with little more than her wits, her beauty, her faith, and a borrowed sword. There may be a re-domestication of Judith at the end, but it is one that leaves traces of the radical sexual warrior and gender troubler that emerge in the spaces and gaps produced by a history out of joint.

Date and Cultural Context

Despite the clear and deliberate historical inaccuracies, these historical references do prove some use in the pursuit of historical questions because they help establish the boundaries for the writing of the book of Judith. Based on the book's references to the people's return to Jerusalem after a period of captivity (Jdt 5:18-19), Judith was written no earlier than the middle of the Persian period (fifth century BCE). Judith also has a very clear boundary for the latest date it could have been written—the mention of Judith by Clement of Rome in his letter to the Corinthians, dated between 95 and 97 CE.[17] Somewhere in the five hundred years or so between the resettlement of Jerusalem during the Persian period and Clement's letter, the book of Judith was composed.

Closer attention to the biblical references and allusions helps to narrow the date of composition even further, as it serves to demonstrate how deeply conversant the author was with biblical texts. As Deborah Levine Gera notes, "The author of Judith was thoroughly acquainted with the Bible and our work is filled with traces of biblical situations and characters, themes and theology, allusions and quotations. Indeed, Judith has been described as a 'symphony of biblical allusions' and virtually every commentator who writes on Judith points to 'the intricate palette of intertextual relations between Judith and biblical writings.'"[18] We will explore in detail some of these "intertextual relations" in the commentary; here in our brief overview of the text's interactions with other texts, we focus on the ones that bear on the dating of Judith.

Judith includes multiple references and allusions to the Torah, the first five books of the Scripture. Judith likens herself to Simeon avenging his raped sister Dinah (9:2 referencing Gen 34), and echoes Moses's Song of the Sea (Exod 15) in her own prayer (Jdt 9) and victory song (Jdt 16). The multiple allusions to the exodus narrative and Moses's story contribute to a characterization of Judith as a kind of female Moses, rescuing her people from foreign domination.[19] Numbers 22–24 is also prominent in

17. Gera, *Judith*, 13.

18. Ibid., 45. Gera cites George T. Montague, *The Books of Esther and Judith* (New York: Paulist Press, 1973), 10; and Jan Willem van Henten, "Judith as Alternative Leader: A Rereading of Judith 7–13," in *A Feminist Companion to Esther, Judith and Susanna*, ed. Athalya Brenner, FCB 7 (Sheffield: Sheffield Academic, 1995), 224. For a thorough explication of biblical influences in Judith, see Gera, *Judith*, 45–56.

19. Jan Willem van Henten, "Judith as a Female Moses: Judith 7–13 in the Light of Exodus 17, Numbers 20 and Deuteronomy 33:8-11," in *Reflections on Theology and*

the composition of Judith. For example, Judith's reprimand of the Bethulian leaders (9:11-27, esp. vv. 12-14) echoes Balaam's warning to Balak (Num 23:19). Achior's speeches to Holofernes (5:5-21) mirror Balaam's dialogue with Balak: both the Ammonite convert and the pagan magician are Gentiles who speak the truth about Israel to hostile foreign leaders.

The book of Judges is also mined by the author of Judith to construct both plot and character—the stories of Ehud, Deborah, and Jael are particularly rich sources. Bagoas's discovering Holofernes's executed corpse resembles Eglon's servants discovering his executed corpse (compare Jdt 13:1; 14:14-18 with Judg 3:23-25). The two situations are also remarkably similar, especially if we understand Ehud as using sexual innuendo to manipulate Eglon into a vulnerable position. The similarities between Judith and Jael (Judg 4–5) are numerous. Both use sexual promise to lure the enemy general into a tent; both take a weapon near at hand and wield it against the man's head; both are celebrated as the "most blessed" in victory songs (Jdt 12:10–13:10; Judg 4:17-22). Margarita Stocker goes as far as to call Jael Judith's "canonical alter-ego,"[20] and Colleen Conway proposes that Judith rewrites Jael in a less sexually and morally ambiguous way.[21] Intertextual interactions continue throughout the historical books with references to Abigail (1 Sam 25), Tamar (2 Sam 13), the wise woman of Tekoa (2 Sam 14), Huldah (2 Kgs 22), and Ruth.

There is hardly a scene in Judith that does not in some way gesture toward another biblical hero or heroine. The figures that are late in the biblical corpus, Esther and Daniel, are particularly noteworthy in terms of our question of date. Both Esther and Judith are title characters who use beauty, charm, and sexual allure to their advantage over powerful men. Both books feature feasts best understood as drinking bouts (Esth 1 and 7; Jdt 12:10-20). Both women fast and then put on their finest clothes and jewelry before they approach the powerful man (Esth 4:16 and 5:1; Jdt 10:3-4). There is no explicit mention of divine providence or assistance—no mention of God at all—in the Hebrew version of Esther and only one direct reference to God's attention in Judith. Even with God's attention, there is nothing miraculous in either text and both can be

---

Gender, ed. Fokkelien van Dijk-Hemmes and Athalya Brenner (Leuven: Peeters, 1994), 33–48.

20. Margarita Stocker, *Judith: Sexual Warrior; Women and Power in Western Culture* (New Haven: Yale University Press, 1998), 144; cf. 13–14.

21. Colleen Conway, *Sex and Slaughter in the Tent of Jael: A Cultural History of a Biblical Story* (Oxford: Oxford University Press, 2017), 27–31.

understood as illustrating the platitude that God helps those who help themselves. Both heroines save their people from annihilation—Esther in the Persian diaspora, and Judith in the context of repatriated Israel. In the Septuagint's version of Esther, the heroine is like Judith in her intense piety, fervent prayers to God, and an interest in kosher food regulations (see especially addition C, chap. 14).

Piety as manifest in both prayers and keeping kosher also links Judith to the book of Daniel. Moreover, the two books share an interest in maintaining separation from "pollution" through avoidance of Gentile foods (Dan 1:8 uses the language of defilement to describe contact with nonkosher food and wine; Jdt 12:2 names eating nonkosher food an "offense"). The foreign king is Nebuchadnezzar in both books, but Nebuchadnezzar's role differs in relation to the plot: Daniel, like Esther, is a Jew living in a foreign court after military conquest, but Judith is living in Israel facing down conquest. Nevertheless, in both stories Nebuchadnezzar has people treat him as if he were a god (Dan 3 may feature a statue of Nebuchadnezzar; Jdt 3:8), and he has a mercurial and dangerous temperament. The final form of Daniel has a definitive date of composition circa 165 BCE, although the passages from Daniel that resemble Judith (the court tales) may have been composed earlier.

All three books—Esther, Daniel, and Judith—have a complex compositional history, which may link them as well. Both Esther and Daniel have a composition history that is multilingual. Esther was composed in Hebrew, but the book has two Greek recensions with additional chapters. Every extant copy of the book of Daniel is a combination of Hebrew and Aramaic; since the Aramaic sections do not correspond with any obvious break in the narrative (such as where the court tales end and the apocalyptic visions begin) the reason for this polyglot is a mystery; Daniel also has an extended Greek version, which contains the story of another heroine, Susanna, who is put in a sexually compromising situation but saved through faith. Judith is extant only in Greek; some evidence suggests a Hebrew original although that is debated, and Jerome claims to have used an Aramaic version for his Latin translation.[22] The questions concerning the original language of Judith, its composition, and translations point to a similar historical context, a time when many in the Jewish community were comfortably multilingual, and both texts

22. Jerome discussed his translation process in the preface to Judith in the Vulgate. See Moore, *Judith*, 95–96.

and people moved back and forth between Israel and various diaspora communities. Such compositional history and linguistic fluidity points to the wider Hellenistic period, as do certain cultural details in Judith like wearing garlands and olive wreaths (Jdt 3:7 and 15:13) and reclining while eating (Jdt 12:15). Other elements—like connections to Daniel—point more narrowly to the Maccabean era.

There are substantial similarities between Judith and the books of 1 and 2 Maccabees. The similarities between the themes, plot, and characters are striking, starting with the parallel names—Judith is the feminine form of Judas (the hero of Maccabees), both of which mean "Jew" or "Judean." They both exhibit a similar piety (see, for example, 1 Macc 3:47-54 where Judas leads a group in fasting and mourning rituals, reading from Torah and prayer) and both defend the temple. Although not otherwise comparable, Nebuchadnezzar in Judith and Antiochus IV (the Greek king against whom the Maccabees fight) have one significant shared trait: they both are declared gods. In fact, in terms of the historical record, Antiochus IV was the first Greek ruler to proclaim himself a god (his title was "Epiphanes" or "God revealed"), and later Greek and Roman emperors certainly followed suit. In addition to proclaiming his own divinity, he was remarkably (by pagan standards) intolerant of other forms of religious expression—like Judith's Nebuchadnezzar.[23] This overlap between the fictional Nebuchadnezzar and the historical Antiochus may be Judith's deliberate conflation of the empires of Assyria and Babylonia, *and* the Greeks.

Moreover, the story of the death of Nicanor (one of the Greek generals sent against Jerusalem) at the hand of Judas (1 Macc 7:39-50) is remarkably close to the sequence of events describing Judith's victory over Holofernes (Jdt 9–16). Gera lists eight points of confluence:

> (1) the hero(ine) prays to God; (2) the chief lieutenant of a powerful and evil king is killed; (3) the enemy army panics and flees; (4) all the surrounding Israelite soldiers attack; (5) they kill and plunder; (6) the enemy's head is chopped off and brought to Jerusalem; (7) the Israelites celebrate their victory; (8) peace descends on the land.[24]

Taking these similarities to be more than just coincidence—and they do appear to be too numerous to be either incidental or coincidental—we

23. Gera, *Judith*, 39.

24. Ibid., 39; see also Moore, *Judith*, 50–51, for more similarities between the two accounts.

must conclude that Judith was written after the books of the Maccabees or that they arose in such identical milieux that the same concerns, themes, elements of plot, and characterization arose independently in them. The ways in which the book of Judith assumes certain institutional structures like the power of the high priest (4:6) and the Jerusalem council (4:6, 8; 11:14) also situate Judith firmly within the time period of the Hasmoneans, the time of Judean independence that begins with the successful revolt against Antiochus IV and ends when the Roman Empire assumes control in 63 BCE.

Situating the story of Judith during the reign of a particular Maccabean ruler such as John Hyrcanus I (135–104 BCE), Alexander Janneus (103–78 BCE), and Salome Alexandra (76–67 BCE) remains hypothetical. From a feminist perspective, the idea that Judith was written under the reign of Salome Alexandra is particularly intriguing. Salome, the widow of Alexander Janneaus, would have presented a model of strong female leadership. She ruled after the unification of Samaria and Judea in 107 BCE and instead of crucifying Pharisees as did her husband, she took them into her court. Judith could have been written as a kind of tribute to this queen or even a piece of political propaganda in support of her rule.[25] The fact that her kingdom fell to the Roman Empire after her death, however, coupled with the book's lack of any clear Roman influence, makes most other commentators cautious to propose such a direct link. Any specific linking of Judith to a Hasmonean ruler rests on too many assumptions about Jewish life in this period.

Geographical appeal is also of little help in finding a more specific date. In the book of Judith, although Bethulia appears to be located in Samaritan territory and Judith summons Samaritans to her cause (4:4), no tensions between Samaritans and Judeans exist. All recognize the piety of Judith's practices, and the temple in Jerusalem is at the heart of the region. Indeed, Judith creates a utopian fantasy space where all of Israel is united—geographically, politically, culturally, and religiously. This collective then fights a foreign invader threatening not just the body of the people but also the sanctity of the temple and the sovereignty of God.

Based on the historical, biblical, and cultural allusions, a date of around 100 BCE seems to be any scholar's best guess for when the book of Judith was composed.

25. See, for example, Gabriele Boccaccini, "Tigranes the Great as 'Nebuchadnezzar' in the Book of Judith," in *A Pious Seductress: Studies in the Book of Judith*, ed. Géza G. Xeravits (Berlin: de Gruyter, 2012), 55–69.

Genre and Structure

Judith has a veneer of historicity and yet is not historical. As a work of fiction, Judith can best be categorized as a Jewish novella akin to other Jewish and non-Jewish stories that arose in the Hellenistic era. Suggesting a more narrow definition, such as folktale, apocalypse, poetic allegory, didactic short story, legend, paradigmatic history, or a type of wisdom literature, does not contribute significantly to interpretation.

The structure of the book, as we have seen, divides into two sections. The first half (chaps. 1–7), a narrative of kings and conquests, features male characters engaged in military battles. Armies of mercenaries conquer fantastically fortified cities. Kings and generals swagger. Tens of thousands of civilians—men, women, children—are slaughtered or enslaved to appease wounded egos. These chapters tell the tale of toxic masculinity run amok. The second half (chaps. 8–16) is a story on a smaller scale, the story of Judith herself. When she finally appears in the book that bears her name (Jdt 8:1), she becomes the center of the narrative. Judith, the widow, triumphs over generals and kings, in a complete inversion of the book's first half. Some scholars have suggested that the two halves were not written together as a unified whole; alternatively, some have argued that the author wrote an imbalanced narrative, a much too long introduction before getting to the real action.[26] Toni Craven has demonstrated definitively, however, that the two sections are linked linguistically and thematically.[27] More than just a long and slow (and, for some, boring) setup for a dramatic entrance by the book's heroine, the first half is essential to the larger project. Repetitions, chiasms, and other carefully constructed correspondences between the two sections demonstrate their complementarity even as they articulate one of the work's larger theological claims: the first half presents Nebuchadnezzar as one claiming to be a god, whereas the second half makes the argument for God's supremacy. In the end, God's agent Judith triumphs over Nebuchadnezzar's agent Holofernes.

The book has a unified structure, carefully and intricately constructed. Achior the Ammonite plays a pivotal role not only in the book's plot but also in its structure and theology. His appearances knit the two halves of

26. See Toni Craven, *Artistry and Faith in the Book of Judith* (Chico, CA: Scholars Press, 1983), 56–58, for a survey of these arguments.

27. Toni Craven, "Artistry and Faith in the Book of Judith," *Semeia* 8 (1977): 75–101; *Artistry and Faith*.

the book together. Achior begins in the Assyrian camp and is the first to voice the theology of the book in his address to Holofernes; Holofernes expels him, and the Bethulians take him in. Judith begins in Bethulia and is the second to voice the book's theology in her address to her town's elders; she leaves Bethulia and is taken into the Assyrian camp. Together Achior's and Judith's movements mirror each other. They come together at the end when Judith reveals Holofernes's head to Achior and he accepts circumcision. Achior and Judith not only share the same theology; together they demonstrate important aspects of the text's construction of gender and ethnicity. In mirror image to one another, both defy expectations of masculinity and femininity, Israelite and foreigner.

Like many other studies, feminist commentary also is eager to skip quickly to Judith. For example, the entry on Judith in the *Women's Bible Commentary* treats chapters 1–7 in one section of two paragraphs, compared to five sections that fill over three pages devoted to chapters 8–16;[28] the vast majority of feminist essays on the book are about the character of Judith. Feminist analysis need not be limited, however, to attention to female characters; rather, feminist questions can be asked about any character and any scenario. Following the path established by Craven's scholarship—a work of rhetorical criticism although Craven also self-identifies as a feminist interpreter[29]—this commentary will treat Judith as a balanced work, giving near-equal consideration to the first chapters as to the last. Not only is equal attention to all of Judith necessary for a full understanding of the theological themes (as Craven argues), but it is also needed for a full understanding of the text's presentations of gender and power.

Canonization and Language

Questions about canonization perpetually swirl around the book of Judith. The narrative is so steeped in scriptural reference and so orthodox in its theology that it seems a perfect candidate for inclusion in the Bible. Yet, as mentioned above, it is currently absent from the Jewish and Protestant canons and accepted into the Catholic and Orthodox canons as a book of deuterocanonical status. Today when one opens a Bible, Judith

28. Denise Dombkowski Hopkins, "Judith," in *Women's Bible Commentary*, ed. Carol A. Newsom, Sharon H. Ringe, and Jacqueline E. Lapsley, 3rd ed. (Louisville: Westminster John Knox, 2012), 386–90.

29. Craven, *Artistry and Faith*, 121.

can be found only in Catholic Bibles (NJB and NABRE, for example), Orthodox Bibles, and comprehensive study Bibles that include the Apocrypha (HarperCollins Study Bible, for example). Other translations of the Scripture prepared by and for Jews or Protestants do not contain the book at all (JPS or NIV, for example). It seems that the question "What to do with Judith?" was not asked first in a feminist context by Pamela Milne[30] but instead has been a recurring query posed when the contours of the canon are established and reestablished.

Evidence from the Septuagint, the Dead Sea Scrolls, and the New Testament indicates that, by the first century CE, a core collection of Jewish Scripture comprised of the Torah, the historical books, and the prophets was widely accepted (although the individual texts were not stabilized, as the various versions of Isaiah, for example, so amply demonstrate). Otherwise, canonical boundaries were fluid and variable; different communities included different books; it is difficult to determine when sacred authority was conferred on a book or if it circulated because of a general popularity. In this environment, the book of Judith was canonical for (at least some) Greek-speaking Jews in diaspora communities. The process that resulted in the Bible as we know it today was gradual, not reaching its final stages until the first century CE, possibly accelerated by the destruction of the Second Temple in 70 CE or maybe even as a reaction to a developing Christian canon.[31] Whereas there are some rabbinic conversations preserved in the Mishnah about the canonical status of the Song of Songs and Qohelet, we have very little information about the process or the criteria used to set the boundaries of what would become the Tanak or the Jewish Bible. We do not know if the rabbis even considered the book of Judith for inclusion. Thus, any consideration of whether the rabbis "rejected" Judith must be tentative. Absence of discussion is not evidence of deliberate exclusion.

In general, it appears that the rabbis preferred the more limited Hebrew canon over the more expansive Greek one (i.e., the Septuagint). The principal objection to Judith, if objections were made at all, might have been that the text did not exist in Hebrew even if there were an earlier Hebrew version.[32] Judith is not present among the Dead Sea Scrolls and

30. Milne, "What Shall We Do with Judith?," 117.

31. See the discussion in Marc Zvi Brettler, "The Canonization of the Bible," in *The Jewish Study Bible*, ed. Adele Berlin and Marc Zvi Brettler, 2nd ed. (Oxford: Oxford University Press, 2014), 2158.

32. That Judith was originally written in Hebrew was the consensus for over a century, based on Anton Scholz's 1885 monograph. See Moore, *Judith*, 66–67.

is not mentioned by the prominent first-century Jewish writers Philo and Josephus. The absence of any reference to Judith in Josephus is noteworthy since Josephus produced many commentaries on biblical texts, including some that were not ultimately included in the Jewish canon. Josephus was particularly interested in beautiful heroines such as Esther, and he drew on both the Hebrew and the Greek versions for his comment on her.[33]

Those arguing for a Hebrew original (or that the LXX version is based on a Hebrew version) advance several arguments, the strongest being the presence of phrases that seem to be wooden, literal translations from the Hebrew. For example, Judith uses the biblical idiom "sons [children] of" to designate ethnic groups, not just Israelites but also at least ten others such as Moabites and even the "sons of the Titans" (Jdt 16:6). The author, however, could easily have imitated Hebrew prose. Craven was among the first to admit that she "was no longer convinced that we should assume a Hebrew original"; she considered instead the possibility that Judith was composed in intentionally Hebraic-sounding Hellenistic Greek.[34] The argument for Greek has gained significant ground in recent years.[35] The Wisdom of Ben Sira may be a helpful analogy, demonstrating the complexity of the evidence of language when examining texts that developed in multilingual contexts. Like Judith, this apocryphal book is extant only in Greek. According to the book's classical Greek prologue, however, Ben Sira's grandson moved from Judea to Egypt where he decided to prepare a translation of the Hebrew original. Here is an example of a Jew moving from an Aramaic-speaking context to a Greek-speaking context (presumably he could speak both fluently) and then translating a Hebrew text into Septuagint Greek. Ben Sira's grandson lived in the Hasmonean period, moving to Egypt in about 132 BCE. A writer familiar with both Hebrew and Greek could have produced an intentionally Hebrew-sounding Greek original in the Hasmonean period, a time of Jewish self-rule and national revival, yet one still taking place within a Hellenistic context.

Setting aside language concerns, many have speculated that the book's content could have precluded canonization. Although some scholars situated the writing of Judith in a Pharisaic milieu, these same scholars also

33. Gera, *Judith*, 11–12.

34. Craven, *Artistry and Faith*, 5.

35. For an excellent review of the argument for a Greek original, see Gera, *Judith*, 79–97.

question if the book is sufficiently compliant with Pharisaic ideology in the first century to warrant inclusion in the canon. Points of possible divergence include the presence of Samaritans among the people of Israel, the acceptance of Ammonite conversion, the absence of a *mikveh* (ritual bath) in Achior's conversion ritual, and the connections to the Maccabean material. Carey Moore, emblematic of this position, frequently references the "Pharisaic piety" of the book yet also concurs that it was probably not canonized because Achior was not immersed in a ritual bath.[36] In other words, the book is thoroughly Pharisaic until suddenly it is not. All of these arguments about what would and would not have been acceptable to Pharisees and their rabbinic inheritors are speculative, especially considering how scant our information is on Pharisaic belief and practice. Most of our information on the Pharisees relies on rabbinic witness such as the Mishnah, which was codified in the third century CE, hundreds of years after the time of the Pharisees. Such arguments also rely on certain Pharisaic stereotypes of rigidity, exclusivity, and legalism. For all of these reasons, it seems unlikely that the failure of Achior to immerse in water after he was circumcised (or any of the other supposedly anti-Pharisaic elements) would have resulted in exclusion from the Bible.

A recurring theme in this conversation about the content of the book is that Judith is somehow "too radical" to be included in the Bible.[37] Her radicalism is most often construed in relation to her gender—for a woman she is shockingly sexual, shockingly mendacious, and shockingly violent. She disrupts too many gender norms and threatens patriarchal hegemony.

There are several problems with this argument. First, it assumes that Greek-speaking Jews and early Christians, who did include Judith, were somehow more "enlightened" in their regard for strong women than their Judean, Hebrew- and Aramaic-speaking brethren. Second, sex, lies, and violence are hallmarks of some of the most lauded biblical heroines. It would be inconsistent to hold Judith to a different moral standard than, say, Jael or Esther. In fact, the Hebrew Bible contains a number of female characters who lie and/or use their sexual allure, and sometimes even sex itself, to achieve their goals—Rebecca (Gen 27), Tamar (Gen 38), Rahab (Josh 2), Shiphrah and Puah (Exod 1), Abigail (1 Sam 25), Ruth, Esther. A few even combine sexual allure with deadly violence. Jael (Judg 4–5), in words bursting with sexual innuendo, invites the general Sisera into

36. Moore, *Judith*, 31, 70, 86–87.

37. Craven's language (*Artistry and Faith*, 117) but many others concur with the sentiment.

her tent. She gives him milk, tucks him in, speaks soothing words—then drives a tent peg into his temple with such force it comes out the other side of his head and pins him to the ground. Jael's deeds are celebrated and inscribed in both prose (Judg 4) and poetry (Deborah's song in Judg 5). Like Judith, all of these women, through their lies and their charms, furthered the will of God. Sexual activity does not bear the same stigma in the Hebrew Bible that it would take on in later (especially) Christian theology. Indeed, in all of these cases, the women's desirability is seen as an advantage, perhaps providentially bestowed. Heroines in the Hebrew Bible not only *may* use their sexuality, but for many that is precisely *how* God uses them to be heroic.

Nor is there anything uniformly pejorative about women who best men. Women, certainly, are seen to be physically not as strong as men are, and they have fewer social options. For a man to be defeated by a woman was shameful. That is, in fact, part of the point of the book of Judith: the general is shamed (and more) "by the hand of a female" (13:15). Given the similarities among Ruth, Esther, and Judith especially (particularly a female protagonist who deploys her sexuality to secure a future for herself and all of Israel) and given that all three books lack explicit supernatural intervention by the deity, it seems unlikely that Judith was considered "too radical" to be included in the Jewish canon on these fronts.

Despite the many and varied arguments attempting to answer the question of Judith's canonical exclusion, the answer may be simply the absence of a Hebrew version and the relatively late date of its composition. We can easily imagine that the Greek additions to Esther would be more acceptable to a rabbinic committee than the Hebrew text—with her prayers, her keeping of distinctly Jewish dietary concerns, and her disgust at having to share the bed of an uncircumcised man—yet, these additions were not included in the canon. One can easily imagine first-century Jews reading the Wisdom of Ben Sirach—with its piety, lauding of the Torah, and resonances with Solomonic wisdom literature—and yet, this book did not make it into the canon either. That Judith was not included in the Jewish canon is probably only a function of its language and date, and it has nothing to do with any concerns over Judith's supposed radicalness.

Reception History: Gender and Power

The character of Judith has frustrated many interpreters. On the one hand, she is unflaggingly devout in her faith in God and her determination to save her people. She possesses laudatory confidence in God's strength and her own capacity to be an instrument of that strength. The text describes her, again and again, as a woman of real piety and courage, all virtues. On the other hand, she deceives, seduces, and kills. There are other assassins in biblical Scripture—Ehud, Jael, Absalom—but none (except maybe Jael) is met with quite as much interpretive hand-wringing as Judith. The more frequent concerns about her character seem to be because she is a woman.

It is difficult to pinpoint the beginning of feminist engagement with the book of Judith, in part because it is difficult to define "feminist." Casting a net that includes anyone arguing for gender equality, whether or not the Bible is their primary focus, Christine de Pizan briefly addresses Judith in her *The Treasure of the City of Ladies* (1405; also called *The Book of the Three Virtues*), the sequel to her masterwork *The City of Ladies* (also 1405). She writes, "It was said of the saintly Judith, praised by all her people: 'You are the glory of Jerusalem; you are the joy of Israel. You are the honor of your people. God gave you the strength of a man, with which you have labored because you have loved chastity.' "[38] De Pizan was also widowed when young and never remarried, so she may also have been influenced by a certain affinity with this biblical heroine. Her situating Judith's strength in the fact that she refrained from sex is not uncommon in interpreters of these early eras, especially Catholic interpreters, whether the author is considered proto-feminist or not.[39]

Judith's reputation began to tarnish starting in the seventeenth century when she was depicted in more seductive, less celebratory ways. For example, in a book titled *The Arraignment of Lewd, Idle, Forward, and Unconstant Women* (1615), Joseph Swetman, an Anglican Englishman about whom we know little more than this treatise, lists Judith as one of the many women who ruined important men by using their feminine wiles.[40] This theme of Judith as femme fatale outpaced more laudatory

38. Christine de Pizan, *A Medieval Woman's Mirror of Honor: The Treasury of the City of Ladies*, ed. Madeleine Pelner Cosman (New York: Persea Books, 1989), 182, as cited in Kathleen M. Llewellyn, "The Example of Judith in Early Modern French Literature," in *The Sword of Judith: Judith Studies across the Disciplines*, ed. Kevin R. Brine, Elena Ciletti, and Henrike Lähnemann (Cambridge: Open Book, 2010), 213, n. 1.

39. The early Christian church fathers lauded Judith as a "chaste exemplar" and a "triumphant liberator." Nicole Tilford, "Judith and Her Interpreters," in *Women's Bible Commentary*, 391.

40. Ibid., 393.

images of Judith so that, by the Victorian era, the image of Judith as a beautiful, sexual, deceptive murderess was firmly established.[41]

Feminist interpretation by self-identified feminists originated, largely, in the milieu of Protestant Christianity, and most early feminist interpreters did not address Judith. For example, Judith does not make any appearances in Elizabeth Cady Stanton's landmark commentary *The Woman's Bible* (1895–1898) although Margarita Stocker suggests that one can read Stanton's perspective on Judith through her interpretation of Jael.[42] If we do see Stanton's analysis of Jael as a cipher for Judith, a sentiment different from de Pizan's emerges. Stanton finds Jael "revolting," her actions more akin to those "of a fiend than of a woman."[43] As much of de Pizan's praise reflects wider trends, so does Stanton's vilification of Jael and, possibly by extension, Judith. Despite de Pizan and Stanton's diametrically opposed conclusions, in both cases, Judith acts in ways that are surprising *for a woman*, and it is this challenge to gender conventions that garners either acclaim or reproach. These voices also underscore just how complex the gender ideology in Judith is, for how is a woman supposed to act? Critics often do not have any clear idea about how to approach this dynamic character who is a sexualized assassin and also devoutly chaste and faithful.

Patricia Montley is among the first modern feminist exegetes of Judith, although she is a playwright, director, and literary scholar, not a biblical scholar. She does not approach the biblical story directly but rather examines the ways that literary works have used the Judith story. Instead of taking a stance at one pole of the interpretive tradition or the other, arguing that Judith is either a lying murderer or an admirable hero, she recognizes that Judith "is a character of ambiguous morals and motives."[44] Instead of treating this ambiguity as a flaw, she maintains, "at the heart of this ambiguity of character is the archetypal significance of the protagonist."[45] The archetypes that Judith embodies are, according to Montley, not only the woman warrior and the femme fatale but also and more important the androgyne. The androgyne is not just a figure who

41. Also see Stocker, *Judith*, 150–51.

42. Ibid., 145.

43. Elizabeth Cady Stanton, *The Woman's Bible*, part 2 (Seattle: Coalition Task Force on Women and Religion, 1974), 20.

44. Patricia Montley, "Judith in the Fine Arts: The Appeal of the Archetypal Androgyne," *Anima* 4 (1978): 38.

45. Ibid., 38.

defies any clear categorization of man or woman; the androgyne harks back to an "original totality" in the human imagination and thus connects us to gods, goddesses, and other primordial figures.[46] It is this participation in the androgyne archetype that makes Judith so attractive to artists and writers and musicians and, we would add, biblical scholars. She simultaneously embodies and transcends male and female, masculinity and femininity. In this way, double entendre and irony—primary literary devices in the book of Judith—are not just about the play of words and the surprises of plot.[47] These literary devices also are manifestations of ethical ambivalence and gender ambiguity.

Despite this strong argument for the recognition of moral ambiguity and gender confusion as a part of feminist reading, many feminist interpreters reproduce the dichotomies manifest in early understandings of Judith, seeing her either as a feminist hero, a "woman who fights with a woman's weapons,"[48] or as a "male-constructed character who functions within the limits of a patriarchal, androcentric context . . . the culmination of a trajectory of misogyny and gynophobia" in the Scriptures.[49] Pamela Milne, representing perhaps the most negative of feminist assessments, even compares Judith's act of beheading to the rash of terrorist beheadings in the twenty-first century.[50]

One of the most positive evaluations of Judith points to another angle through which to view her actions. Grounding her reading in liberation theology, Z. C. Narito argues that the book of Judith empowers powerless women to organize and fight against systems of domination and oppression.[51] To build a peaceful and just society, she argues, sometimes violence is necessary to achieving this goal. The book of Judith provides an ethical model for oppressed peoples—the weak can employ any means necessary to defeat the strong, especially when God is on their side. Narito demonstrates the power of Judith in Christian liberation ethics where

46. Ibid., 39.

47. For a survey of irony in Judith, see Moore, *Judith*, 78–85.

48. Elisabeth Schüssler Fiorenza, *In Memory of Her: A Feminist Theological Reconstruction of Christian Origins* (New York: Crossroad, 1984), 117.

49. Pamela J. Milne reflecting on her past work on Judith in "A Self-Response: What Would I Do with Judith Now?," in *A Feminist Companion to Tobit and Judith*, 139.

50. Ibid., 140.

51. Z. C. Narito, "The Book of Judith," in *Women of Courage: Asian Women Reading the Bible*, ed. Oo Chung Lee, Man Ja Choi, Sun Ai Lee-Park, Elli Kim, Mirza Rodriguez, and Debra Goodsir (Seoul: SaDange, 1992), 53–62.

a strict adherence to conventional mores is a luxury only the powerful few can afford.

A liberation theology perspective, however, reveals an additional ethical problem. Judith may be oppressed in relation to Assyrian military might, but she is in her own community a wealthy widow with enormous social capital. She is also a slave owner.[52] That she exhibits a high degree of trust toward her slave and frees her at the end of her life does not militate against the moral problem the situation bespeaks. It is perhaps the height of unintended irony that the woman who defends her people against the Assyrian's threat of enslavement does so with her own slave by her side.

Who is Judith—chaste exemplar, triumphant liberator, sexual warrior, femme fatale? Victim, perpetrator, or avenger? There is no single answer to this question. Instead, Judith is, in the words of Mieke Bal, "a locus of confusion, 'Judith' as a topos of thought and representation challenges so many of our most dearly held certainties."[53] We will see that Judith's character takes shape at the convergence of many different kinds of confusions, most especially gender and moral confusion. The confusion challenges many conventional categories. For this reason, she constantly surprises those who encounter her, both in and out of the text.

Is Judith a feminist text? Feminist interpreters are often divided in their answer to this question. Yet, we contend, with other feminist readers like Helen Efthimiadis-Keith, that unequivocally positive and unequivocally negative assessments of Judith "can lead feminist biblical interpreters to engage in the same meaning-closing endeavours as had characterized the androcentric interpretations we have been contesting." Moreover, "such meaning-closing endeavours flout the very feminist ethics upon which one could rightly expect them to be based, namely justice, care, autonomy, and the self. . . . [T]hey show a profound level of disrespect towards the text/s, the interpreters who write commentaries, and the various publics that such interpreters may have."[54] A feminist ethical approach will not necessarily calm the worries or ease the frustrations of readers; in fact, it may exacerbate them. Yet, this sort of reading will

52. Jennifer A. Glancy, "Judith the Slaveholder," in *A Feminist Companion to Tobit and Judith*, 200–211, is a notable exception to this interpretive silence.

53. Mieke Bal, "Head Hunting: 'Judith' on the Cutting Edge of Knowledge," in *A Feminist Companion to Esther, Judith and Susanna*, 266.

54. Helen Efthimiadis-Keith, "Judith, Feminist Ethics, and Feminist Interpretation," in *A Feminist Companion to Tobit and Judith*, 161.

entail the openness to difference, respect for multiple positions, and care for others that feminism demands.

Reading Judith

Feminist interpretation of Scripture has many dimensions and not all feminist interpreters agree, but all feminist readings share a basic commitment to the equality of all people. Therefore, our analysis pays careful attention to gender ideologies embedded in the story. We shall expose ideologies that promote inequality, such as stereotyping or the normalizing of violence against women. Ideologies that promote equality, such as the subversion of gender expectations or support for women leaders, are highlighted. In most cases, however, we find that biblical texts are a complicated mix of ideologies, and it becomes the feminist interpreter's role to assess the ways in which the varying ideologies interact. Such an enterprise is not just an intellectual exercise, but for the feminist interpreter it is a form of activism; textual ideologies are rarely confined to the pages that contain them but continue to have very real effects in the world.[55] Reading Judith matters.

In the commentary that follows, we will be reading Judith carefully alongside other interpreters; feminist, gender, and queer theories; and art and literature. We are also reading Judith alongside each other. We approach the text from our own perspectives as two biblical scholars with similar training and interests although different areas of expertise—Jennifer works mostly with Hebrew Bible texts and Rob with early Christian literature. We met in 2000 when we were graduate students; we began writing together a few years later. Now, we are married. Our work fully integrates into other aspects of our life, and so we have found ourselves talking about Judith as we are eating dinner or buying groceries or driving in the car. We do not, however, write at the same time. For this commentary, Jennifer wrote the proposal, Rob wrote the first draft during his sabbatical in 2017, and Jennifer completed the manuscript during her sabbatical the next year. We then exchanged sections back-and-forth as we have worked on refining our ideas and editing our text. Neither of us came to Judith through our religious upbringings; Rob grew up in Protestant communities, whereas Jennifer's background is Jewish.

55. See Jennifer L. Koosed, *Reading the Bible as a Feminist*, Brill Research Perspectives (Leiden: Brill, 2017), for a concise definition of feminist interpretation of Scripture.

We both first read Judith in the biblical studies classroom. Working on this commentary, however, has given us the opportunity to speak about Judith in many different religious contexts. We have had speaking engagements at the synagogue where we are members, at the local Jewish Federation, and at several Protestant churches. Those talks always end with someone asking, why isn't this book in our Bible? No matter the context, Judith is a story that engages and inspires, and we have enjoyed the time we have had with this intrepid character.

This reading is not a line-by-line commentary;[56] rather, we will read each narrative section as a whole. The first chapter addresses Judith 1–4, chapters describing Nebuchadnezzar's war against King Arphaxad and the nations to his west, culminating (from the perspective of the plot) in the threat to Judah. As in many war stories, these chapters are almost entirely about the emotions (the entire campaign is fueled by Nebuchadnezzar's rage [Jdt 1:12]), plans, and actions of men.

In chapter 2, focused on Judith 5–6, Achior the Ammonite who informs Holofernes about the Jews takes center stage. Much like Rahab in Joshua 2, Achior is the foreigner with a strong faith in the God of Israel and in God's covenant with the Jewish people. Achior, exiled from the Assyrian camp and eventually fully received into the Israelite side through circumcision, offers a site for masculinity studies and an opportunity to study ethnicity and nationalism in the book of Judith.

Chapter 3 covers Judith 7–9. The town is on the verge of surrender when, finally, Judith is introduced. Judith is introduced like no other biblical heroine, with an extended genealogy. Judith proceeds to deliver a rousing speech—pious, patriotic, and courageous—to the magistrates and citizens of Bethulia. She ends by proclaiming that she is going to do something about the siege and that God will work through her to overcome their enemies. After she gets the blessing of the magistrates to do as she will, she turns her attention to God and offers a prayer, also pious, patriotic, and courageous. This chapter begins the analysis of the character of Judith, especially of her gender presentation and the way sexuality shapes both character and plot.

Chapter 4 addresses Judith 10–11, where the core of the plot finally commences. Judith executes her plan. These next few sections have received extensive feminist attention. Judith uses her feminine beauty and persuasive speech to lull Holofernes into trusting her. In this chapter,

56. For an excellent line-by-line commentary, see Gera, *Judith*.

we engage questions feminists have asked about the text: Is the book of Judith good or bad for women? Does Judith break gender stereotypes; act with strength, intelligence, and independence; and hence provide a liberating role model for women? Or does the book reinforce patriarchal ideologies? Is Judith just another femme fatale who uses her beauty and sexuality in ways that are dangerous to, and ultimately denigrated by, men? Feminist criticism can, and sometimes does, destabilize the very notion of gender; queer theory, to which we appeal in this chapter, always foregrounds such destabilization. When Judith takes off her sackcloth and puts on beautiful clothes, she is demonstrating what Judith Butler calls gender performance. Through putting on the proper dress, jewelry, and mannerisms of "woman," Judith is demonstrating the very "unnaturalness" of the category "woman."

Another focus of this chapter is the role of Judith's unnamed slave. The narrative is replete with the rhetoric of slavery, with the threat of slavery, and with the use of slavery. Judith's slave takes many of the same risks as her owner does when she accompanies her into the enemy camp, but she rarely receives equal consideration in the commentaries. Judith and her slave may share the same biological sex, but their different class positions result in their embodying very different gender roles and expectations.

Judith's plot comes to fruition, and in chapter 5 we address Judith 12:1–13:10. Our heroine wisely uses her piety to establish a routine in the Assyrian camp that will ultimately let her escape after she beheads Holofernes. She cleverly uses double entendre to manipulate Holofernes into believing that she has consented to have sex with him. We examine the sexualized violence of this passage and continue to discuss the feminist debate about Judith. This chapter will also continue to build a queer reading by arguing that Judith plays the woman she is not (or is she?) in a form of drag. Because the scene of Judith cutting off the head of Holofernes is frequently depicted in art (especially in the 1500s–1700s), we will bring the paintings of Artemisia Gentileschi and others into the analysis. Many of these paintings also depict Judith's slave, so we will also examine the history of her reception in art.

Our final chapter turns to Judith 13:11–16:20. Judith returns triumphantly to Bethulia—the Jewish widow has protected the virgin/Bethulia by cutting off the head of her attacker. Achior and Judith come face-to-face, and her display of Holofernes's head compels him first to faint and then to be circumcised. The Assyrians find Holofernes's decapitated body, grow fearful, and run away. Israelites fall upon the fleeing Assyrian army, slaughtering them by the thousands; meanwhile others loot the abandoned Assyrian camps. The campaign ends in the glory of blood and booty. We will return here to the ideologies of masculinity, particularly the ways male sexuality is constructed and constrained and the ways male violence frames the story of Judith. Male violence is not, however, given the last word. In a strange phallic display, the women of Bethulia are given long branches; they then dance and sing and lead the men in a parade in honor of Judith. After three months of celebration, Judith returns home, refuses marriage, and lives to the age of 105. Finally, she sets her slave free, dies, and is buried with her husband Manasseh. Is this a final domestication of Judith or does she remain a dangerous subversive presence by refusing marriage?

In our conclusion, we return to the overarching feminist questions raised by the book of Judith, questions that include issues of ethnicity and class as well as feminist activism. Rather than make a final pronouncement about Judith's status as a feminist hero, we will continue to complicate the question.

As you read our work, you will be reading alongside other interpreters. Our commentary includes seven contributing voices—seven other readers whose views about Judith will be interspersed with the commentary proper, incorporating competing perspectives. Some of these interpreters are biblical scholars; others are not. Some have religious investments in the text; others read Judith as literature with no regard for divine inspiration or sacred authority. These pieces will sometimes complement what we write, and sometimes these pieces will contradict what we write. Feminist commentary does not speak in a unified voice; it is multifaceted and polyvocal because, at base, feminism is about the equality and the inclusion of everybody. Feminism and therefore feminist commentary reflect the whole human community. We are but nine people reading the book of Judith. We present our readings to you. Now, add your voice to ours. What do *you* do with Judith?

Judith 1:1–4:15

The Masculine Machinations of War

Nebuchadnezzar's War (1:1–3:9)

The book of Judith opens when the crushing cogs of global war (at least, war that encompasses the known spaces of civilization that the biblical text imagines) begin to grind as the result of honor and pride among a few elite men.

In the clash of empires recounted in the first three chapters of Judith, we hear nothing of the thousands of people whose lives were upended and ended during every battle. Soldiers, most of them civilians, expected to join armed conflicts whenever need arises, are a part of this nameless, faceless, voiceless mass, but the ravages of war are not confined to the soldiers who carry out the orders of these powerful and distant men. The violence spills out and covers the land. Men and women, young and old, soldier and civilian—all are subject to its destruction.

Thus is the logic of empire: the often-arbitrary decisions of a very few privileged men (and sometimes women) affect the lives—indeed, end the lives—of so many nameless people. Nebuchadnezzar acts initially because of his desire for more glory. When his interests are not supported by lesser kings, he acts because of his pride and anger. His actions consume people in Israel simply because they are in the way; their cities and nation lie along the easiest route for his Assyrian armies to get to their

Jdt 1:1-16

1:1It was the twelfth year of the reign of Nebuchadnezzar, who ruled over the Assyrians in the great city of Nineveh. In those days Arphaxad ruled over the Medes in Ecbatana. 2He built walls around Ecbatana with hewn stones three cubits thick and six cubits long; he made the walls seventy cubits high and fifty cubits wide. 3At its gates he raised towers one hundred cubits high and sixty cubits wide at the foundations. 4He made its gates seventy cubits high and forty cubits wide to allow his armies to march out in force and his infantry to form their ranks. 5Then King Nebuchadnezzar made war against King Arphaxad in the great plain that is on the borders of Ragau. 6There rallied to him all the people of the hill country and all those who lived along the Euphrates, the Tigris, and the Hydaspes, and, on the plain, Arioch, king of the Elymeans. Thus, many nations joined the forces of the Chaldeans.

7Then Nebuchadnezzar, king of the Assyrians, sent messengers to all who lived in Persia and to all who lived in the west, those who lived in Cilicia and Da-

victims. Nebuchadnezzar is not a god, but for the tens of thousands of people whose lives he irrevocably altered, without ever having seen or known them, he may as well have been.

Nebuchadnezzar's Campaign against Arphaxad (1:1-16)

Nebuchadnezzar was the ferocious emperor of the Babylonians, responsible for the destruction of the temple and the subsequent exile of thousands of Judeans in 586 BCE; he was not, contrary to the opening verse of the book, the emperor of the Assyrians involved in a campaign against the Israelites after their return from exile (see Achior's speech, which recounts the exile and the return in 5:19). Nineveh, "the great city," was the capital of the Assyrian Empire built up by Sennacherib during his reign (705–681 BCE) but destroyed by Nebuchadnezzar's father Nabopolassar in 612 BCE. Nineveh was a notorious watchword in the ancient Near East, a shorthand for brutality (for example, the entire book of Nahum is an oracle against Nineveh, especially 3:1, 19; Nineveh is also Jonah's focus). Even though Nebuchadnezzar and Nineveh are not historically linked, here they are brought together as if Hitler ruled over the gulag. Ecbatana was a grand city and the Median capital, but Arphaxad is otherwise unattested. The author of Judith could not be more clear that what follows is a work of fiction; it is as if the book began with the opening, "Once upon a time . . ."

mascus, Lebanon and Antilebanon, and all who lived along the seacoast, [8]and those among the nations of Carmel and Gilead, and Upper Galilee and the great plain of Esdraelon, [9]and all who were in Samaria and its towns, and beyond the Jordan as far as Jerusalem and Bethany and Chelous and Kadesh and the river of Egypt, and Tahpanhes and Raamses and the whole land of Goshen, [10]even beyond Tanis and Memphis, and all who lived in Egypt as far as the borders of Ethiopia. [11]But all who lived in the whole region disregarded the summons of Nebuchadnezzar, king of the Assyrians, and refused to join him in the war; for they were not afraid of him, but regarded him as only one man. So they sent back his messengers empty-handed and in disgrace.

[12]Then Nebuchadnezzar became very angry with this whole region, and swore by his throne and kingdom that he would take revenge on the whole territory of Cilicia and Damascus and Syria, that he would kill with his sword also all the inhabitants of the land of Moab, and the people of Ammon, and

The author continues to build the fantasyland, brick by brick. The hewn stone walls of Ecbatana are magnificent but not historical. Although ancient Ecbatana has not been carefully excavated since it is still inhabited (the contemporary city is called Hamadan and is located in Iran), there are no signs of such great fortifications. Herodotus tells of elaborate and colorful concentric walls that ringed the city, built by Deioces in about 700 BCE, but these may be as fictional as Ecbatana's walls in Judith. Apparently, descriptions of Ecbatana were prone to exaggeration.[1] The purpose of the construction details in verses 2-4 is not to provide historical data but to inspire awe and set up a contrast. King Arphaxad had great power and wealth; his cities were impressively fortified and his armies terrible. Yet, Nebuchadnezzar will defeat him. How do the little provinces of Samaria and Judea stand a chance? The more awesome Arphaxad's forces are, the more fearsome Nebuchadnezzar.

"Then King Nebuchadnezzar made war against King Arphaxad" (1:3); their armies clashed on the plain bordering Ragau, with all the neighboring peoples joining the Assyrian forces. Next, Nebuchadnezzar summons to the fight all the peoples in the west—from Lebanon to Jerusalem, from Egypt to Ethiopia. The book is replete with geographic details, but much like its historical challenges, it has geographical inconsistencies and inaccuracies

1. Deborah Levine Gera, *Judith*, CEJL (Berlin: de Gruyter, 2014), 118–19.

Jdt 1:1-16 (cont.)

all Judea, and every one in Egypt, as far as the coasts of the two seas.

[13]In the seventeenth year he led his forces against King Arphaxad and defeated him in battle, overthrowing the whole army of Arphaxad and all his cavalry and all his chariots. [14]Thus he took possession of his towns and came to Ecbatana, captured its towers, plundered its markets, and turned its glory to disgrace. [15]He captured Arphaxad in the mountains of Ragau and struck him down with his spears, thus destroying him once and for all. [16]Then he returned to Nineveh, he and all his combined forces, a vast body of troops; and there he and his forces rested and feasted for one hundred twenty days.

as well. Just as what appear to be historical "facts" are often fictions, so too are many of the geographic particulars because the author is pursuing goals other than topographical accuracy. Although the contours are correct, there are numerous questions about the precise location of the place names listed in verses 7-10. The larger point nevertheless obtains: Nebuchadnezzar has influence over a great sweep of territory. Already in ten short verses, almost every conceivable type of feature—hills, rivers, plains, seacoasts—is named. All are under Nebuchadnezzar's dominion. Or, at least, so he thinks. He attempts to rally this vast and variegated area with all of its peoples to his cause. They do not, however, rally. Instead, they "refuse to join him" (literally: "disregard his word"). In the Hebrew texts of the Bible, this phrase is used only in relation to God or God's messengers (Num 15:31; 2 Sam 12:9; 2 Kings 19:21).[2] Considering the author's biblical literacy, the phrase here could be the first instance of one the primary themes of the book: the competition between God and Nebuchadnezzar, between the God of Israel and the man who would be proclaimed god of all the world.

Nebuchadnezzar, with his divine aspirations, expected his word to command multitudes. Yet, people refuse to join his war because they do not fear him. The implication is that he is not a god; he is only a man, and not as much of a man as he thinks. His messengers return in disgrace and Nebuchadnezzar rages (1:11-12). Although the entire episode and the subsequent action it compels can be understood as the opening sally in the rivalry between God and Nebuchadnezzar, we also recognize how the plot is predicated on emotions (fear, anger, shame) all deeply embedded in ideologies of masculinity.

2. Ibid., 127.

The Assyrian Army

For the first fourteen chapters in the book of Judith, the Assyrian army is synonymous with invincibility, brutality, ruthlessness, devastation, terror, and unprecedented victories.[3] That changes suddenly in the last two chapters. How, then, in the final analysis, is the Assyrian army remembered? The answer is terse: it is remembered ignominiously and with ridicule. The story of its fall proves fascinating.

As a vast secondary character, the army serves as a nameless, limitless crowd of faces, tents, and weapons. In literary terms, its thousands function as a unit.[4] The army, however, is a flat, static, one-dimensional character because it does not develop or change during the story.[5] The Assyrian army functions well as a killing, burning, and looting machine.

And the majority of the chapters of the book of Judith provide overwhelming textual verification that the Assyrians deserve their world renown as skilled killers. This army knows well how to slaughter, pillage, and loot; it prefers to leave no survivors.

The vast Assyrian army—numbering at first 120,000 and then ballooning to 170,000 (Jdt 2:15, 7:2)—successfully slashes and smashes its way west from Nineveh. In a cut-and-burn pattern, the Assyrian army seems to have zigzagged its way in record time from Nineveh to the Great Sea. But the narrator records an impossibility. From Nineveh, Holofernes's army travels three hundred miles in three days to Bectileth (Jdt 2:21)! Furthermore, this impossible feat takes place on foot!

Why does the narrator offer this? Possible explanations are these: the narrator does not know geography or cities, or the narrator is confused, or the verses are out of order.[6]

I offer another view: I think the narrator presents this impossibility as humor, as yet another indication that the book of Judith is not an accurate historical tale but a moral folk tale.

Robin Gallaher Branch

3. The army is an agent of physical conflict; see Joseph Lostracco and George Wilkerson, *Analyzing Short Stories*, 7th rev. ed. (Dubuque, IA: KendallHunt, 2008), 19.

4. Robin Gallaher Branch and Pierre Jordaan, "The Significance of Secondary Characters in Susanna, Judith and the Additions to Esther in the Septuagint," *Acta Patristica et Byzantina* 20 (2009): 402.

5. Lostracco and Wilkerson, *Analyzing Short Stories*, 14.

6. Carey A. Moore, *Judith*, AB 40 (Garden City, NY: Doubleday, 1985), 137.

The importance of masculinity to the characterizations and the plot of Judith is signaled by people's response to Nebuchadnezzar's martial summons. Nebuchadnezzar is "one man" (1:11), and the word "man" (ἀνήρ) thrusts us into an analysis of men and masculinity in the text and in the world that produced the text. "Masculinity" describes the ways in which any given culture defines and delimits the proper behavior of a man; as one part of a binary opposition, masculinity is always also intertwined with femininity—the ways in which any given culture defines and delimits the proper behavior of a woman. There is never a single version of masculinity (or femininity) in any given culture; rather, masculinities are differently defined depending on other identity positions (race, religion, ethnicity, class) as well as dominant and subordinate masculinities.

Feminist interpretation has always analyzed the ideologies of femininity but generally has regarded men only insofar as they relate to the women; hence, the nearly nonexistent feminist analysis of the book of Judith's first seven chapters. Whereas this focus on women provides a necessary corrective in the history of biblical interpretation, ultimately women and femininity can be understood only with equal attention to men and masculinity. In addition, feminist scholars risk reinscribing some of the very ideas they critique when they look only at women in discussions of gender and sexuality; without an equal and concomitant examination of masculinity, men will still emerge as the neutral party against which all others are defined. For these reasons and more, feminist interpreters do well also to employ the lens of masculinity studies.[7]

The context of war is essential to the constructions of gender that the book of Judith presents. As Caryn Reeder summarizes:

> A particularly influential construction of masculinity, and thus also femininity, in the Greco-Roman world was shaped by warfare. From Homer to Polybius to Tacitus and beyond, to be a man meant to face the enemy and fight with courage. Alternatively, being a woman (or womanish) was equated with inactivity and cowardice. Men fought while women remained in the home, weaving, weeping, and waiting for the men to return. This conception of masculinity and femininity

7. For more on the importance of masculinity studies for feminist interpretation, see Jennifer L. Koosed, "Moses, Feminism, and the Male Subject," in *The Bible and Feminism: Remapping the Field*, ed. Yvonne Sherwood (New York: Oxford University Press, 2018), 223–39. See also Rhiannon Graybill, *Are We Not Men? Unstable Masculinity in the Hebrew Prophets* (New York: Oxford University Press, 2016), 11–12.

> reflected the broader gender dichotomies of the Greco-Roman world. Men had the power, and thus enacted the violence of war; women and womanish men were powerless victims of that violence. As a result of this construction of gender, warfare itself became gendered. The victors won recognition as real men—but the defeated were emasculated, denigrated to the level of "women."[8]

The equation between masculinity and war (and martial defeat with failed masculinity) is also clear in the Hebrew Bible and other ancient Near Eastern texts.[9] In these contexts, Nebuchadnezzar is the representation of hegemonic masculinity, a sociological term that names the ideal form of masculinity, the one that ranks above all other gender expressions, in any given culture. As the emperor and commander of the army, Nebuchadnezzar is the most powerful man in his male-dominated society. By the end of chapter 1, he will have defeated the Medes even with their extraordinary martial array and Ecbatana's imposing fortifications. The narrator recounts the victory as if Nebuchadnezzar alone were responsible. At the beginning of verse 13 we hear of the king and "his forces," but the plural soon slips into the singular: "Thus *he* took possession of his towns and came to Ecbatana, captured its towers, plundered its markets, and turned its glory into disgrace" (1:14; emphasis ours). The battles against Arphaxad culminate with the Median king's own capture and death, seemingly, again, at the hands of Nebuchadnezzar alone: "He captured Arphaxad in the mountains of Ragae and struck him down with his spears, thus destroying him once and for all" (1:15). Nebuchadnezzar appears to absorb his entire army into himself—collapsing the many into a single masculine pronoun. The image is of terrifying strength and overwhelming violence that consumes everything in its wake. This is what it means to be a man—powerful, strong, death-dealing.

It is, in fact, violence that defines, establishes, and perpetuates the male-dominated society in both the text and the world. Male domination is manifest not just in men's control over women but also in some men's control over other men. Just as the male-female hierarchy is maintained by violence and the threat of violence, so too is the male-male hierarchy.

8. Caryn A. Reeder, "Gender, War, and Josephus," *Journal for the Study of Judaism in the Persian, Hellenistic and Roman Period* 46 (2015): 67–68.

9. Harold C. Washington, "Violence and the Construction of Gender in the Hebrew Bible: A New Historicist Approach," *BibInt* 5 (1997): 330–31. See also Cynthia R. Chapman, *The Gendered Language of Warfare in the Israelite-Assyrian Encounter* (Winona Lake, IN: Eisenbrauns, 2004).

In these patriarchal systems, all men, but especially elite men, secure enormous capital. "In such a context, violence or its threat become a means to ensure the continued reaping of privileges and exercise of power. It is both a result and a means to an end."[10] In martial contexts, the violence is extreme: real men kill.[11]

Yet, to return to verse 11, even in this portrait of the apex male, a chink appears in the armor. The provinces to the west are called but refuse to come; they are summoned but refuse to be afraid. They call Nebuchadnezzar "one man" and so strip him of the multitudes he commands and leave him vulnerable and alone. Since Nebuchadnezzar can conquer only through other people's bodies, when those bodies refuse to comply with his commands, he has nothing. His power is not intrinsic or biological but instead external to him, constructed and conferred on him by his society. Likewise, his masculinity does not derive from some deep inner core of identity, but it is also external to him, in relation to others. Ironically, the hallmark of Nebuchadnezzar's masculinity is his ability to control multitudes, but since his masculinity is external to him, it is really, ultimately, out of his control.

Along with power and privilege, Nebuchadnezzar also has an immense sense of entitlement. The refusal of the western provinces to rally to his battle cry threatens his power as well as his sense of self. How dare they say no? Nebuchadnezzar responds with rage and the promise of death to those who disobey (1:12).[12] In the Hebrew Bible, anger is an emotion ascribed exclusively to God and men; women are never angry.[13] Writing in a contemporary context but in words that resonate with the Hebrew evidence, Michael Kaufman notes, "Many of our dominant forms of masculinity hinge on the internalization of a range of emotions and their

10. Michael Kaufman, "The Seven P's of Men's Violence," in *Men's Lives*, ed. Michael S. Kimmel and Michael A. Messner, 9th ed. (Boston: Pearson, 2013), 544.

11. Susanne Scholz uses the phrase "real men kill" to describe the men in the book of Judges in "Judges," in *Women's Bible Commentary*, ed. Carol A. Newsom, Sharon H. Ringe, and Jacqueline E. Lapsley, 3rd ed. (Louisville: Westminster John Knox, 2012), 119.

12. Herodotus's *History*, book 7, opens with King Darius of Persia smarting from his defeat at the famous battle of Marathon. As a result, he was "now even more full of wrath and more resolved to march upon Greece" (*The History*, trans. David Grene [Chicago: University of Chicago Press, 1987], 466).

13. Ellen van Wolde, "Sentiments as Culturally Construed Emotions: Anger and Love in the Hebrew Bible," *BibInt* 16 (2008): 14.

redirection into anger."[14] For an alpha male, most emotions are unacceptable, but rage is not only allowed but a marker of his dominant masculinity.[15] A man's rage fuels the fire of violence. Nebuchadnezzar vows, in language that positions him as the only actor, to kill every inhabitant of Cilicia, Damascus, Syria, Moab, Ammon, Judea, and Egypt (Jdt 1:12).

An additional component of this complex of masculinity, power, and violence is the concept of honor. Honor and shame systems were a part of many ancient Near Eastern and Mediterranean societies and play a role in the texts that these societies produced; these systems were also gendered. When Nebuchadnezzar's messengers return from the west, they are not only "empty-handed" but also "in disgrace" (1:11). The refusal creates humiliation—a particular form of masculinized honor is at stake. Issues of honor and shame will continue to surface in Judith as the threat to the temple is considered a matter of honor[16] and as military defeat is construed as emasculating and denigrating (see Reeder's citation above). Hence, the genocidal threat against the different peoples of the west is seemingly excessive, but it is actually commensurate with the threat the west's refusal represents. The entire patriarchal system with its gender ideologies and hierarchies is at stake.

Before Nebuchadnezzar can avenge his honor, he must first, through his proxy Holofernes, carry out the original military campaign, the one in which the west refused to participate. The campaign against King Arphaxad is a rousing success as the Medes are not only defeated but also "disgraced" (Jdt 1:14). The chapter ends with Nebuchadnezzar

14. Kaufman, "Seven P's of Men's Violence," 545.

15. In the Greco-Roman context, anger had a different gendered valence. By the first century CE, the hallmark of masculinity was self-control, and anger, even the anger of an emperor in a time of war, was unacceptable. Instead, women were understood to be prone to anger. See Colleen Conway, *Behold the Man: Jesus and Greco-Roman Masculinity* (Oxford: Oxford University Press, 2008), 24, 27, 163. As Stephen D. Moore and Janice Capel Anderson argue about 4 Maccabees (written in the first century), since self-control is an essential element of Greco-Roman masculinity, the king Antiochus's inability to rule his anger compromises his masculinity. ("Taking It Like a Man: Masculinity in 4 Maccabees," *JBL* 117 [1998]: 253–55.) If the association with masculinity and self-control predates the first century, Nebuchadnezzar's anger in Judith may also be a critique. In chapter 1, Nebuchadnezzar loses his head metaphorically; in chapter 10, his agent will make the metaphor literal.

16. Ellen Juhl Christiansen, "Judith: Defender of Israel—Preserver of the Temple," in *A Pious Seductress: Studies in the Book of Judith*, ed. Géza G. Xeravits (Berlin: de Gruyter, 2012), 72, 79.

and his men celebrating this victory with feasting (really, drinking) for 120 days (1:16). Real men work hard and then play hard. Then, as now, "power" is expressed by the ability to provide pleasure without regard to consequence. The excessive victory celebrations foreshadow the means of Nebuchadnezzar's defeat and add an ironic twist. The Assyrian victory is celebrated with drink; it will be drink that will bring the Assyrians down.

Nebuchadnezzar's Campaign against the West (2:1–3:10)

Sometime after the victory against Arphaxad and, presumably, after recovering from the hangover that would have resulted from four months of imbibing, Nebuchadnezzar decides it is time to fulfill his vow of revenge. The western campaign begins. This military assault starts in Nebuchadnezzar's eighteenth year, perhaps coincidentally, perhaps a subtle way of invoking for readers the real bloodbath the historical Nebuchadnezzar ordered when the Babylonians invaded Jerusalem, also in the eighteenth year of his reign (Jer 32:1; 52:29). The fictional Nebuchadnezzar calls all of his advisers together to plot the destruction of everyone who disobeyed him, a disobedience that all agree is wicked and worthy of the punishment of death (Jdt 2:1-3).

Holofernes is now introduced. He is the chief general, second only to Nebuchadnezzar, and he will act for Nebuchadnezzar for the rest of the book. Nebuchadnezzar commissions him with a long speech that echoes divine speech: "Thus says the Great King, the lord [κύριος] of the whole earth" (2:5). The speech is also full of graphic violence as Nebuchadnezzar paints a picture of world domination: "I am coming against them in my anger, and will cover the whole face of the earth with the feet of my troops, to whom I will hand them over to be plundered" (2:7). He declares this in an image that makes each soldier an emanation of his rage and his control—he sends the soldiers *and* he hands over their victims. The wounded will fill the ravines, and the dead will clog the rivers; the living will be captured and sent away to the very ends of the earth (2:8-9). Nebuchadnezzar ends by swearing, not by some other god, but by his own power and kingdom (as he will do again in 1:12). In biblical literature, there is no king who swears in a comparable way—the formula is used only by God (God swears by God's own life in Num 14:21 and Ezek 5:1, for example; God swears by God's own holiness in Amos 4:2).[17]

17. Gera, *Judith*, 145.

Jdt 2:1–3:10

2:1In the eighteenth year, on the twenty-
second day of the first month, there was
talk in the palace of Nebuchadnezzar,
king of the Assyrians, about carrying out
his revenge on the whole region, just
as he had said. 2He summoned all his
ministers and all his nobles and set be-
fore them his secret plan and recounted
fully, with his own lips, all the wicked-
ness of the region. 3They decided that
every one who had not obeyed his com-
mand should be destroyed.

4When he had completed his plan,
Nebuchadnezzar, king of the Assyrians,
called Holofernes, the chief general of
his army, second only to himself, and
said to him: 5"Thus says the Great King,
the lord of the whole earth: Leave my
presence and take with you men con-
fident in their strength, one hundred
twenty thousand foot soldiers and
twelve thousand cavalry. 6March on
against all the land to the west, because
they disobeyed my orders. 7Tell them
to prepare earth and water, for I am
coming against them in my anger, and
will cover the whole face of the earth
with the feet of my troops, to whom I
will hand them over to be plundered.
8Their wounded shall fill their ravines
and gullies, and the swelling river shall
be filled with their dead. 9I will lead them
away captive to the ends of the whole
earth. 10You shall go and seize all their
territory for me in advance. They must
yield themselves to you, and you shall
hold them for me until the day of their
punishment. 11But to those who resist
show no mercy, but hand them over to
slaughter and plunder throughout your
whole region. 12For as I live, and by the
power of my kingdom, what I have spo-
ken I will accomplish by my own hand.
13And you—take care not to transgress

Nebuchadnezzar never explicitly deifies himself; it is Holofernes who will later make such deification explicit. Nevertheless, the king does use language in ways that subtly imply his divine status. Holofernes's later declarations are not just examples of the enthusiasm of a loyal subject.

Nebuchadnezzar's last words in the book of Judith command Holofernes to be obedient, and his language again is reminiscent of God's ordering of obedience (2:13; see, for example, Num 22:18). He then retreats from the story, becoming a distant power whose will is made manifest through his agents. The stage is now set for Nebuchadnezzar and YHWH to commence their proxy war, battling through the actions of their representatives, Holofernes and Judith, respectively.

Holofernes, now center stage, prepares for war. Consistent with the book's historical and geographical inaccuracies, the author uses hyperbolic numbers for the retinue that follows Holofernes into battle: 120,000

Jdt 2:1–3:10 (cont.)

any of your lord's commands, but carry them out exactly as I have ordered you; do it without delay."

[14]So Holofernes left the presence of his lord, and summoned all the commanders, generals, and officers of the Assyrian army. [15]He mustered the picked troops by divisions as his lord had ordered him to do, one hundred twenty thousand of them, together with twelve thousand archers on horseback, [16]and he organized them as a great army is marshaled for a campaign. [17]He took along a vast number of camels and donkeys and mules for transport, and innumerable sheep and oxen and goats for food; [18]also ample rations for everyone, and a huge amount of gold and silver from the royal palace.

[19]Then he set out with his whole army, to go ahead of King Nebuchadnezzar and to cover the whole face of the earth to the west with their chariots and cavalry and picked foot soldiers. [20]Along with them went a mixed crowd like a swarm of locusts, like the dust of the earth—a multitude that could not be counted.

[21]They marched for three days from Nineveh to the plain of Bectileth, and camped opposite Bectileth near the mountain that is to the north of Upper Cilicia. [22]From there Holofernes took his whole army, the infantry, cavalry, and chariots, and went up into the hill country. [23]He ravaged Put and Lud, and plundered all the Rassisites and the Ishmaelites on the border of the desert, south of the country of the Chelleans. [24]Then he followed the Euphrates and passed through Mesopotamia and destroyed all the fortified towns along the

troops; twelve thousand archers; innumerable camels, donkeys, mules, sheep, oxen, goats; rations for everyone; gold and silver. These vast numbers of men, animals, provisions, and riches "cover the whole face of the earth to the west" (2:19), "like a swarm of locusts, like the dust of the earth" (2:20). It confounds the imagination to picture so many under the direction of a single man.

Holofernes marches these multitudes from Nineveh to the plain of Bectileth in only three days to reach the first victims of Nebuchadnezzar's wounded ego. Although Bectileth is unknown, upper Cilicia is not, and the distance from Nineveh to upper Cilicia is about three hundred miles—impossible to traverse in three days, especially for a massive army. Whereas some commentators see here proof of a corrupted text or the writer's ignorance of geography,[18] we find another example of exag-

18. Moore, *Judith*, 137–38, 145.

brook Abron, as far as the sea. 25He
also seized the territory of Cilicia, and
killed everyone who resisted him. Then
he came to the southern borders of Ja-
pheth, facing Arabia. 26He surrounded
all the Midianites, and burned their
tents and plundered their sheepfolds.
27Then he went down into the plain of
Damascus during the wheat harvest,
and burned all their fields and destroyed
their flocks and herds and sacked their
towns and ravaged their lands and put
all their young men to the sword.

28So fear and dread of him fell upon
all the people who lived along the sea-
coast, at Sidon and Tyre and those who
lived in Sur and Ocina and all who lived
in Jamnia. Those who lived in Azotus
and Ascalon feared him greatly.

3:1They therefore sent messengers
to him to sue for peace in these words:
2"We, the servants of Nebuchadnez-
zar, the Great King, lie prostrate be-
fore you. Do with us whatever you will.
3See, our buildings and all our land and
all our wheat fields and our flocks and
herds and all our encampments lie be-
fore you; do with them as you please.
4Our towns and their inhabitants are
also your slaves; come and deal with
them as you see fit."

5The men came to Holofernes and
told him all this. 6Then he went down
to the seacoast with his army and sta-
tioned garrisons in the fortified towns
and took picked men from them as
auxiliaries. 7These people and all in the
countryside welcomed him with gar-
lands and dances and tambourines.
8Yet he demolished all their shrines
and cut down their sacred groves; for
he had been commissioned to destroy
all the gods of the land, so that all na-
tions should worship Nebuchadnezzar
alone, and that all their dialects and
tribes should call upon him as a god.

9Then he came toward Esdraelon,
near Dothan, facing the great ridge of
Judea; 10he camped between Geba
and Scythopolis, and remained for a
whole month in order to collect all the
supplies of his army.

geration and error designed to invoke the fantastic. Geographic errors continue: the path of the army zigs and zags, crosses and then recrosses the Euphrates, approaches the coast from two different and mutually exclusive directions. As they go, they slaughter, burn, and plunder. Far from distracting a knowledgeable reader, the geographic oddities add to the campaign's characterization. This slaughter is fast and furious; it is also manic, as the army destroys everything in its frenzied path. The path of the army is erratic, just like an angry abuser lashing out in unpredictable ways. One emotion elicits another—the people to the west finally fear Nebuchadnezzar (2:28).

Judith and Columbus's Mistaken Journeys

Two verses from Judith make a surprising appearance in a compilation of biblical texts by Christopher Columbus, called *Libro de las Profecías*. In making a case to restore the goodwill of the Spanish crown to finance further voyages to discover a maritime route to Asia, Columbus began the production of an extravagant publication to prove the theological necessity for these voyages. Drawing largely on his medieval theological mind-set, Columbus equates the route to the east with gaining the economic wealth needed to finance the reconquest of Jerusalem ahead of the end of the age. Biblical geography provides Columbus with both the theological and the navigational arguments about maritime routes. From his reading of the Bible, Columbus is convinced that the "islands of the Indies" lie slightly west of Asia. He draws on Judith largely for its mention of "Tharsis" as reflected in the Latin Vulgate 2:12, 13 (Jdt 2:21, 23). These verses are among the several that Columbus piles together to prove his point that "Tharsis" is a city but mostly referred to as an island in the Bible. Along with Jonah 1:3, he uses Judith 2:12, 13 (Vulg) to prove it is a city.[19] Although there are several textual problems with these verses and newer translations do not regard Tarsus as the referent in this verse, Columbus's concerns here are to use ancient geography as represented in the Bible as incontrovertible proof of global topography. In doing so, he also is fascinated with the narrative of the king of Assyria's military conquests over a broad swath of territory. The wealth of the city and its geography are important for his argument. That "Tharsis" is a wealthy city, worthy enough to be pillaged by the king, proves his point of the necessity of the Christian imperialism he advocates to the Spanish crown. The picture of imperialism achieved by military and economic mechanisms pulls these problematic verses from Judith into Columbus's attention.

Steed Vernyl Davidson

To this point in the narrative, Holofernes is little more than an agent of his lord and king. He has yet to speak, and the actions ascribed to him are, for the most part, under the direction of Nebuchadnezzar. Insofar as he is Nebuchadnezzar's agent, he shares in much of the portrait of mas-

19. Delno C. West and August Kling, *The Libro de las Profecías of Christopher Columbus* (Gainesville: University of Florida Press, 1991), 243.

culinity derived from the king. Masculinity becomes a form of currency in this gendered economy. It can be transferred and traded in trust, even if it must also be carefully budgeted, secured, and maintained. Obeying his lord and in so doing receiving Nebuchadnezzar's masculinity, Holofernes becomes another example of hegemonic masculinity. He commands a vast army and so becomes the subject of a concentrated array of verbs denoting death and destruction. The actions were taken by his whole army, but the verbs are singular, as if Holofernes alone accomplished the deeds. In just five verses (2:23-27), he ravaged and plundered and destroyed and seized and killed and burned and plundered again and burned some more; he destroyed and sacked and ravaged and put all the young men to the sword. The sheer number of verbs furthers the construction of masculinity present in the book of Judith: real men command, real men act, and real men kill.

The people are afraid. They send messengers to Holofernes and prostrate themselves; they proclaim themselves slaves of Nebuchadnezzar and hand over to him all that they possess (3:1-4). The language is of utter abjection, even feminization. Still, Holofernes does not speak but responds with action. He moves down the coast, and the people meet him with celebrations, presumably because they believe that he has accepted their surrender (3:6-7). Holofernes is seeking, however, not just their subjugation; not even surrender can stop the rage of Nebuchadnezzar. The goal of the military intrusion is political submission *and* theological capitulation; all of the peoples' holy places are demolished "so that all nations should worship Nebuchadnezzar alone" and call him god (3:8). The contrast between the dancing people, playing tambourines and throwing flowers, with the army still not sated is startling. Again, Holofernes is the subject of a number of verbs of destruction: he "demolished" and "cut down" (3:8), "plundered" and "destroyed" (4:1).

Although not explicitly stated in Nebuchadnezzar's commission (2:5-13), Holofernes announces that he has been commanded to establish the worship of his king (3:8), which also elevates his own worth, for now he is second only to a god. In contrast to more typical polytheistic arrangements, Nebuchadnezzar is not one god among many but the only god (henotheism if not actually monotheism), a move that puts him in direct opposition to YHWH, who also demands exclusive worship (see, for example, Exod 20:2). Certain forms of monotheism lead to dualistic hierarchies that manifest also in the human community and foment violence against others. Hence, feminist theologians have approached monotheism with caution, offering both critique and correction. Monotheism can promote an all-encompassing unity that honors the diversity within; monotheism can promote an exclusivist doctrine that demands conformity and uses violence to enforce that conformity.[20] Especially dangerous is exclusivist monotheistic theology wedded to state imperial power, as we see here in Nebuchadnezzar's war, as we see in our own time with the rise of Christian nationalism in the United States.

The victory over the peoples of the coasts is complete. After this great victory, Holofernes and his men rest and resupply (3:10). Our attention now turns to the Israelites, who, for the first time in the story, are more than just another people on the list bound for destruction. Now, we hear their voices.

Fear is a powerful motivator, and the narrative is imbued with fear. As Deborah Levine Gera notes, "Almost everyone in Judith is afraid and acts out of fear."[21] Fear of the Lord is a biblical theme; it is a virtue that leads to righteous living, it defines the proper attitude one should have before God, and it includes such sentiments as awe and respect (see, for examples, Exod 1:17; Lev 19:14; and Prov 1:7). Nebuchadnezzar also commands an obedience born in fear, but this fear is contrasted with a proper fear of God. The plot begins with a lack of fear (1:11) that results in a failure to comply; the Assyrian response is ruthless violence. The military assault produces the fear that was initially missing. "Fear and dread" fall on all the people of the seacoast (2:28). Soon, hearing the reports, the people of Israel will also be afraid (4:2; 7:4). Imperial powers frequently use their military forces as a mechanism of control: "State terrorism [is] the intentional use or threat of violence by state agents or their proxies against individuals or groups who are victimized for the purpose of intimidating or frightening a broader audience."[22] This violence can be directed at people in other states or against the state's own people. The victims are the vehicles for "the communicative power of

20. For an early exchange about the power and peril of monotheism from a feminist perspective, see Marcia Falk, "Toward a Feminist Jewish Reconstruction of Monotheism," *Tikkun* 4 (July–August 1989): 53–56; and Lawrence S. Hoffman, "A Response to Marcia Falk," *Tikkun* 4 (July–August 1989): 56–57.

21. Gera, *Judith*, 127.

22. Richard Jackson, Eamon Murphy, and Scott Poynting, "Introduction," in *Contemporary State Terrorism: Theory and Practice*, ed. Richard Jackson, Eamon Murphy, and Scott Poynting (New York: Routledge, 2010), 3. See also Timothy Howe and Lee L. Brice, eds., *Brill's Companion to Insurgency and Terrorism in the Ancient Mediterranean* (Leiden: Brill, 2016).

violence";[23] a key element of Nebuchadnezzar's revenge is the terror that ripples out from the epicenter of his violent attacks.

Israel's Responses (4:1-15)

In chapter 4, the narrative focuses on one particular people: Israelites living in Judea. Nebuchadnezzar's horde has swarmed the hill country, conquered cities, and left desolation behind. The people of Israel hear and are afraid. They express their worry for Jerusalem and its temple; the threat of the destruction and desecration of their holy items terrifies them, and this fear is set in the context of their having recently returned from exile and reconsecrated their holy items (4:1-3). The focus on the reconsecration of the temple instead of the rebuilding that took place immediately after the return from exile may be another signal that the book of Judith was written in a Maccabean context. The language of "reconsecration" is similar to the language used in 1 Maccabees 4:38, which describes the rededication of the temple after the victory of the Maccabees over Antiochus IV. It is as if the return from the Babylonian exile (533 BCE) has been conflated with the rededication of the temple after Antiochus IV's desecration (165 BCE). The social context of Judith is the space where one lives after a hard-won victory over an existential threat.

The Judeans send word to the surrounding environs including to Samaria: "So they sent word to every district of Samaria, and to Kona, Beth-horon, Belmain, and Jericho, and to Choba and Aesora, and the valley of Salem" (4:4). This verse displays again the book's deliberate geographical idiosyncrasies. Out of the eight places listed, only three can be located.[24] While some scholars again search tirelessly for clues that would indicate their exact locations, others simply attribute the list to the author's fertile imagination. The mix of known and unknown, real and imagined, is an aspect of the author's approach to the fantastic. The inclusion of Samaria, and, even more, the positioning of Judith's hometown Bethulia in Samaria (4:6), is an interpretive crux since Samaria was a separate territory inhabited by Samaritans and not Judeans. Tensions between Judeans and Samaritans were exacerbated by the fact that their religious beliefs and practices were remarkably similar, but the Samaritans had their own cultic center (Mount Gerizim rather than

23. Jackson, Murphy, and Poynting, "Introduction," 3.
24. Gera, *Judith*, 172–74.

Jdt 4:1-15

4:1When the Israelites living in Judea heard of everything that Holofernes, the general of Nebuchadnezzar, the king of the Assyrians, had done to the nations, and how he had plundered and destroyed all their temples, 2they were therefore greatly terrified at his approach; they were alarmed both for Jerusalem and for the temple of the Lord their God. 3For they had only recently returned from exile, and all the people of Judea had just now gathered together, and the sacred vessels and the altar and the temple had been consecrated after their profanation. 4So they sent word to every district of Samaria, and to Kona, Beth-horon, Belmain, and Jericho, and to Choba and Aesora, and the valley of Salem. 5They immediately seized all the high hilltops and fortified the villages on them and stored up food in preparation for war—since their fields had recently been harvested.

6The high priest, Joakim, who was in Jerusalem at the time, wrote to the people of Bethulia and Betomesthaim, which faces Esdraelon opposite the plain near Dothan, 7ordering them to seize the mountain passes, since by them Judea could be invaded; and it would be easy to stop any who tried to enter, for the approach was narrow, wide enough for only two at a time to pass.

8So the Israelites did as they had been ordered by the high priest Joakim and the senate of the whole people of

Mount Zion in Jerusalem), priesthood, and Pentateuch. In a strange twist, then, Judeans call to Samaritans for help in defending the temple (4:5), and Judith the "Jew" lives in a Samaritan town.

The fragmentary telescoping of historical references in the book of Judith, and in chapter 4 in particular, reminds readers of Israel's multiple tribulations. Since the Assyrian assault, exacerbated by the Babylonian exile and beyond, the people of Israel struggled with issues surrounding community boundaries: intermarriage, conversion, ritual precision. Questions concerning who is (or is not) a part of the community appear in a range of Persian and Hellenistic literature (e.g., Ezra–Nehemiah, Ruth, Esther and its additions) and will reappear in Judith as well, as our heroine lives in Samaria, she keeps kosher, and the Ammonite Achior converts. In addition, the issue of profanation of the temple is neither a trivial nor distant memory to Judith's original community. Questions of God's fidelity and intervention in national affairs and problems around Israel's relationship to other nations continued to arise in the Hasmonean restoration. Judith's first audience was the inheritors of a land hard-won through armed rebellion, the purpose of which was to secure the liberties not only of self-governance but also of religious ritual. Many, no doubt,

Israel, in session at Jerusalem. [9]And
every man cried out to God with great
fervor, and they humbled themselves
with much fasting. [10]They and their
wives and their children and their cattle
and every resident alien and hired la-
borer and purchased slave—they all
put sackcloth around their waists.
[11]And all the Israelite men, women,
and children living at Jerusalem pros-
trated themselves before the temple
and put ashes on their heads and
spread out their sackcloth before the
Lord. [12]They even draped the altar with
sackcloth and cried out in unison, pray-
ing fervently to the God of Israel not
to allow their infants to be carried off
and their wives to be taken as booty,
and the towns they had inherited to be
destroyed, and the sanctuary to be pro-
faned and desecrated to the malicious
joy of the Gentiles.

[13]The Lord heard their prayers and
had regard for their distress; for the
people fasted many days throughout
Judea and in Jerusalem before the
sanctuary of the Lord Almighty. [14]The
high priest Joakim and all the priests
who stood before the Lord and minis-
tered to the Lord, with sackcloth around
their loins, offered the daily burnt offer-
ings, the votive offerings, and freewill
offerings of the people. [15]With ashes on
their turbans, they cried out to the Lord
with all their might to look with favor on
the whole house of Israel.

believed they had done the impossible—defeating the Greeks—only by God's aid, and that aid was bestowed on them because of covenantal loyalty. Yet, now that hostilities were over and Jewish rule restored, pressures of economic rebuilding and governance meant that some sort of negotiated space needed to be constructed between Israel and the other nations.

Jews living among those nations were wrestling with fraught questions of their own. Jews were building lives among pagans, entering a period of relative tolerance and economic freedom. Yet they needed to determine how best to maintain Jewish identity and their connection to the new Hasmonean state. Although the book of Judith is set in Israel, it reflects many of the tensions experienced in the diaspora.

Judean/Samaritan relations also find expression in Judith. The author places Bethulia in the territories of Samaria yet leaves all of the tensions between Judea and Samaria unremarked; these Samaritan territories instead rally to the high priest's call to arms. Rather than identifying the inhabitants of Samaria as somehow other—which is how both communities regarded each other ever since the Assyrian conquest, mutual hostilities evident in Ezra–Nehemiah, John 4, and Luke 9—the book of Judith assumes either friendly Samaritans or Jewish settlements in Samaria.

Alternatively, since the text never actually names the people who live in Samaria "Samaritans," the text may erase the Samaritans altogether by assuming everyone who lives in Samaritan territory is actually Jewish. Either way, the text asserts a unity that did not exist in reality.

The temple authorities and the high priest Joakim (4:6-7) devise the plan for saving Jerusalem, a plan dependent on this unity. The political organization this passage assumes, one where the high priest wields considerable power, resonates within the historical context of the Hasmonean rule. Priest-kings directed the people not just liturgically but also in terms of economic, political, and martial matters; a senate also made decisions and directed action (see 4:8). During the Hasmonean era, a ruling council (γερουσία), translated here as "senate," was formed, and it continued to have liturgical and political power until the destruction of the second temple (this group of men is also called the Sanhedrin).[25] In the book of Judith, the high priest and the senate in Jerusalem order the people to fortify the cities, store provisions, and seize the mountain passes to cut off entry to the plains. The people obey.

Joakim[26]

Joakim appears twice (Jdt 4:6-8; 15:8-10). A remote leader and a flat character in the sense that he does not grow or change during the course of the story, Joakim leads via letter from Jerusalem. Mieke Bal observes that narration presents a point of view, a certain way of seeing, an angle, if you will, on events as they are presented—whether historical, factual, or fictitious.[27] Here Joakim's letter presents a point of view of alarm, haste, fear, and worship. Although obviously not a soldier, Joakim does lead according to his skillset and vocation. He and others wear sackcloth around their loins, put ashes on their turbans, and cry out "to the Lord with all their might to look with favor on the whole house of Israel" (4:14-15). His activities dominate chapter 4. Joakim's genius as a figurehead is to lead an already religious people into national penitence and supplication by example.

25. Gera, *Judith*, 178–79.

26. This section takes material from Robin Gallaher Branch, "Joakim, Uzziah, and Bagoas: A Literary Analysis of Selected Secondary Characters in the Book of Judith," *OTE* 25 (2012): 57–83; see esp. 65–67, 79.

27. Mieke Bal, *Narratology: Introduction to the Theory of Narrative* (Toronto: University of Toronto Press, 1985), 100.

Weeks later, when the coast is clear and the Assyrians are routed and slain, Joakim and the Israelite council visit Bethulia (15:8). The text makes it plain they come to see for themselves "the good things the Lord had done for Israel, and to see Judith and to wish her well" (15:8). Significantly, Joakim and his delegation are unlike other men in the tale who, upon first sight of Judith, are struck by her beauty. The clerics remain textually silent about this aspect of Judith; instead, Joakim loads Judith with accolades reserved for Israel's heroes—and for God.

In my many readings of the book of Judith, I have wondered this: When all is said and done, is Joakim a coward? My musings and answers go back and forth. On the one hand, there is no evidence the people of Bethulia wished he were on site with them; furthermore, there is no evidence that he made any attempt to come until the Assyrians were defeated. On the other hand, while Joakim did not send water from Jerusalem to Bethulia, maybe that was impossible because of the presence of the Assyrians and the presence of the children of Esau and the people of Moab (7:8). Yet, it would seem that the Bethulians controlled some sort of access to the passes. What I found clear was this: In a siege, Joakim lacked the capacity to strategize or to plan an attack. Those are telling deficiencies in a leader. Joakim's gift seems to be the ability to pontificate, write orders, and make pronouncements.

The text, however, clearly validates his gift of pronouncements, for these pronouncements validate Judith. In one voice he and the members of the Israelite council bless and laud Judith. Note this singular honor: they come to the conqueror; the conqueror does not go to Jerusalem. Theirs is a public blessing. They give Judith accolades surpassing virtually any other person in Scripture, accolades that touch on those reserved for God: "*You* are the glory of Jerusalem, *you* are the great boast of Israel, *you* are the great pride of our nation! *You* have done all this with *your* own hand" (15:9-10a; italics added). Usually, God receives the credit for battle, and this does happen in 15:8. Elsewhere, however, as in the Song of Moses and Miriam and in Deborah's Song, all credit for the victory goes to God (Exod 15:1-21; Judg 5). By Joakim's decree, Judith and God share the credit in this story.

Robin Gallaher Branch

Fanciful geography in this chapter conveys levels of symbolic meanings. The passes described as so narrow they will permit only two people at a time (4:7) do not exist, but narrow passes are a feature of a number of Greek stories, including Herodotus's account of Thermophilae.[28] The town of Bethulia is called on explicitly to block these mountain passes (4:6). The narrative situates Bethulia south of Esdraelon and near Dothan, in the hill country of Samaria, strategically located atop a hill that controls the pass to Jerusalem. Bethulia is, however, an unknown appellation, and there is no known town that matches all of these geographical criteria. Bethulia seems best understood as a fictional town of symbolic import. The Greek "Bethulia" sounds like the Hebrew בתולה ("virgin" or "young woman"). Israel is sometimes called בתולת בת־ציון ("virgin daughter of Zion") in the Bible (2 Kgs 19:21; Lam 1:15 uses a similar appellation). It is not unusual for a city or state to be personified as a woman, and the designation "virgin daughter of Zion" carries connotations of tenderness and affection. In this way, Bethulia may also stand in for the whole people. The hilltop location indicates a place often associated with shrines and connection with God.[29] The symbolic virgin needs protecting from the Assyrian army, but she also needs to block her passes to prevent the storming of Jerusalem. The threatened violation of the community body through military conquest is figured as the threat to a woman's body through rape.

As they rush to follow Jerusalem's commands, we also see the people calling on God (4:9-12). First, "every man of Israel cried out to God" (4:9), thus establishing a patriarchal frame for what is otherwise a collective lament. Next, men with "their wives and their children and their cattle," Israelite and non-Israelite, paid worker and slave alike, clothe themselves in sackcloth, cover their head with ashes, and repeatedly entreat God for salvation. Finally, in Jerusalem, the people prostrate before the temple, covering the altar with sackcloth as if it too were in great distress (4:12). These verses recall the repentance of the city of Nineveh as described in the book of Jonah where the entire city— "human beings and animals" (Jonah 3:8)—fast and wear sackcloth to avert the destruction of God. Calamity is a great equalizer, affecting all living creatures alike, no matter one's ethnicity, class status, or species classification. Together they are all vulnerable bodies; together they all desire safety; together they all cry out for salvation. Again, though, the focus comes back to the men. The men express concern about "their infants" and "their wives," who will be taken away as booty to be raped and to be enslaved (4:12). They are

28. Gera, *Judith*, 178.

29. Toni Craven, *Artistry and Faith in the Book of Judith* (Chico, CA: Scholars Press, 1983), 76.

worried about the loss of their cities but also the loss of their honor as their defeat would be celebrated by "the malicious joy of the Gentiles" (4:12). The assault to family (particularly the raping of wives and the loss of children, presumably to be enslaved and therefore also subject to rape) is a breach of individual male honor, much like the desecration of the temple is a loss of collective (again, male) honor.

Chapter 4 in the book of Judith is setting up several of the book's ideological theses. The first concern is faithfulness and its relationship to God's promise of deliverance. The second is that God will use seemingly powerless people (in this case, a widow) to effect salvation. Judith presents an inversion of conventional authority and power, which is also an inversion of conventional, hegemonic masculinity as represented by the Assyrian king and general. Simply challenging hegemonic masculinity is not alone a feminist stance, however, especially if we understand feminism as addressing issues of gender alongside other important identity positions like class, ethnicity, sexuality, religion. The patriarchal frame keeps reminding the reader that free Israelite men, their cries and concerns, are really the focus of the story.

Our feminist lens, however, helps us shift our focus to bring other figures into sharper relief. We wonder about the slaves. They have put on sackcloth. Are they also praying that the wives of their owners be spared the degradation of slavery? There is an unintended irony created by the images of slaves crying out to avert their own owners' enslavement. The textual myopia over the issue of slavery is one of the issues that complicates the book's feminist legacy. We see a similar unintended irony in the lament of the cattle.[30] The cattle wear sackcloth, a garment made of the skins of other animals' hides, generally goat or camel, as they participate in the entreaties to God to prevent the death of their human compatriots. The priests then amp up their sacrificial schedule, offering "the daily burnt offerings, the votive offerings, and freewill offerings" (4:14), all rituals that involve the killing and immolation of animals in

30. Interrogation of the ways the human community treats the nonhuman community fits into the feminist purview, especially given the interrelatedness of environmental degradation, animal cruelty, and the abuse of women. See Carol J. Adams, *The Sexual Politics of Meat: A Feminist-Vegetarian Critical Theory* (New York: Continuum, 2015) for an analysis of how misogyny and animal abuse are impulses of the same patriarchy. Ken Stone's biblical interpretive work also focuses on the interrelatedness of gender, sexuality, and animal ideologies; for a recent example, see Stone, "Affect and Animality in 2 Samuel 12," in *Reading with Feeling: Affect Theory and the Bible*, ed. Fiona C. Black and Jennifer L. Koosed (Atlanta: SBL Press, 2019), 13–36.

order to get the attention of God. Thus, the cattle participate in prayers that involve the wearing of dead animals and the burning of dead animals in order to prevent not more dead animals but more dead humans (the ones who have been killing all the animals). Just as the Assyrian assault may not ultimately matter to those already enslaved (and may bring a grim satisfaction in seeing the slave owner become the slave), the Assyrian threat may not matter much to the animals either—they are dead either way.

God does respond to the people's entreaties. The book of Judith notes that God "heard their prayers and had regard for their distress" (4:13). Such notice is reminiscent of other situations where God hears and responds, for example, Exodus 2:23-25; Numbers 20:16 and 21:3; and Deuteronomy 26:7 (the later three examples all using the same phrasing in the LXX that we find in Judith). Unlike the situations in Exodus, Numbers, and Deuteronomy, however, where God's response is salvific action (for example, in Exodus God goes on to commission Moses and send the plagues), God does not directly act to bring about salvation in Judith. From this point on, we must infer God's actions, for God neither speaks nor produces any miraculous events.

After the note that God has heard, the narrative shifts focus to Joakim and the Jerusalem priests who, in their sackcloth and ashes, sacrifice continuously to God and continue to cry out. The chapter ends with another ironic moment since the people cannot know if God had earlier noticed their desperation, hears them now, or will act. The irony continues, as it does in the book of Esther, where the faithful reader, rather than the narrator, finds divine intervention in the plot.

Judith 5:1–6:21

Achior, a Different Kind of Man

War Council: Achior Speaks (5:1-24)

Chapter 5 opens with Holofernes learning of the Israelite preparation for war (5:1). What impression might battle-ready Israelites make on Assyria's vast army? These locals could not have represented any real threat. For Holofernes, the problems are inconvenience and dishonor. Nebuchadnezzar initiated the western campaign in order to preserve his honor and to punish dissident kings along the imperial borders. Holofernes is enraged (5:2) to discover resistance among the people of Israel, not because of any tactical concern but to preserve honor, punish disobedience, and spread terror.

Neither Nebuchadnezzar nor Holofernes had a grievance against the Israelites until they closed the passes southward to Jerusalem. The real motivation for Holofernes's anger—and the expression of this anger is the first time the narrative depicts his voice—seems to be Israelite impertinence. In fortifying their cities, these Israelites delay the inevitable and deny him proper deference. It is not the military threat that enrages Holofernes but, as with Nebuchadnezzar, it is the failure to fear.

In many ways, Holofernes here repeats Nebuchadnezzar's gender performance. Rather than naturally arising out of particular bodies with particular reproductive capacities, gender is culturally delineated and defined. We, then, learn to express gender through a complicated

Jdt 5:1-24

5:1 It was reported to Holofernes, the gen-
eral of the Assyrian army, that the people
of Israel had prepared for war and had
closed the mountain passes and forti-
fied all the high hilltops and set up bar-
ricades in the plains. 2 In great anger he
called together all the princes of Moab
and the commanders of Ammon and
all the governors of the coastland, 3 and
said to them, "Tell me, you Canaanites,
what people is this that lives in the hill
country? What towns do they inhabit?
How large is their army, and in what
does their power and strength consist?
Who rules over them as king and leads
their army? 4 And why have they alone,
of all who live in the west, refused to
come out and meet me?"

5 Then Achior, the leader of all the
Ammonites, said to him, "May my lord
please listen to a report from the mouth
of your servant, and I will tell you the
truth about this people that lives in the
mountain district near you. No false-
hood shall come from your servant's
mouth. 6 These people are descended
from the Chaldeans. 7 At one time they
lived in Mesopotamia, because they
did not wish to follow the gods of their
ancestors who were in Chaldea. 8 Since
they had abandoned the ways of their
ancestors, and worshiped the God of
heaven, the God they had come to
know, their ancestors drove them out
from the presence of their gods. So
they fled to Mesopotamia, and lived

interplay of our bodies and our experiences, with societal expectations and cultural ideas. Gender performance is the way we express our gender through myriad behaviors: gestures, dress, hairstyle, comportment, desires, occupation, emotions, relationships (romantic, familial, public).[1] Holofernes learns to perform a certain kind of hegemonic masculinity through mirroring Nebuchadnezzar's violence and rage, especially in chapters 2 and 3; Nebuchadnezzar establishes the script that Holofernes follows. But he is also his own agent, and as the plot progresses, we will see Holofernes augment the arrogance, violence, and rage he copies from the king. As with with any performance, the audience has an important role. Individuals must present a particular gender identity, but this presentation must be recognized in order to be complete. The other nations must recognize Nebuchadnezzar and Holofernes as men through obedience and deference, otherwise their masculinity—and all of the systems of power and privilege predicated on their masculinity—is at risk.

1. Judith Butler, *Gender Trouble: Feminism and the Subversion of Identity* (New York: Routledge, 1990), 22–25.

there for a long time. [9]Then their God
commanded them to leave the place
where they were living and go to the
land of Canaan. There they settled,
and grew very prosperous in gold
and silver and very much livestock.
[10]When a famine spread over the land
of Canaan they went down to Egypt
and lived there as long as they had
food. There they became so great a
multitude that their race could not be
counted. [11]So the king of Egypt became
hostile to them; he exploited them and
forced them to make bricks. [12]They
cried out to their God, and he afflicted
the whole land of Egypt with incurable
plagues. So the Egyptians drove them
out of their sight. [13]Then God dried up
the Red Sea before them, [14]and he led
them by the way of Sinai and Kadesh-
barnea. They drove out all the people
of the desert, [15]and took up residence
in the land of the Amorites, and by their
might destroyed all the inhabitants of
Heshbon; and crossing over the Jor-
dan they took possession of all the hill
country. [16]They drove out before them
the Canaanites, the Perizzites, the Je-
busites, the Shechemites, and all the
Gergesites, and lived there a long time.

[17]"As long as they did not sin against
their God they prospered, for the God
who hates iniquity is with them. [18]But
when they departed from the way he
had prescribed for them, they were ut-
terly defeated in many battles and were
led away captive to a foreign land. The
temple of their God was razed to the

Challenges to power are challenges to entrenched, elaborate and pervasive networks and to gender codes and norms, each presented as absolute and even natural. To defy these norms (successfully) is a challenge not just to political and martial order but also to the social and natural orders. The defiance of (as opposed to deference to) Holofernes, likewise, is a challenge to the gendered authority he represents. The Israelites constitute a minor force. To assert independence or to defend oneself against a more powerful authority is to attack the roots of the gendered identity of that authority, even implicitly "feminizing" those forces and their general.

Holofernes demands to know these people, their size, their strength, their rulers. He approaches the problem presented by their intransigence in the only terms he knows—political hierarchy and military power: "How large is their army, and in what does their power and strength consist? Who rules over them as king and leads their army?" (5:3). These may be important questions for a general to ask; however, they are not the most appropriate questions now, and they will not be answered, at least not in the way that Holofernes anticipates. He can see the world

Jdt 5:1-24 (cont.)

ground, and their towns were occupied by their enemies. [19]But now they have returned to their God, and have come back from the places where they were scattered, and have occupied Jerusalem, where their sanctuary is, and have settled in the hill country, because it was uninhabited.

[20]"So now, my master and lord, if there is any oversight in this people and they sin against their God and we find out their offense, then we can go up and defeat them. [21]But if they are not a guilty nation, then let my lord pass them by; for their Lord and God will defend them, and we shall become the laughingstock of the whole world."

[22]When Achior had finished saying these things, all the people standing around the tent began to complain; Holofernes' officers and all the inhabitants of the seacoast and Moab insisted that he should be cut to pieces. [23]They said, "We are not afraid of the Israelites; they are a people with no strength or power for making war. [24]Therefore let us go ahead, Lord Holofernes, and your vast army will swallow them up."

only through his own hegemonic masculine positionality. His questions reach crescendo as he notes the affront: "And why have they alone, of all who live in the west, refused to come out and meet me?" (5:4). His rage at resistance mirrors Nebuchadnezzar's rage at refusal (1:12), and both call a council to address the insult (5:2 and 2:2). During Nebuchadnezzar's council, only he speaks. In Holofernes's council, another man takes center stage.[2]

Studies that examine the norms of masculinity in the Bible and the biblical world have been growing in number.[3] Masculinity in ancient

2. According to Herodotus's *History*, Darius of Persia, to avenge his honor, amassed an army to invade Greece and Egypt. When he died, his son Xerxes took up the defense of the family's (and the nation's) honor. Xerxes subdued Egypt and then looked to Athens. Before invading, he calls a council of generals; Xerxes, seeking the benefits of more land, is also motivated by "honor, vengeance, and requital" (*The History*, trans. David Grene [Chicago: University of Chicago Press, 1987], 469). His advisers praise his plan, until Artaphrenes advises him to consider Darius's loss at Marathon. These Greeks, he says, are unlike the other nations. They are free and resolute. Further, "Do you see how it is always the greatest houses and the tallest trees that the god hurls his bolts upon? For the god loves to thwart whatever is greater than the rest" (472). Xerxes, enraged by Artaphrenes's council, has him exiled and proceeds with his plan. As in Judith, he fails just as his adviser predicted.

3. For a brief yet comprehensive review of the assessment of masculinity in biblical studies, see Peter-Ben Smit, *Masculinity and the Bible: Survey, Models and Perspectives*, Brill Research Perspectives (Leiden: Brill, 2017).

Near Eastern, early Greek, and early Roman society was often linked with issues of public display, honor, and deference to power, as we have seen with the Assyrian king and his general. Yet, masculinity in any given culture is not singular. In addition to hegemonic masculinity, the masculinity of the elite, cultures also produce a range of alternative masculinities. As a book written in the Hasmonean era, Judith emerges in the confluence of Hellenistic imperialism and Jewish nationalism; its cultural context is complicated and thus so are its gender ideologies. The Assyrian leaders represent a particular kind of masculine ideal, but it is not the only kind of masculinity in the book, nor is it triumphant in the end since the Assyrians will be defeated in a rout. When Achior, the Ammonite leader, steps forward to respond to Holofernes's questions, another kind of man takes center stage. As Ovidiu Creangă notes, "The presence of an alternative masculinity may have less to do with a subordinate man's difficulty or inability of embodying the hegemonic standard and more with the hegemony's partial rejection in certain strata of society."[4] Achior will present to the readers of Judith another way of being a man. In chapter 5, the dialogue between him and Holofernes is also a contrast in masculinities. As the plot progresses, Achior with be paired with Judith and they will work together not only to defeat the Assyrians but also to reconfigure gender and power.

Achior the Ammonite

The Bible identifies character in terms of words and actions. Achior displays heroic qualities. He exhibits bravery, courage, honesty, skill with words,[5] and a breadth of character that enables him to grow and change. Achior's character is first revealed in his long speech.

Stepping forward to answer Holofernes's questions about the Israelites, Achior presents a detailed assessment of Israel's history, the Israelites themselves, and their God (Jdt 5:5-21). Achior's account renders sound theological insights and reasoned professional and military advice. Both are surprising because

4. Ovidiu Creangă, "Introduction," in *Hebrew Masculinities Anew*, ed. Ovidiu Creangă (Sheffield: Sheffield Phoenix, 2019), 11.

5. His diction, his choice of words, in particular displays his character. See Joseph Lostracco and George Wilkerson, *Analyzing Short Stories*, 7th rev. ed. (Dubuque, IA: KendallHunt, 2008), 35.

they come from the leader of the Ammonites, the hereditary enemies of the Israelites who are descended from the incestuous union of Lot and his younger daughter (Gen 19:38). As a leader of men, Achior is a keen and trained observer. His life depends on his ability to observe his foe, and the foe often has been Israel. When Holofernes offers in open forum to hear about these presumptuous upstarts, Achior bases his answer on his observations over decades.

In essence, he tells Holofernes this: avoid these people. They have a mighty God. Only if they have sinned will they be defeated; only then their God will desert them. The consequence of this defense will be disaster for you. The Assyrian army will be defeated and become the laughingstock of the known world (Jdt 5:20-21). While Achior's tone and manner are measured and respectful, the immediate reactions to his speech are not.[6]

Achior's comrades will have none of it![7]

Perhaps playing to the mood of his commanders, Holofernes expels Achior (Jdt 6:10). Humiliating Achior publicly, Holofernes strips him of rank and command. Holofernes, already established in the text as a bully, openly shames Achior before his comrades and predicts his death by sword and spear when next they meet (Jdt 6:5-6).

Yet within days Achior's words hold true.

The character of Achior reminds readers that the book of Judith is a moral tale, indeed, a folk tale. If it were a fairy tale, Achior would somehow save Judith's life and they would wed and live happily ever after. But the book of Judith contains moral absolutes and as such showcases the character of God.

Robin Gallaher Branch

Achior is the leader of the Ammonite contingent within the Assyrian army. Ammonites have a long biblical history. The eponymous ancestor of the Ammonites is Ben-ammi, son of Lot and his youngest daughter (Gen 19:38). In other words, Achior is the descendent of a bastard who was the product of drunken incestuous rape of a man by a woman. It is unlikely that the Ammonites told this story when recounting their own origins. Rather, such a story should be understood not as historical

6. For insights on tone, see ibid., 49–60.

7. Narrative characters may view the same situation differently. See Mieke Bal, *Narratology: Introduction to the Theory of Narrative* (Toronto: University of Toronto Press, 1985), 105.

recollection but as Israelite insult (incest insults still carry power, hence, the sting of being called a "mother fucker"). Problems with Ammonites continue. Deuteronomy 23:3-6 precludes Ammonites along with Moabites from entering the Israelite community because of their lack of hospitality to the wilderness generation. Treatment of Achior's Ammonite ethnicity is thus comparable to the presentation of Ruth's Moabite ethnicity. Reading the book of Ruth against the backdrop of Genesis 19 and Deuteronomy 23:3-6, we find an argument for inclusion of Moabites by the Israelite community. We should proceed with caution, however, and not assume prejudices that are not clearly in the text. Although the book marks Ruth's Moabite identity repeatedly, never does it do so in a derogatory way. The same applies to Achior. In the book of Judith, his Ammonite identity is a neutral marker that takes on negative connotations only when we read his story alongside Genesis 19 and Deuteronomy 23. It is possible that the book is mounting an argument for the inclusion of Ammonites into the Israelite community; it is also possible that the original audience never considered Achior's Ammonite identity a problematic barrier to overcome.[8]

In this first of several long speeches in the book of Judith, Achior does not actually answer what Holofernes asked. From Achior's perspective, Holofernes has asked the wrong questions. Instead of giving the general the tactical information he demands, Achior reviews Israel's sacred history and asserts Israel's favored and protected status. The size and strength of their army is immaterial; what matters is their faith in their God. His review recollects that of Rahab (Josh 2:9-13, compare especially Josh 2:10 and Jdt 5:13), another foreigner who exhibits strong faith in Israel's God, even stronger faith than certain Israelites hold.

Achior begins by noting that because Holofernes's opponents "abandoned the ways of their ancestors" by rejecting idolatry and polytheism, the Chaldeans drove them from their ancestral home. Thus, they came to Mesopotamia to worship freely their one God (5:6-8). Although Achior does not name Abraham, we can hear echoes of his story, especially as it is recounted in postbiblical accounts. For example, in Jubilees, Abraham turns from idolatry and converts to the worship of the true God, thus he has to leave his home (Jub. 11–12). Leaving one's ancestral home and forsaking one's ancestral traditions is positively portrayed by Achior; he will soon follow the same model.

8. We will return to this discussion of Achior's ethnic identity in chapter 7.

Achior's review continues. Once the Chaldeans expelled the people and they settled in Mesopotamia, prosperity followed. Then, famine drove them into Egypt. Similarly, they prospered until the Egyptian king "became hostile to them" (Jdt 5:11). Hearing the people cry out in distress, God subjected the Egyptians to the plagues and, in response, the Egyptians drove out the Israelites. From Egypt through the wilderness and into Canaan, the Israelites drive out the inhabitants and take possession of the land (Jdt 5:9-16). After this buildup, Achior arrives at the climactic theological proclamation: "As long as they did not sin against their God they prospered, for the God who hates iniquity is with them. But when they departed from the way he had prescribed for them, they were utterly defeated" (5:17-18a). And then the historical review turns, for now Achior describes, without naming the conquering empire or ruler, Babylon's destruction of Jerusalem, the temple, and the subsequent exile (5:18a). Voicing the view of the Deuteronomistic Historian, he portrays the destruction of the temple and the exile as a consequence of the Israelites turning away from God. Finally, Achior states that when they turn back to God, God returns them to Zion. The phrase "but now" (5:19) suggests that this was a recent return (cf. 4:3).

There are several noteworthy features to Achior's speech. First, Achior mentions no patriarch, nor is Moses named. Neither specific heroes nor specific enemies matter. The focus of this sacred review is on the nation and its relationship with God.[9] Individuals serve only as instruments or intermediaries. Second, the absence of details that would anchor the review more firmly in history establishes a pattern of sin-punishment-repentance-restoration that is true in every era. Achior is speaking not just of the past but also of an eternal design that always obtains. Third, Babylon is not named as the empire responsible for the most recent disaster. There is a "delicate irony"[10] here as Achior recounts the very real destruction of Jerusalem by the historical Nebuchadnezzar to the proxy of the fictive Nebuchadnezzar poised to destroy the fictive Jerusalem. Fourth, Achior's review ignores the earlier Assyrian conquest of the north. In conjunction with the story's geography where Samaria is a seamless part of Israel, there is no division between north and south even in past histories.

9. Deborah Levine Gera, *Judith*, CEJL (Berlin: de Gruyter, 2014), 201.

10. Ibid., 215.

Achior has advice for the general: If we determine that the people have committed some sin, we may strike. If they are not guilty, then it would be foolish to campaign against them; their God will protect them, and we will be "the laughingstock of the whole world" (5:21). In his final statement, Achior does not worry about military defeat because of the horrific loss of life that would accompany such defeat; instead, for Achior, the worst imaginable consequence of a military loss to the Israelites is the humiliation the Assyrians will suffer. Achior thus ends his sacred review by expressing the same anxiety about humiliation that motivated Nebuchadnezzar and Holofernes. The Assyrians through Holofernes are headed for an even worse humiliation than Achior imagines because of the gender ideologies in play.

Achior's speech may not seem like a masculine performance in the same way that Holofernes's violence and rage does. Presumably, Achior is a strong military leader (he is the top Ammonite general), but it is not his martial prowess that is on display here. Rather, it is his intelligence and his persuasive speech. Nevertheless, his speech is a masculine performance, one that is "differently masculine rather than non-masculine."[11] In an early and influential analysis of biblical masculinity, using King David as the paragon, David J. A. Clines names such mental and verbal abilities as hallmarks of ideal masculinity in the Bible.[12] Brian DiPalma also focuses on displays of knowledge in his proposal that an alternative form of masculinity, one that was still powerful but not linked to martial violence, developed in the Persian period. Using the evidence of the court tales of Daniel (Dan 1–6), DiPalma names this form of masculinity "scribal masculinity."[13] Holofernes is strong and violent; Achior is intelligent and persuasive. In his courage before Holofernes's rage and in his speaking truth to Holofernes's power (albeit couched in deferential address), Achior presents an alternative model of masculine authority, one that relies on words instead of swords.

11. We take this phrase from Brian DiPalma's analysis of Daniel in the court tales. Brian Charles DiPalma, "Scribal Masculinity and the Court Tales of Daniel," in *Hebrew Masculinities Anew*, 231.

12. David J. A. Clines, *Interested Parties: The Ideology of Writers and Readers of the Hebrew Bible* (Sheffield: Sheffield Academic, 1995), 216–29. Clines also lists physical strength and violence, beauty, strong friendships with other men, the absence of women, and musicality as markers of ideal masculinity in the Hebrew Bible.

13. DiPalma, "Scribal Masculinity and the Court Tales of Daniel," 235. Notably, Daniel and his compatriots are also favorably compared to Nebuchadnezzar.

Many past studies have regarded Achior as a marginal figure, unnecessary and even distracting to the main action. Yet, scholarly consensus has been building toward a more robust appreciation for the many ways Achior contributes to structure, plot, and characterization. Building on Toni Craven's work, Carey Moore argues that Achior is "a crucial figure for uniting both sections of the book";[14] A. D. Roitman, who published the first detailed analysis of Achior, points out an "intriguing structural relationship and a subtle complementarity between Achior and Judith";[15] and in her Jungian analysis, Helen Efthimiadis-Keith even finds that Achior is the "effective protagonist" of the narrative and "the most important character of the book from a psychological point of view."[16] For us, Achior does not displace Judith as the book's protagonist, but his characterization and role in the plot does link him with Judith, as both Roitman and Efthimiadis-Keith argue. As Achior is contrasted with Holofernes in his masculine display, he is also "designed thematically as well as functionally as the mirror image of Judith, being a kind of double or 'alter ego.' In some ways, the Ammonite leader is the masculine/pagan version of the feminine/Jewish Judith."[17] Whereas Roitman suggests that this mirroring could be a result of the book's promotion of proselytism, we argue that an equally important facet of the pairing is the book's promotion of certain ideas about gender. Through contrast and concert, Judith and Achior present alternative versions of masculinity and femininity, ones that will ultimately defeat the masculinity embodied by Nebuchadnezzar and Holofernes.

Achior finishes his review, and the officers in the council erupt, as do "all the people standing around the tent" and "all the inhabitants of the seacoast and Moab" (5:22). Together, they call for Achior to be "cut to pieces" (5:22), or, in English idiom, "torn limb from limb." Achior's words have clearly not convinced anyone; they serve only to increase rage. The fate of the Assyrians and their supporters is sealed, and there can be no lingering question about divine justice. These Gentiles are

14. Carey A. Moore, *Judith*, AB 40 (Garden City, NY: Doubleday, 1985), 59.

15. Adolfo D. Roitman, "Achior in the Book of Judith: His Role and Significance," in *"No One Spoke Ill of Her": Essays on Judith*, ed. James C. VanderKam, EJL 2 (Atlanta: Scholars Press, 1992), 32.

16. Helen Efthimiadis-Keith, *The Enemy Is Within: A Jungian Psychoanalytic Approach to the Book of Judith* (Leiden: Brill, 2004), 406; see also 317–21 for a fuller summary of her position.

17. Roitman, "Achior in the Book of Judith," 38.

no longer ignorant of God or of God's redeeming acts and devotion to Israel. Although they have been informed, they still assert, "We are not afraid of the Israelites; they are a people with no strength or power for making war" (5:23). In their response, they return to Holofernes's original questions, which focused on leadership and military might, questions Achior never answered. Instead of heeding Achior's implicit warning—that there is no need to itemize their infantry because their faith is the true measure of their strength—the people assume that the Israelites are unprepared for the war they are bringing down on their own heads. Consequently, they will suffer the fate they deserve for their defiance; Assyria will devour them.

War Council: Holofernes Responds (6:1-13)

Holofernes responds much like the others do, with incredulity and anger. Now his question is not "who are the Israelites" but "who are you, Achior," to say such things. Holofernes also provides his own theological retort: there is no god but Nebuchadnezzar and so Israel's God cannot save them (6:2). His reference to Achior's "prophecy" calls to mind such Gentile prophets who speak Israelite truth to non-Israelite power like Balaam (Num 22). Like these other pronouncements, it is Achior's words that will come to pass, not Nebuchadnezzar's words, despite the insistence of his most loyal general.

Holofernes declares that the Israelites will be destroyed "as one man" (6:3). The Greek is ἄνθρωπος, which could be translated as "person" or "human." Yet, the translators seem to sense the underlying gendered nature of the national conflict. Rhetorically, the war is being waged on two fronts. First, it is a war about theological supremacy. Who is the real god: Nebuchadnezzar or YHWH? Second and related, it is a war of masculinity. Rhetorically, all of the people in Israel will be reduced to a single man, their collective masculinity reduced to the smallest fraction of the whole. In this way, they will be overwhelmed by the strength and violence (and manliness) of the Assyrian army.

Holofernes continues to rage as he paints the picture of Israel's horrific defeat: mountains drunk with blood, fields full of corpses (6:4). Such oratory resembles conquest narratives in Assyria (see, for example, Shalmaneser III's descriptions of military campaigns) and may seem like hyperbolic boasting; however, clashes of armies do leave piles of mutilated, bloody dead bodies. Holofernes's threat is real, even with its rhetorical flourish where he vows to erase the Israelites' footprints. He

Jdt 6:1-13

[6:1]When the disturbance made by the people outside the council had died down, Holofernes, the commander of the Assyrian army, said to Achior in the presence of all the foreign contingents:

[2]"Who are you, Achior and you mercenaries of Ephraim, to prophesy among us as you have done today and tell us not to make war against the people of Israel because their God will defend them? What god is there except Nebuchadnezzar? He will send his forces and destroy them from the face of the earth. Their God will not save them; [3]we the king's servants will destroy them as one man. They cannot resist the might of our cavalry. [4]We will overwhelm them; their mountains will be drunk with their blood, and their fields will be full of their dead. Not even their footprints will survive our attack; they will utterly perish. So says King Nebuchadnezzar, lord of the whole earth. For he has spoken; none of his words shall be in vain.

[5]"As for you, Achior, you Ammonite mercenary, you have said these words in a moment of perversity; you shall not see my face again from this day until I take revenge on this race

swears that the Assyrian victory will come to pass, all in the name of his god, King Nebuchadnezzar, "lord of the whole earth" (6:4). Although Holofernes accuses Achior of playing the prophet (6:2), the reader knows that Achior is not playing; he is, indeed, theologically interpreting the present moment correctly.

Holofernes then turns to punish Achior for his lack of faith in Nebuchadnezzar and his daring to suggest that the Israelite God may be stronger than he is. He avers that Achior "shall not see my face again from this day until I take revenge on this race" (6:5). The irony is evident, although its full force will not be apparent until Judith pulls Holofernes's head from a bag and shows it to Achior (14:6). Holofernes wants to humiliate Achior by making him witness the failure of his words. Only when Achior sees the Israelites' defeat will Holofernes personally oversee his death. Therefore, he orders his slaves to bind Achior and drop him outside of an Israelite town. Having defended them, he can die with them.

The focus and verbal play on the word "face" continues as Holofernes sarcastically tells Achior not "to look downcast" (literally: "don't let your face fall") at the prospect of expulsion from the camp (6:9). His words mirror, even mimic, Nebuchadnezzar's speech in chapter 2, but he shifts from affirming Nebuchadnezzar's word to asserting the truth of his own (compare 2:12 to 6:4 and 6:9). This speech also displays a certain unintended irony. What Holofernes intended to be a painful and ignominious death will become the very means of Achior's salvation.

that came out of Egypt. [6]Then at my
return the sword of my army and the
spear of my servants shall pierce your
sides, and you shall fall among their
wounded. [7]Now my slaves are going
to take you back into the hill country
and put you in one of the towns beside
the passes. [8]You will not die until you
perish along with them. [9]If you really
hope in your heart that they will not
be taken, then do not look downcast!
I have spoken, and none of my words
shall fail to come true."

[10]Then Holofernes ordered his
slaves, who waited on him in his tent,
to seize Achior and take him away to
Bethulia and hand him over to the Isra-
elites. [11]So the slaves took him and led
him out of the camp into the plain, and
from the plain they went up into the hill
country and came to the springs below
Bethulia. [12]When the men of the town
saw them, they seized their weapons
and ran out of the town to the top of
the hill, and all the slingers kept them
from coming up by throwing stones at
them. [13]So having taken shelter below
the hill, they bound Achior and left him
lying at the foot of the hill, and returned
to their master.

The slaves do as ordered and carry Achior out of the camp. As they approach the town, the men of Bethulia run out and throw stones down upon their enemy. Holofernes's slaves tie up Achior and run (6:11), thus deviating from the command to deliver him directly to "one of the towns" (6:7). The slaves' disobedience in the face of Israelite challenge is the first sign of Holofernes's loss of control. If he cannot even rule his slaves, what will happen with his soldiers? Achior is now between the two camps, neither Assyrian nor Israelite. His crossing from one to the other presages Judith's own crossing in chapter 10. Yet, whereas Judith will return to her village and her people, Achior will never return to either Assyrian camp or Ammonite people.

The narrative does not give access to Achior's feelings. In stark contrast to the previous chapter, Achior neither speaks nor acts. His body moves us from the Assyrian camp into the fortified village of Bethulia; his reactions to this move must wait.

Achior Enters Bethulia (6:14-21)

The men defending the spring come down to Achior, untie him (the Vulgate depicts him tied to a tree and many painters follow the Vulgate's lead), and take him up to Bethulia. There is a marked contrast in Achior's positionality; the Assyrian slaves throw him down at the foot of the hill, and the Israelite soldiers stand him up and take him up the hill. Achior is

Jdt 6:14-21

[14]Then the Israelites came down from their town and found him; they untied him and brought him into Bethulia and placed him before the magistrates of their town, [15]who in those days were Uzziah son of Micah, of the tribe of Simeon, and Chabris son of Gothoniel, and Charmis son of Melchiel. [16]They called together all the elders of the town, and all their young men and women ran to the assembly. They set Achior in the midst of all their people, and Uzziah questioned him about what had happened. [17]He answered and told them what had taken place at the council of Holofernes, and all that he had said in the presence of the Assyrian leaders, and all that Holofernes had boasted he would do against the house of Israel. [18]Then the people fell down and worshiped God, and cried out:

[19]"O Lord God of heaven, see their arrogance, and have pity on our people in their humiliation, and look kindly today on the faces of those who are consecrated to you."

[20]Then they reassured Achior, and praised him highly. [21]Uzziah took him from the assembly to his own house and gave a banquet for the elders; and all that night they called on the God of Israel for help.

making not just a physical move but a metaphorical one as well, moving from the low point of bound prisoner of the Assyrians to the high point of inclusion in the Israelite community. The Israelites take Achior to principal citizens of Bethulia: "Uzziah son of Micah, of the tribe of Simeon, and Chabris son of Gothoniel, and Charmis son of Melchiel" (6:16). All the young men and women accompany them to see the show. Bethulia's women play an equal role in all public displays. We have already seen them praying and fasting (4:10); here they participate in the town meeting; later they will greet the returning Judith (13:13) and dance in her honor (15:12). Although the presence of women in public can be inferred in many biblical stories, only Judith names them explicitly as full participants in public assemblies.

Uzziah, the only official to speak, questions Achior (6:15). There is something ironic in his name. Uzziah is Hebrew for "the Lord is my strength"; although a theological principle emphasized in the book, Uzziah does not live up to his name. He appears weak, indecisive, and lacking in faith. The strength of God will manifest in another: Judith. Moreover, Uzziah is a member of the tribe of Simeon, as are Judith and her husband, as the reader will be informed in chapter 8. The reference may portend that Uzziah, like his ancestor Simeon in regard to Dinah (Gen 34), will seek to recover his city and its honor; however, again, Judith will take up that task instead.

In response to Uzziah's questions, Achior tells the assembly what had happened in Holofernes's council (6:17). This is the only verse in chapter 6 where Achior is the subject of the verb; even so, the narrator offers only indirect speech. Achior's story causes the people of Israel to fall down in worship and to call out: "O Lord God of heaven, see their arrogance, and have pity on our people in their humiliation, and look kindly today on the faces of those who are consecrated to you" (6:19).

The people then reassure and praise Achior, and the elders throw him a feast or, more accurately, a drinking party (πότος). Drinking parties punctuate the narrative (1:16; 6:21; 12:10), even as they alternate with fasts both voluntary and involuntary (4:9; 7:21-22; 8:6). The drinking parties in Judith seem to be another expression of masculine power since they are thrown by kings, generals, and elders. In this instance, the drinking party is also the occasion of an all-night prayer session.

Judith 7:1–9:14

Judith Takes Center Stage

The War Begins (Judith 7:1-32)

When the narrative switches from the world of kings and emperors and massive hordes to villages, farmers, and rural hilltop outposts, our attention shifts from the lofty rhetoric of power and pride to the small village of Bethulia, filled with people who fear, feel thirst, faint, cry. Holofernes's army swarms the hills and valleys. The Bethulians teeter on the edge of death. Their worries are about survival overlaid across the ever-present threat of enslavement and rape.

Chapter 7 of Judith "has the largest cast of characters to be found in the book."[1] Yet the precise numbers, names, and locations are, as in the rest of the book, largely fictitious. Each element is carefully crafted to build this fiction with an aura of verisimilitude.

Assyria and Bethulia Prepare for Battle (7:1-18)

Holofernes immediately makes good on his promise to overwhelm Israel. The next day, he orders the move against Bethulia. The army breaks camp and repositions itself in the same plain beside the same spring where the slaves had dumped Achior. The numbers are massive—170,000 warriors and twelve thousand cavalrymen with all of their attending foot soldiers (7:2). Holofernes is clear: my army is bigger than

1. Deborah Levine Gera, *Judith*, CEJL (Berlin: de Gruyter, 2014), 235.

Jdt 7:1-18

[7:1]The next day Holofernes ordered his whole army, and all the allies who had joined him, to break camp and move against Bethulia, and to seize the passes up into the hill country and make war on the Israelites. [2]So all their warriors marched off that day; their fighting forces numbered one hundred seventy thousand infantry and twelve thousand cavalry, not counting the baggage and the foot soldiers handling it, a very great multitude. [3]They encamped in the valley near Bethulia, beside the spring, and they spread out in breadth over Dothan as far as Balbaim and in length from Bethulia to Cyamon, which faces Esdraelon.

[4]When the Israelites saw their vast numbers, they were greatly terrified and said to one another, "They will now strip clean the whole land; neither the high mountain nor the valleys nor the hills will bear their weight." [5]Yet they all seized their weapons, and when they had kindled fires on their towers, they remained on guard all that night.

[6]On the second day Holofernes led out all his cavalry in full view of the Israelites in Bethulia. [7]He reconnoitered the approaches to their town, and visited the springs that supplied their water; he seized them and set guards of soldiers over them, and then returned to his army.

[8]Then all the chieftains of the Edomites and all the leaders of the Moabites and the commanders of the coastland came to him and said, [9]"Listen to what we have to say, my lord, and your army will suffer no losses. [10]This people, the Israelites, do not rely on their spears but on the height of the mountains where

your army. In fact, it seems to be growing as it has approached Bethulia—in 2:15 the text counts 120,000 warriors and now there are 170,000. The narrator repeatedly stresses the size (in both width and breadth) of the army, numbers of men, how much land they cover, and their armaments (see also 7:18). Such vast numbers invoke from the Israelites a terror they express in gastronomical metaphor—literally, the Israelites worry that the enemy army "will lick the face" (ἐκλείξουσιν οὗτοι τὸ πρόσωπον) of the whole land (7:4; our translation). "Devouring" is more than just killing; it is also incorporation, a fear of being consumed by the enemy and therefore being made a part of the enemy, a kind of genocide. The villagers arm themselves, take to their watchtowers, and prepare to defend their town (7:5).

On the second day, Holofernes makes another martial display by parading his cavalry in front of the villagers. He also takes the time to gather military intelligence and, strategically, to capture the water supply. Yet, after taking council with his officers of the Edomites, the Moabites, and the coastlands, Holofernes decides to wait for the actual attack.

they live, for it is not easy to reach the tops of their mountains. 11 Therefore, my lord, do not fight against them in regular formation, and not a man in your army will fall. 12 Remain in your camp, and keep all the men in your forces with you; let your servants take possession of the spring of water that flows from the foot of the mountain, 13 for this is where all the people of Bethulia get their water. So thirst will destroy them, and they will surrender their town. Meanwhile, we and our people will go up to the tops of the nearby mountains and camp there to keep watch to see that no one gets out of the town. 14 They and their wives and children will waste away with famine, and before the sword reaches them they will be strewn about in the streets where they live. 15 Thus you will pay them back with evil, because they rebelled and did not receive you peaceably."

16 These words pleased Holofernes and all his attendants, and he gave orders to do as they had said. 17 So the army of the Ammonites moved forward, together with five thousand Assyrians, and they encamped in the valley and seized the water supply and the springs of the Israelites. 18 And the Edomites and Ammonites went up and encamped in the hill country opposite Dothan; and they sent some of their men toward the south and the east, toward Egrebeh, which is near Chusi beside the Wadi Mochmur. The rest of the Assyrian army encamped in the plain, and covered the whole face of the land. Their tents and supply trains spread out in great number, and they formed a vast multitude.

His officers reason that the Bethulians, lacking water, will surrender. "They and their wives and children will waste away with famine" (7:14) while not a single Assyrian soldier will be killed. More, they regard the Bethulians as at fault: the troops will pay "them back with evil because they rebelled" and did not immediately surrender (7:15). How quickly we have moved from Holofernes's vow to fill the earth with bloody and mutilated bodies (6:4). Now, he decides to destroy his opponents with patience. Corpses will pile up nevertheless, but without blood, without mangled flesh. Indeed, they will bloat and then fester. Given the contrast in the plan of attack, we must ask: since when do generals care if some of their soldiers are killed for their own greater glory? Is Holofernes himself afraid of a little blood? A very different model of conquest emerges, one that does not quite stand up to the portrait of brutal masculinity in the last chapter, but the rhetoric of war rarely coheres with the realities of strategy.

The chieftains also recommend that men be stationed on top of the nearby mountains to guarantee that "no one" escapes (7:13). The dramatic irony is clear—not one *man* (ἄνδρα) will leave the town's gates, but two *women* will. Salvation will come by the hand of a woman.

Suffering Under Siege (7:19-32)

Faced with hundreds of thousands of Assyrian soldiers covering every hill and filling every valley, the people of Bethulia lose their courage. Such failure of nerve is exacerbated by physical deprivation. They hold out for thirty-four days with water rations, thirty-four days of having some water but never enough. We can imagine this siege taking place in late summer or early fall—after the crops have been harvested (see 4:5) but before the rainy season has begun. The weather would be hot and dry, the sky a brilliant blue, and the sun intense on the Samaritan hilltop. As no person can move freely in and out of the city, no objects can either. There is nowhere to dispose of garbage and human waste. There is nowhere to bury the bodies once people start to die. The garbage and the excrement and the corpses become additional sites for the proliferation of disease. There are biblical descriptions of such sieges in 2 Kings 6 (recounting Aram's siege of Samaria) and 2 Kings 25 and Lamentations (describing the Babylonian siege of Jerusalem). There are also descriptions of the suffering of men, women, and children during sieges in Greek histories (Aeneas Tacticus, "On Siegecraft"). In more contemporary times, photographs and films of ghettos from the Nazi era may help us imagine the scene. Siege warfare is citizen assault, chemical weaponry, and terrorism, all in one.

Imagining the material conditions of siege and the consequent emotional anxiety and anguish, we should not judge the response of the Israelites too harshly for losing their courage (7:19). The narrator reports that the children lie in a stupor, while women and young men faint from thirst (7:22). All the people—men, women, and children—gather around the town's elders to demand a solution (7:23).

Uzziah[2]

In contrast to Holofernes who makes life-changing decisions on insufficient information, Uzziah encourages people to give him information. First, he listens to Achior the Ammonite. Second, he listens to his constituents, the people of Bethulia. Third, he listens to Judith's assessment of the situation from her theological perspective. Fourth, he listens to her reprimand.

2. This section takes material from Robin Gallaher Branch, "Joakim, Uzziah, and Bagoas: A Literary Analysis of Selected Secondary Characters in the Book of Judith," *OTE* 25 (2012): 57–83.

Jdt 7:19-32

19The Israelites then cried out to the
Lord their God, for their courage
failed, because all their enemies had
surrounded them, and there was no
way of escape from them. 20The whole
Assyrian army, their infantry, chariots,
and cavalry, surrounded them for thirty-
four days, until all the water contain-
ers of every inhabitant of Bethulia were
empty; 21their cisterns were going dry,
and on no day did they have enough
water to drink, for their drinking water
was rationed. 22Their children were list-
less, and the women and young men
fainted from thirst and were collaps-
ing in the streets of the town and in
the gateways; they no longer had any
strength.

23Then all the people, the young
men, the women, and the children,
gathered around Uzziah and the rulers
of the town and cried out with a loud
voice, and said before all the elders,
24"Let God judge between you and us!
You have done us a great injury in not
making peace with the Assyrians. 25For
now we have no one to help us; God has
sold us into their hands, to be strewn

Part of listening is evaluation. He evaluates Achior's speech, judges it sound, organizes a banquet for him, and invites him to stay in his house (6:21). That Uzziah offers hospitality to a Gentile and a traditional enemy of Israel is indeed remarkable; his action marks him as graciously hospitable. His character is further displayed in a positive light when he evaluates Judith's reprimand, without anger or self-justification, and presents reasons for his actions (8:28). He talks with Judith in a way indicating his respect for her wisdom, style of leadership, and piety. He may even be acknowledging her as his superior in several ways.

Significantly, the text finds nothing unusual in Uzziah's action of listening to a woman and accepting her direction. Uzziah commends Judith as one known for wisdom. His acknowledgment of her wisdom shows that Uzziah willingly shares responsibility for governing the town. In contrast to Nebuchadnezzar and Holofernes, he is not a pompous, know-it-all leader. Uzziah displays humility. He looks for advice and seeks prayer from Judith (8:31a).

Robin Gallaher Branch

God can seem absent, even hostile, in the midst of such suffering; faith in God's providential care can waver. The people assess their situation theologically. Affirming the basic Deuteronomistic worldview—that suffering is divine punishment for sin—they believe that God has sold

Jdt 7:19-32 (cont.)

before them in thirst and exhaustion.
26Now summon them and surrender
the whole town as booty to the army of
Holofernes and to all his forces. 27For it
would be better for us to be captured by
them. We shall indeed become slaves,
but our lives will be spared, and we shall
not witness our little ones dying before
our eyes, and our wives and children
drawing their last breath. 28We call to
witness against you heaven and earth
and our God, the Lord of our ances-
tors, who punishes us for our sins and
the sins of our ancestors; do today the
things that we have described!"

29Then great and general lamenta-
tion arose throughout the assembly, and
they cried out to the Lord God with a
loud voice. 30But Uzziah said to them,
"Courage, my brothers and sisters! Let
us hold out for five days more; by that
time the Lord our God will turn his mercy
to us again, for he will not forsake us ut-
terly. 31But if these days pass by, and no
help comes for us, I will do as you say."

32Then he dismissed the people to
their various posts, and they went up
on the walls and towers of their town.
The women and children he sent home.
In the town they were in great misery.

them into the hands of the Assyrians (7:25). Accentuating this connection to Deuteronomy, the people call on heaven and earth to witness their situation (7:28), a phrase used only in Deuteronomy (Deut 4:26; 30:19; and 31:28: "I call heaven and earth to witness"). Consequently, they wish to surrender, for slavery is preferred to death.

Much like in chapter 4, where the language of distress vacillates between the cries of all the people and the cries of the men, chapter 7 is similarly confusing. The passage begins with all the people, even explicitly naming the presence of men, women, and children (7:23). Yet, in the middle of their reported speech, the focus suddenly shifts to the men as they anticipate the agony of watching their wives and children die (7:27). Whose voices are we really hearing? In contrast to chapter 4, the men here seem to accept slavery as a better fate than death, precisely the opposite of their earlier prayer where they fervently implored God to avert the fate of slavery (4:12). History is strewn with the bodies of people who chose death over slavery, as history also bears testimony to those who bore slavery's degradation in order to live. The people of Bethulia are on the horns of this dilemma. These passages in chapters 4 and 7 also echo a number of other biblical passages where Israelites complain to a leader and propose an alternative fate that mere chapters ago they abhorred. For example, having just risked everything to escape slavery, in Exodus 14:12 the Israelites declare that it would be better to return to

Egypt as slaves than to die in the desert (see also Num 14:2-3). Exodus 17 also functions as an important intertext.[3] In Exodus 17, the Israelites are faint with thirst, for they lack water, and they complain to Moses because of their fear of death, especially the death of their children (see also Num 20:1-13). These textual echoes of Exodus invite the question, what Moses will arise to save the people this time?

Uzziah is the first to respond to the people's cries. He attempts to rally his people by shouting, "Courage, my brothers and sisters!" (7:30; note that the translators have chosen to translate the Greek ἄδελφοι ["brothers"] inclusively), but Uzziah is no Moses.[4] Uzziah pleads for patience and a delay of five days before he promises to surrender. Beyond a vague "God will turn his mercy to us again" (7:30), it is unclear what Uzziah hopes to accomplish during his five-day stall (although in 8:31 Uzziah will say that he hopes God will send rain to fill the cisterns). He dismisses the people (λαός) to stand their posts and the women and children to return home (7:32). As the passage begins with a certain confusion about who is speaking, it ends with a similar confusion about who Uzziah is addressing, since he begins his speech by addressing his "brothers" and ends by sending the "people" back to their defensive positions and the women and children back to their homes. Part of the confusion is endemic to the Greek words that can be used to indicate either male persons or all people; part of the confusion is the result of a laudable but sometimes problematic commitment to gender-inclusive language on the part of the English translators.

Uzziah is not the leader the people need. The situation and the language of the Bethulians invite not only (unfavorable) comparison between Uzziah and Moses but also comparison between God's actions in the wilderness and God's actions here. Following Jan Willem van Henten's analysis, Deborah Levine Gera identifies a type scene with the following structure: "(1) the people react strongly to a difficult situation, crying aloud; (2) they converge on the chief leader(s); (3) they voice their angry complaints; (4) the leader turns to God, (5) who resolves the crisis."[5] As with all type scenes, how and where the narrative both conforms to and deviates from the common structure hold interpretive

3. Jan Willem van Henten, "Judith as Alternative Leader: A Rereading of Judith 7–13," in *A Feminist Companion to Esther, Judith and Susanna*, ed. Athalya Brenner, FCB 7 (Sheffield: Sheffield Academic, 1995), 233–36.

4. Gera, *Judith*, 245.

5. Ibid.

implications. Here the fifth element is altered. In the wilderness, God is always present, leading the people as a cloud of smoke by day and a pillar of fire by night, and Moses regularly engages in intimate communion with the deity. In Bethulia, God's presence can only be inferred. Instead of the direct intervention of God, the widow Judith appears to answer the people's prayers. Judith combines the saving actions of both God and Moses,[6] thus suggesting that God works through people to effect salvation.

Enter Judith (Judith 8:1–10:8)

Chapters 1–7 establish the theological themes, the situation that drives the plot, the characterization of all major and minor figures save for the title character, and the ideologies of masculinity that fuel both plot and characterization (and thus signal, in part, the book's ideologies of femininity as well). The first part of the book also builds dramatic tension. By the end of this section we have reached the story's emotional nadir; the people are on the verge of dying from thirst and thus on the verge of surrendering to enslavement by the Assyrians. Their hope is extinguished; their misery immense. All despair—except one.

Introducing Our Heroine (8:1-8)

"Once Judith takes the stage in chapter 8, she shares it with others but surrenders it to no one."[7] Her name (the feminine form of "Jew"[8]) signals that she will be, in some way, the representative of her people.[9] Her name also indicates that she is a counterpart to Judas (the masculine form of "Jew") Maccabeus, especially given the similarities between her victory

6. Van Henten sees Uzziah as a failed Moses and Judith as a successful Moses ("Judith as Alternative Leader," 238).

7. Toni Craven, *Artistry and Faith in the Book of Judith* (Chico, CA: Scholars Press, 1983), 62.

8. It is common to note that Judith means "Jewess." As Amy-Jill Levine writes, however, "*Jewess* perpetuates the almost abandoned practice of gendering people according to ethnic, religious, and racial categories." See "A Jewess, More and/or Less," in *Judaism Since Gender*, ed. Miriam Peskowitz and Laura Levitt (New York: Routledge, 1996), 149.

9. See Anne-Mareike Wetter, *"On Her Account": Reconfiguring Israel in Ruth, Esther, and Judith* (London: T&T Clark, 2015), 156–240 for an in-depth analysis of Judith as representing Israel.

Jdt 8:1-8

8:1 Now in those days Judith heard about these things: she was the daughter of Merari son of Ox son of Joseph son of Oziel son of Elkiah son of Ananias son of Gideon son of Raphain son of Ahitub son of Elijah son of Hilkiah son of Eliab son of Nathanael son of Salamiel son of Sarasadai son of Israel. 2 Her husband Manasseh, who belonged to her tribe and family, had died during the barley harvest. 3 For as he stood overseeing those who were binding sheaves in the field, he was overcome by the burning heat, and took to his bed and died in his town Bethulia. So they buried him with his ancestors in the field between Dothan and Balamon. 4 Judith remained as a widow for three years and four months, 5 at home where she set up a tent for herself on the roof of her house. She put sackcloth around her waist and dressed in widow's clothing. 6 She fasted all the days of her widowhood, except the day before the sabbath and the sabbath itself, the day before the new moon and the day of the new moon, and the festivals and days of rejoicing of the house of Israel. 7 She was beautiful in appearance, and was very lovely to behold. Her husband Manasseh had left her gold and silver, men and women slaves, livestock, and fields; and she maintained this estate. 8 No one spoke ill of her, for she feared God with great devotion.

and his over Nicanor. She may be the female version of this liberator; she may also function as a critique of the way the Hasmonean family seized political and religious power after their victory over the Seleucids.[10] The ways in which the text may gesture toward the Maccabees (either through emulation or critique) is picked up in medieval Jewish writings and menorahs in which Judith is associated with the Hanukkah story.

Chapter 8 begins with the longest genealogy of any biblical woman—sixteen generations (8:1). In fact, few biblical men have genealogies that rival hers. Genealogies, even ones of historical figures, are never just factual. Genealogies always also communicate political, sociological, literary, and religious meanings. Like the use of history and geography, the genealogy contributes to the ways in which the author builds the story's fictional world. All of the names appear in other biblical genealogies and in other stories, although never in this order or in these relationships. Judith's forefathers share names with judges (Gideon), prophets (Elijah), advisers (Joseph), and Levites (Merari). Many names are associated with different tribes of Israel (for example, Joseph is the father of both Ephraim and Manasseh; Nathanael is of the tribe of Issachar according

10. Van Henten, "Judith as Alternative Leader," 244–45.

to Num 1:8).[11] Ultimately, her lineage traces back to a man named Israel. Although probably not the eponymous ancestor of the whole people, this final name in Judith's genealogy certainly suggests Jacob/Israel. The genealogy evokes many different figures and many different roles, all of which help to characterize the heroine. Judith channels the whole heritage and strength of Israel and is the manifestation of Israel's highest ideals.

Like many biblical women, Judith is also introduced as a wife (8:2). In striking contradistinction from the androcentric genre of genealogy, however, her husband Manasseh lacks a genealogy of his own, and his position is presented in relation to Judith's family. We receive only a brief note that her husband was also a member of her tribe and family (both are from the tribe of Simeon, as we learn in 9:2). The narrative quickly moves to the most salient fact about Manasseh: he is dead. Judith's husband had died three years earlier, killed by heat exhaustion as he oversaw the harvest of his barley fields (8:2-3). Judith's husband was a wealthy landowner but he had a weak constitution. Fainting and dying from heatstroke connotes a fragility not becoming a man. In fact, the only other character that dies of heatstroke in the Bible is a child (2 Kings 18–20). He too is overcome while in the fields (watching the harvest with his father); then he is carried to his mother and dies in her arms. Such a death casts doubt on Manasseh's vigor and therefore casts doubt on his masculinity. The strength of the family lies elsewhere.

After summarily dispensing with her husband, the text returns to Judith, and the following descriptions of her widowhood, piety, beauty, and wealth are also unusual in biblical narrative. At the time of the story, Judith had been a widow for three years and four months (Jdt 8:4). In other words, forty months, a number linking her to Noah's forty days in the ark and Moses's forty years in the wilderness. Astute readers know that, as the period of forty nears its end, salvation is on the horizon.

During these past forty months, Judith has been living a life of extreme piety. She lives in a tent on her roof, wears sackcloth in addition to her widow's weeds, and fasts every day except the days before and of the Sabbath, the new moon, and other festivals (8:5-6). Her status as a widow has also conferred on her great wealth since she inherited from her husband "gold and silver, men and women slaves, livestock, and fields," all of which she manages on her own (8:7). She is also a slave-owner,

11. See ibid., 248, for the full list of tribal associations.

not just to the woman who will soon accompany her on her quest and later be freed, but also to untold numbers of other human beings. We will explore this aspect of her character more below.

Even with her austerity, Judith is still extremely beautiful. Thus, she is smart and capable on top of being pious, beautiful, and wealthy. The author wraps up Judith's introduction by noting how admired she is by her community: "No one spoke ill of her, for she feared God with great devotion" (8:8). Her people admire her, yet their esteem seems restrained; instead of telling the reader how the other Bethulians felt or what they thought about Judith, the text simply indicates that the people have refrained from negative words. By linking their forbearance with Judith's fear, there is an implication that only her piety has kept her from the gossips' lips.[12] For the first time, the word "fear" (φοβέομαι) in this verse refers to the reverence one has for the deity, and it will be contrasted to the fear the people feel (or sometimes don't feel) for Nebuchadnezzar and Holofernes (see 1:11; 2:28; 4:1).

Judith has separated herself from the people in Bethulia because of both circumstance (her wealth must put her in the upper echelons of the class hierarchy) and personal decision (she lives on her roof and eschews public appearances). Judith is a representation of the people and separate from them at the same time, an ideal woman but different from all the other women in Bethulia. There is a certain ambiguity in her characterization, an ambiguity that will deepen as the story continues.[13]

Even her status as widow is one of ambiguities. Judith's widowhood is essential for the plot because it gives her both the freedom of movement and the sexual experience she needs to seduce Holofernes (prostitutes are also free and sexually experienced, but they do not have social standing). Widowhood also has special status in biblical law and story. Because of the material circumstances of widows in ancient Israel (husbands confer economic support and protection), widowhood is an especially vulnerable position. Therefore, widows are a protected class (see Exod 22:20-21; Deut 24:17). The extra attention widows receive in the legal codes also translates theologically as God is said to pay particular attention to the widows and particular attention to how others in positions of power treat

12. Gera, *Judith*, 269.

13. Denise Dombkowski Hopkins, "Judith," in *Women's Bible Commentary*, ed. Carol A. Newsom, Sharon H. Ringe, and Jacqueline E. Lapsley, 3rd ed. (Louisville: Westminster John Knox, 2012), 386–87.

the widows (Deut 10:18 and 14:29; Ps 68:5). Widows are simultaneously vulnerable *and* protected by God.

Widowhood is also a metaphor. For example, Jerusalem is a widow in Lamentations (1:1), and all of Israel is a widow in Isaiah (54:4-8). In both cases, no husband has died (and who would that husband be? God?), but the metaphor works because the city and the people find themselves in a particular kind of helplessness wedded to a particular kind of fierce divine protection (or at least hope of protection). Judith represents both this acute vulnerability and this special protection as a literal widow and as a figure of all of Israel. Judith is a widow, but she is also wealthy, wise, enterprising, self-reliant, and strong. Israel may be the smaller and weaker state in the ancient Near East's political arena, but it has a strong Rock and Redeemer.

Judith Confronts the Elders (8:9-36)

Judith's power and respect, separate from and above the townspeople, are confirmed by her first actions: she hears, she sends, she summons (8:9-10). She hears a report that the people of Bethulia are displeased with the town's leadership; she has heard that thirst is a driving factor in this dissatisfaction; she has heard of Uzziah's promise to surrender in five days. These notices not only confirm that Judith was absent from the meeting with the elders but also imply that she does not share the thirst prompting the urgency of the situation. Her voluntarily fasting may have prepared her for the deprivation caused by the lack of water. Alternatively, she may have resources not shared among the general population (she will later bathe in water [10:2]). Either way, her distinct position in the town enables her to send her slave to summon the elders to her home.

Judith has male slaves (8:7), but one female slave has earned her confidence in ways similar to Abraham's slave (Gen 24:2) and the enslaved Joseph in Potiphar's house (Gen 39:4). Judith's slave also finds a parallel to Bagoas, the eunuch who waits upon and councils Holofernes (Jdt 12:11). Yet, Bagoas has a name, a voice, and independent action. Judith's slave is anonymous, silent, and only obeys her mistress's command. The Greek (and Latin) word used most frequently for this woman is ἅβρα (seven times, including here in 8:10); later works of art, music, and literature sometimes convert the common noun to a proper noun and name her Abra. Whereas the impulse to name this anonymous woman is a humanizing one, consistent with the function of many creative reimaginings, and contributor Jessica Jernigan will name her such while discussing paintings that depict her, we will not do so when discussing

Jdt 8:9-36

9 When Judith heard the harsh words
spoken by the people against the
ruler, because they were faint for lack
of water, and when she heard all that
Uzziah said to them, and how he prom-
ised them under oath to surrender the
town to the Assyrians after five days,
10 she sent her maid, who was in charge
of all she possessed, to summon Uz-
ziah and Chabris and Charmis, the el-
ders of her town. 11 They came to her,
and she said to them:

"Listen to me, rulers of the people
of Bethulia! What you have said to the
people today is not right; you have
even sworn and pronounced this oath
between God and you, promising to
surrender the town to our enemies un-
less the Lord turns and helps us within
so many days. 12 Who are you to put
God to the test today, and to set your-
selves up in the place of God in human
affairs? 13 You are putting the Lord Al-
mighty to the test, but you will never
learn anything! 14 You cannot plumb the
depths of the human heart or under-
stand the workings of the human mind;
how do you expect to search out God,
who made all these things, and find out
his mind or comprehend his thought?
No, my brothers, do not anger the Lord
our God. 15 For if he does not choose to
help us within these five days, he has
power to protect us within any time he
pleases, or even to destroy us in the
presence of our enemies. 16 Do not try
to bind the purposes of the Lord our
God; for God is not like a human being,
to be threatened, or like a mere mortal,
to be won over by pleading. 17 There-

her role in the book of Judith. Calling her "Slave" collapses her personal identity with her socio-economic reality and, ultimately, further degrades her. Slaves were generally denationalized, striped of their country, culture, and kinship ties; they were made into "blank slates" for the benefit of their owners.[14] Besides her sex (woman) and legal status (slave, albeit one elevated over the other slaves), no other identifying information about Judith's slave is given to the reader.

Assessing Judith's slave is complicated. Some commentators deny that she is indeed a slave because of her close relationship with her mistress.[15] Translations also obscure her slave status by calling her Judith's "maid" (as the NRSV does and as Robin Gallaher Branch will in her contribution below). Yet, the text is quite clear that the woman who manages Judith's estate is also a part of that estate, otherwise Judith would not have had

14. Catherine Hezser, *Jewish Slavery in Antiquity* (Oxford: Oxford University Press, 2006), 27–28.

15. See, for example, Helen Efthimiadis-Keith, *The Enemy Is Within: A Jungian Psychoanalytic Approach to the Book of Judith* (Leiden: Brill, 2004), 249.

Jdt 8:9-36 (cont.)

fore, while we wait for his deliverance, let us call upon him to help us, and he will hear our voice, if it pleases him.

[18]"For never in our generation, nor in these present days, has there been any tribe or family or people or town of ours that worships gods made with hands, as was done in days gone by. [19]That was why our ancestors were handed over to the sword and to pillage, and so they suffered a great catastrophe before our enemies. [20]But we know no other god but him, and so we hope that he will not disdain us or any of our nation. [21]For if we are captured, all Judea will be captured and our sanctuary will be plundered; and he will make us pay for its desecration with our blood. [22]The slaughter of our kindred and the captivity of the land and the desolation of our inheritance—all this he will bring on our heads among the Gentiles, wherever we serve as slaves; and we shall be an offense and a disgrace in the eyes of those who acquire us. [23]For our slavery will not bring us into favor, but the Lord our God will turn it to dishonor.

[24]"Therefore, my brothers, let us set an example for our kindred, for their lives depend upon us, and the sanctuary—both the temple and the altar—rests upon us. [25]In spite of everything let us give thanks to the Lord our God, who is putting us to the test as he did with our ancestors. [26]Remember what he did with Abraham, and how he tested Isaac, and what happened to Jacob in Syrian Mesopotamia, while he was tending the sheep of Laban, his mother's brother.

to free her at the end of the story (16:23). Many commentators argue that the relationship between the two women is a mutually supportive, genuine friendship, despite the mistress-slave hierarchy.[16] We do not have sufficient data about the lives of enslaved persons in the Hellenistic period to make reasonable conjectures about how Judith and her slave could have regarded one another; in fact, there is not a single primary source from a slave's perspective.[17] We may tentatively use cross-cultural comparisons, some of which indicate that slaves and owners could feel mutual affection for one another. Evidence, though, also suggests that these personal bonds only partially or temporarily mitigated the brutality of the legal and economic relationship.[18]

16. See, for example, Craven, *Artistry and Faith*, 121. Craven even discusses the slave as Judith's employee, hired to manage her household (118).

17. Hezser, *Jewish Slavery in Antiquity*, 13. Information about slaves during the Greco-Roman period comes from literary sources and legal documents, neither of which provides direct access into what slaves thought about their lives.

18. Jennifer Glancy draws on the witness of slaves and slave owners from the nineteenth-century American South in order to glean insight into the possible personal

[27]For he has not tried us with fire, as he did them, to search their hearts, nor has he taken vengeance on us; but the Lord scourges those who are close to him in order to admonish them."

[28]Then Uzziah said to her, "All that you have said was spoken out of a true heart, and there is no one who can deny your words. [29]Today is not the first time your wisdom has been shown but from the beginning of your life all the people have recognized your understanding, for your heart's disposition is right. [30]But the people were so thirsty that they compelled us to do for them what we have promised, and made us take an oath that we cannot break. [31]Now since you are a God-fearing woman, pray for us, so that the Lord may send us rain to fill our cisterns. Then we will no longer feel faint from thirst."

[32]Then Judith said to them, "Listen to me, I am about to do something that will go down through all generations of our descendants. [33]Stand at the town gate tonight so that I may go out with my maid; and within the days after which you have promised to surrender the town to our enemies, the Lord will deliver Israel by my hand. [34]Only, do not try to find out what I am doing; for I will not tell you until I have finished what I am about to do."

[35]Uzziah and the rulers said to her, "Go in peace, and may the Lord God go before you, to take vengeance on our enemies." [36]So they returned from the tent and went to their posts.

In the Greco-Roman world, among both Jews and Gentiles, slavery was taken for granted. It was such an integral part of the social and economic order that it was considered natural, divinely authorized. As a metaphor, slavery even shaped the ways in which the Jewish people understood their relationship to their God. Although the biblical laws in Leviticus and Deuteronomy limit the power a slave owner could wield over a slave, "in the Jewish Greek writings of the Hellenistic and early Roman period the distinction between Jewish and non-Jewish slaves is almost completely absent and the biblical rules concerning Hebrew slaves' manumission in the seventh year of their service is ignored."[19] Jewish slave owners seemed to share the general cultural attitudes about slaves, and this is reflected in the book of Judith. As feminist commentators, however, we cannot simply accept the ideology presented in the text. Judith's position as a slave owner would have been unremarkable

---

relationship between Judith and her slave ("Judith the Slaveholder," in *A Feminist Companion to Tobit and Judith*, ed. Athalya Brenner-Idan and Helen Efthimiadis-Keith, FCB 20, 2nd ser. [London: Bloomsbury T&T Clark, 2015], 204).

19. Hezser, *Jewish Slavery in Antiquity*, 31–32.

in her own time, but, for us, more than any other aspect of her character, her ownership of other human beings damages her feminist legacy.

The Maid

Judith figures prominently in European art in the last millennium, especially the fourteenth through the seventeenth centuries. Judith interacting in some way with Holofernes is a favorite subject of these paintings and usually the scene involves his death.

In the baroque oil by Artemisia Gentileschi (1593–1656), Holofernes seems to be struggling as a buxom Judith pulls his hair back and applies his sword directly under his chin. A woman, presumably the maid, holds him down while the deed is done.

Another painting of Judith and Holofernes by Andrea Mantegna (1431–1506) shows Judith at Holofernes's tent door looking warily over her shoulder. A stooped, aged maid, barefoot, holds the sack as Judith deposits the general's head.

Perhaps the most famous painting of Judith is indeed a study in heads—three heads, to be exact. The painting by Cristofano Allori (1577–1621) seems to be from a lens angle looking up. Judith looks down directly at the viewer. She is glorious, regally robed and sashed. In her right hand she grasps the hirsute head of Holofernes by his dark hair. His eyes are closed. His beard covers the grotesqueness of what probably was an open mouth.

She holds the head away from her, perhaps lest it soil her voluminous gown with gore. Behind Judith and looking only at Judith is a woman in an attractive cowl headdress, presumably the maid. The maid's face shows concern for her mistress. Judith's face is unreadable; perhaps it shows detachment, perhaps resignation, perhaps shock that the assassination succeeded so easily.

The painting by Allori reflects best the text of the book of Judith. Allori's maid is handsome; some would call her refined and lovely. Mantegna's maid seems old and wizened, too old to survive until Judith is 105; Gentileschi's version is inaccurate because the maid is not present during the assassination. Also, Allori's maid pictorially gives this telling insight: the maid's focus (here and arguably throughout her life) is Judith.

Let's look at the maid in detail.[20]

20. Portions of this selection come from my earlier work on Judith in *Bible History Daily*. See Robin Gallaher Branch, "Judith: A Remarkable Heroine, Parts 1 and 2," https://www.biblicalarchaeology.org/daily/people-cultures-in-the-bible/people-in-the-bible

The maid cares for the physical needs of her mistress—food and clothing—and acts as chaperone and attendant. The maid's presence validates Judith's tall tale to Holofernes and the assembled Assyrian soldiers. Her dutiful presence as attendant and (powerless) chaperone adds the necessary mystique and credibility a great lady needs when claiming she flees in distress from her doomed city into the Assyrians' welcoming presence because the Assyrians "are about to eat them up!" (10:12).

Although the text gives no indication that the maid knew Judith's complete plans or was asked to accompany her, I think Judith's character indicates she would not order someone to come with her on what could be a death mission. I believe she asked her maid, and the maid, meeting her eyes and with her head held high, nodded yes. I believe they prayed together. These beliefs fall well within the boundary of imagination the biblical narrative text offers—and allows—its readers.

In modern terms, both Judith and her maid are enemy agents bent on the destruction of Israel's foe. Both are heroines.

The maid provides insights on how Judith relates to other women and how other women relate to her. The text affirms repeatedly that Judith relates well to other women. The unnamed women of Bethulia express no hint of jealousy toward her beauty, wealth, piety, and accomplishments. Indeed, they arguably identify with her! She inspires them. They sing her praises and dance in her honor (15:12). Judith and the women crown themselves with garlands (15:13). Judith then leads the women first, with the men following, in a celebratory victory dance, just as Miriam the prophet led the women after the victory at the Sea of Reeds (Exod 15:20-21). In both stories, a mighty foe bent on the destruction of God's covenant people falls.

Robin Gallaher Branch

Judith's power is not just over her human property; she also wields power over the town elders. She summons them through her slave and they respond without question. As her first actions confirm her power and authority, so do her first words. Without any deferential address she commands the elders to listen to her and then comes directly to the point: "What you have said to the people today is not right" (9:11). Judith

/judith-a-remarkable-heroine/; https://www.biblicalarchaeology.org/daily/people-cultures-in-the-bible/people-in-the-bible/judith-a-remarkable-heroine-part-2/ (first published 2012; updated August 12, 2016).

may not leave her own house, but she is certainly well informed about what happens in her town.

Judith then begins the narrative's second extended speech, as eloquent and impassioned as Achior's earlier discourse (5:5-21). She accuses the elders of putting God to the test and even setting themselves up in the place of God (Jdt 9:12). This accusation is theological, so much so that Carey Moore notes, "With some justification, one might describe Judith as the sole female theologian in the OT."[21] Her harsh rhetoric echoes Holofernes's angry retort after Achior's speech, "Who are you?" or, colloquially, "Who do you think you are?" (6:2).

Judith's argument is twofold. First, God is superior in terms of knowledge. People do not even understand other people, let alone the ways in which God thinks and reasons: one "cannot plumb the depths of the human [ἄνθρωπος] heart or understand the workings of the human mind" (8:14). The Greek ἄνθρωπος is grammatically masculine yet is typically translated with the inclusive English "human." Like the other places in Judith where we have already noted an ambiguity in the use of this term, however, there may be something intentionally androcentric in Judith's critique of the male elders and *their* inability to discern other men's thoughts and feelings. They lack the wisdom and discernment to do so, but Judith can understand other people and, more, the mind of God.

Judith's second point is that God has complete freedom (8:15-17). Regardless of what actions the people take or do not take, God can decide to save or to destroy. God can be neither threatened nor cajoled. God's freedom is central to Judith's theology. Judith does not discount prayer. She still advocates waiting and praying, while also acknowledging that God may hear and decide to help—or not (8:17).

In the next part of her speech, she addresses the theological perspective earlier voiced by Achior and the elders. God punishes Israel, particularly for the sin of idolatry, by using other nations as God's whip (8:19). Not all threat, however, is prompted by sin. God can also use other nations to test Israel. Judith avers that her entire generation of Israelites is not guilty of idolatry (8:18). Rather, they are on the verge of another crime—permitting Jerusalem and its temple to be desecrated (8:21). Were the Assyrians to break through the Bethulians' defense and conquer Jerusalem, then the people will have failed their God. The slavery that will result from Assyria's conquest will be the means of their divine punishment, full of shame and disgrace (8:23).

21. Carey A. Moore, *Judith*, AB 40 (Garden City, NY: Doubleday, 1985), 186.

Judith here touches on the thorny problem of interpreting political events in light of the Deuteronomistic perspective on suffering. A simple theodicy—suffering is a result of sin—can never explain a complex world. Monotheism in general makes explaining suffering more difficult as life's vicissitudes cannot be attributed to the actions of evil (or even just capricious) supernatural beings; all must come from the one God. In addition to the Deuteronomistic perspective, other voices are present in the biblical Scripture. The prophets denounce the sins of social injustice (see Amos 2:6-7); the blameless Job suffers because he is tested (Job 2); the sage who wrote Ecclesiastes offers no explanation but simply affirms that sometimes the wicked prosper and the good suffer (Eccl 8:14). Judith adds her voice to the ongoing search for meaning in light of suffering in the world. For her, God tests the righteous through suffering, but God's testing is also a mark of divine favor and not wrath or disregard (8:27). Yet, if the people fail this test, the resulting Assyrian victory will be, indeed, God's punishment. No matter how sinless a people lives (and, Judith avers, the people have been sinless for generations [8:18]), trouble may come when God decides to test. What can a people, then, do to remain safe and secure? Remain faithful and fight. There is no other option.

Judith ends her theological oration with words of wisdom—"the Lord scourges those who are close to him" (8:27)—a sentiment expressed in Proverbs 3:12; Job 5:17; and Psalm 94:10, 12. The claim is meant to strengthen the hearts of those in Bethulia, but it is also perilously close to a dynamic of domestic abuse. The cycle of abuse often involves a toxic knot of violence, victim blaming, and love. When people hit members of their family, their violent acts are often accompanied by words of love, even claims that the battery is because of the love ("I hit you because I love you").[22] The suggestion of domestic abuse here again underscores how challenging it can be to explain why good people suffer in this world.

Judith pauses in her speech and Uzziah responds with praise. Uzziah's presence is sudden, as he is missing from the list of the summoned elders (8:10; most translations, including the NRSV, add his name). His absence earlier may be the result of scribal error or a deliberate dismissal of his leadership. Uzziah says that, as usual, Judith has spoken words both true and wise. Nevertheless, since the people are dying of thirst, he cannot violate his oath (8:30). Uzziah seems to be dodging responsibility and

22. Renita J. Weems explores the dynamic of domestic abuse in the rhetoric of the prophets in *Battered Love: Marriage, Sex, and Violence in the Hebrew Prophets*, OBT (Minneapolis: Fortress, 1995).

evading Judith's critique. He insists he is not testing God; the people made him promise to surrender, and now his hands are tied. Instead of engaging Judith, Uzziah asks her to pray for rain (8:31). The suggestion can be regarded as either logical or misguided. On the one hand, rainfall, essential for survival in the Near East, was associated with the storm god Ba'al. Even YHWH encompasses some of Ba'al's attributes, and prayers for rain are common in the Bible.[23] Ora Brison suggests that asking Judith to pray for rain is an acknowledgment of her status as a divine intermediary with "spiritual and magical abilities for causing rainfall."[24] On the other hand, rain, even if it comes, will be only a temporary salve. Uzziah's request may be a respectful petition to a great spiritual leader, but his response to Judith may also be condescending, even sarcastic. God has not listened to our prayers or the entreaties of the entire town, but somehow God will listen to you, oh great and mighty Judith?[25]

Uzziah is weak leader, deflecting responsibility and hiding behind a vow, but at least he speaks. None of the other elders respond. In this passage, Judith is more the "real man" in the sense of performing masculinity. She commands and theologizes; she speaks and acts. This upsetting of gender expectation, another ironic element, also has comic aspects: there is something amusing in the image of elders rushing to a widow's house only to be schooled and scolded.

Judith ignores Uzziah's request for prayer, for she moves into the next part of her speech without acknowledging his response. She begins again with a command to listen and then predicts that she is "about to do something that will go down through all generations of our descendants" (8:32). She will not inform anyone of the details of her plans; she states only that she and her slave will leave the town and that she will do so that very night. Before Uzziah can make good on his promise to surrender, Judith vows to be the instrument of God's deliverance (8:33-34). In 8:33, the motif of her "hand" ("The Lord will deliver Israel by my hand") first appears. Her "hand" becomes the metonymy signaling the power of these actions.

23. As a storm god, one of Ba'al's titles was "Rider of Clouds." This title is appropriated for YHWH in Ps 68:4, for example: "Sing to God, sing praises to his name; lift up a song to him who rides upon the clouds—his name is the Lord—be exultant before him." Examples of prayers for rain include Zech 10:1 and Ps 135:7. Elijah prays for drought and then rain to prove the power of God in 1 Kings 17–18; James 5:18 recounts Elijah's prayers.

24. Ora Brison, "Judith: A Pious Widow Turned *Femme Fatale*, or More?," in *Feminist Companion to Tobit and Judith*, 186.

25. Moore, *Judith*, 184.

Judith's power comes from her prayers and her actions, both grounded in her wisdom. The narrative associates Judith with wisdom in several ways. Of the eight biblical figures deemed "wise," three are women (Abigail in 1 Samuel 25, the woman from Tekoa in 2 Samuel 14, and the woman from Abel Beth-Maacah in 2 Samuel 20), and Judith combines several elements from each. As Deborah Levine Gera notes, "All three of the wise biblical women manage to avert a crisis of bloodshed by means of their eloquence and persuasive powers, manipulating the powerful men whom they address and deflecting their anger."[26] Judith's wisdom also draws on the portrait of Woman Wisdom and the Strange Woman in Proverbs. As Claudia Camp and Gale Yee both argue, these two female figures in Proverbs share numerous characteristics, including working outside of their homes, verbal eloquence, and association with banquets and hospitality.[27] As Gera points out, Judith does as well.[28] There are also parallels between Ben Sirach's description of the wise man and the portrait of Judith (Sir 6:34; 8:9; 39:5).[29] Judith combines piety with quick-witted speech and decisive action, all under the mantle of wisdom. This approach is a recommendation for Jewish survival in the face of larger and stronger enemy nations.

Uzziah did not seem swayed by Judith's wisdom earlier; now he and his fellow elders comply with her request. They neither ask further questions nor engage Judith in more conversation. They are content to let her handle the situation as she sees fit. Closing the scene with little more than a platitude, Uzziah and the other rulers state, "Go in peace, and may the Lord God go before you, to take vengeance on our enemies" (8:35). Considering that she has just proposed leaving the safety of her fortified town to venture forth into enemy-occupied territory with only her slave, presumably without any real weapon, the sanguine response of the elders is striking. The men cede authority to this widow and her slave. Again, gender expectations are reversed in an ironic twist. Their response may be an expression of confidence; their response may be

26. Gera, *Judith*, 288. See also Sidnie White Crawford, "Esther Not Judith: Why One Made It and the Other Didn't," *BR* 18 (2002): 22–31, 45.

27. Gale Yee, " 'I Have Perfumed My Bed with Myrrh': The Foreign Woman (*'iššа zārâ*) in Proverbs 1–9," *JSOT* (1989): 53–68; Claudia Camp, *Wisdom and the Feminine in the Book of Proverbs* (Sheffield: Sheffield Academic, 1981), 129–33.

28. Gera, *Judith*, 289.

29. Linda Bennett Elder, "Judith's *Sophia* and *Synesis*: Educated Jewish Women in the Late Second Temple Period," in *Biblical and Humane: A Festschrift for John F. Priest*, ed. Linda Bennett Elder, David L. Barr, and Elizabeth Struthers Malbon (Atlanta: Scholars Press, 1996), 53–69.

something more sinister, a desire simply to be rid of her. A few (male) commentators note that Judith may have been a challenging neighbor. For example, David Noel Freedman remarks in private correspondence cited in Carey Moore's commentary, "The elders may have been quite willing to let Judith go and be lost. Pious and virtuous as she was, she may have been a pain in the neck to the leadership."[30] The elders' response bespeaks exasperation with her strong personality and her bossy ways. At least one scholar suggests that this may be the real reason for Manasseh's speedy demise as well—it was his escape from a trying wife.[31] Whether or not the elders' reaction to Judith is shaped by sexist attitudes about strong women who seize the mantle of leadership, these commentators' remarks certainly do betray sexist perspectives.

Judith Prays and Prepares for Battle (9:1-14)

Once the elders leave, Judith does pray—but not for rain. Her appeal to God, "artfully arranged," reworks a number of motifs from the Hebrew Scriptures.[32] Judith's prayer coincides with the public evening incense offering in the temple. As the incense smoke rises, pleasingly, to God, so may her prayer. She prostrates herself, uncovers the sackcloth she always wears (presumably underneath her widow's clothing), and puts ashes on her head (9:1). These are all outward manifestations of distress, seen across biblical literature and mentioned already in 4:11. According to some manuscripts (Syriac, Old Latin, and other Greek versions), Judith tears her clothes, which may be an indirect allusion to Absalom's sister and David's daughter Tamar who tears her clothes, puts ashes on her head, and cries after she is raped by Amon, the crown prince and her half brother (2 Sam 13:19).[33] An allusion to Tamar as Judith prepares to supplicate God is consistent with the content of her prayer, which immediately references rape (9:2-3).

Rape overhangs the narrative in Judith even before this direct reference. One of the most frequent consequences of defeat in warfare is rape. Rape is a powerful expression of dominance where the victor not only

30. David Noel Freedman in Moore, *Judith*, 184.

31. Morton S. Enslin and Solomon Zeitlin, *The Book of Judith* (Leiden: Brill, 1972), 42.

32. Géza G. Xeravits, "The Supplication of Judith (Judith 9:2-14)," in *A Pious Seductress: Studies in the Book of Judith*, ed. Géza G. Xeravits (Berlin: de Gruyter, 2012), 177. Xeravits presents a close reading of the prayer, 163–77.

33. Gera, *Judith*, 301.

Jdt 9:1-14

9:1 Then Judith prostrated herself, put
ashes on her head, and uncovered the
sackcloth she was wearing. At the very
time when the evening incense was
being offered in the house of God in
Jerusalem, Judith cried out to the Lord
with a loud voice, and said,
2 "O Lord God of my ancestor
Simeon, to whom you gave a sword to
take revenge on those strangers who
had torn off a virgin's clothing to de-
file her, and exposed her thighs to put
her to shame, and polluted her womb
to disgrace her; for you said, 'It shall
not be done'—yet they did it; 3 so you
gave up their rulers to be killed, and
their bed, which was ashamed of the
deceit they had practiced, was stained
with blood, and you struck down slaves
along with princes, and princes on their
thrones. 4 You gave up their wives for
booty and their daughters to captivity,
and all their booty to be divided among
your beloved children who burned with
zeal for you and abhorred the pollu-
tion of their blood and called on you for
help. O God, my God, hear me also,
a widow.

enters into the territories and towns of the vanquished but enters into their very bodies. Rape establishes the new hierarchy as the one who penetrates ranks above the one who is penetrated, and this hierarchy is gendered as rape is also a performance of hegemonic masculinity. When the men of Israel fear the capture and enslavement of their wives and children (4:12), they are also expressing worry about rape since those taken as war booty are subject to sexual violence as an aspect of their enslavement.[34]

Judith delivers a fierce prayer that is more battle cry than humble entreaty, beginning with an appeal to "the God of my ancestor Simeon" (9:2). This is not just a nod to an ancestor; rather, it is an evocation of Genesis 34, where Simeon and his brother Levi avenge the rape of their sister Dinah by killing Shechem and his associates. Judith's memory of this story diverges in several ways from the Genesis account. In Judith's

34. Sexual violence is not just incidental but integral to the gender dynamics of war. See Harold C. Washington, "Violence and the Construction of Gender in the Hebrew Bible: A New Historicist Approach," *BibInt* 5 (1997): 324–63. See also Gwynn Kessler, "Teaching Rape, Slavery, and Genocide in Bible and Culture," in *Rape Culture and Religious Studies: Critical and Pedagogical Engagements*, ed. Rhiannon Graybill, Meredith Minister, and Beatrice Lawrence (Lanham, MD: Lexington Books, 2019), 55–72, who discusses sexual violence, the enslavement of women, and war; and Naomi Steinberg, "Social Death as Gendered Genocide: The Fate of Women and Children," *BibInt* 26 (2018): 23–42.

Jdt 9:1-14 (cont.)

[5]"For you have done these things and those that went before and those that followed. You have designed the things that are now, and those that are to come. What you had in mind has happened; [6]the things you decided on presented themselves and said, 'Here we are!' For all your ways are prepared in advance, and your judgment is with foreknowledge.

[7]"Here now are the Assyrians, a greatly increased force, priding themselves in their horses and riders, boasting in the strength of their foot soldiers, and trusting in shield and spear, in bow and sling. They do not know that you are the Lord who crushes wars; the Lord is your name. [8]Break their strength by your might, and bring down their power in your anger; for they intend to defile your sanctuary, and to pollute the tabernacle where your glorious name resides, and to break off the horns of your altar with the sword. [9]Look at their pride, and send your wrath upon their heads. Give to me,

version, rather than being absent, God directs Simeon's vengeance by handing him the sword. According to Judith, God had declared that the rape "shall not be done"; yet, as Judith correctly states, "they did it" (9:2). The retribution of Simeon is righteous and just. Her description of the rape is also far more graphic than the one Genesis provides. Here the "strangers" attack Dinah—whom Judith calls only "the virgin"—by tearing her clothes off (ἔλυσαν μήτραν; "loosed" or "broke the womb"), exposing her thighs (most likely a euphemism for her genitalia), and polluting her womb, presumably with illicit semen. The rape is both violent and shameful. Since the rape is understood not as the brutal act of an individual but as the collective act of a community ("strangers," not Shechem, raped Dinah in Judith's account), the rape also is a national/ethnic destruction and humiliation. The gendered and sexual dynamics of honor and shame are at play.[35]

Judith's account of Simeon's attack is equally graphic. God arranges that the beds of the Shechemites be stained with their own blood, their slaves and princes slaughtered, their wives and daughters taken as booty (9:3-4). God through Simeon avenges Dinah's disgrace. The grammar is complex and difficult in verses 2 and 3, perhaps enacting through grammar the violence of the scene. These verses contain a concentration of images that foreshadow Judith's own salvific acts: deception, seduc-

35. Ellen Juhl Christiansen, "Judith: Defender of Israel—Preserver of the Temple," in *A Pious Seductress*, 79.

a widow, the strong hand to do what I
plan. [10]By the deceit of my lips strike
down the slave with the prince and the
prince with his servant; crush their arrogance by the hand of a woman.

[11]"For your strength does not depend on numbers, nor your might on
the powerful. But you are the God of
the lowly, helper of the oppressed,
upholder of the weak, protector of the
forsaken, savior of those without hope.
[12]Please, please, God of my father, God
of the heritage of Israel, Lord of heaven
and earth, Creator of the waters, King
of all your creation, hear my prayer!
[13]Make my deceitful words bring wound
and bruise on those who have planned
cruel things against your covenant, and
against your sacred house, and against
Mount Zion, and against the house your
children possess. [14]Let your whole nation and every tribe know and understand that you are God, the God of all
power and might, and that there is no
other who protects the people of Israel
but you alone!"

tion, blood, beds, pollution. As Simeon and Levi trick the Shechemites by promising Shechem can marry Dinah if the men submit to circumcision (Gen 34:13-15), Judith too will use deception to get close to the enemy in order to strike him when he is in a vulnerable and physically incapacitated state. The bed of the Shechemites "is stained with blood" (9:3), first because of the breaking of Dinah's hymen, then by the cutting of their own penises, and finally because of Simeon's slaughter. Judith too will stain her enemy's bed with his own blood. In a gender reversal, she will be the one to avenge and avert the shame of the virgin, in this case, her town Bethulia.

In her prayer, Judith recounts the fate of the Shechemite wives and the daughters more explicitly than Genesis 34: "You gave up their wives for booty and their daughters to captivity" (9:4). These women suffer the same fate that the people of Bethulah fear: to be taken away as a piece of property. Judith expresses no empathy for these women but instead celebrates and exhibits a crass disregard for the violence against them.[36]

Conversely, there is no celebration in Genesis; rather, the earlier text condemns the actions of Simeon and Levi. Their father Jacob rebukes them (Gen 34:30) and in his deathbed speech repeats his negative evaluation of their attack (Gen 49:5-7). God sanctions Jacob's verdict, since the deception and slaughter of the Shechemites is the reason that (the tribes

36. Amy-Jill Levine, "Sacrifice and Salvation: Otherness and Domestication in the Book of Judith," in *A Feminist Companion to Esther, Judith and Susanna*, 211.

of) Levi and Simeon lose their share in the land. Judith is silent about Levi but holds up Simeon as a model of righteous, divinely directed response. Judith herself identifies with Simeon (and not Dinah, despite that she too is a woman threatened with rape from a foreign power), but then she pivots and interjects, "O God, my God, hear me also, a widow" (9:4). She ends this first part of the prayer by drawing attention to her own vulnerable status, perhaps even more vulnerable than that of Dinah, who had both father and brothers to protect and avenge her.

The second part of the prayer begins with a paean to God's providence. God designed everything that has happened, is happening, and will happen (9:5-6). After this theological interlude, Judith returns to her present situation. She describes the Assyrians' mighty forces, their pride in their army, and their trust in their own strength. Yet, they are not invincible: "They do not know that you are the Lord who crushes wars: the Lord is your name" (9:7, citing Exod 15:3 LXX; see also Jdt 16:2). Her characterizing God as the one who crushes wars puts God in direct opposition to the portrait of Nebuchadnezzar as the one who wages wars (1:5, 13). Judith Lang draws the comparison sharply by noting that the word "power" (κράτος; 9:8) describes both the Assyrian rulers and God, but what constitutes this power is very different. Power for the Assyrian rulers is human power, especially their military power, which "is always associated with fear, terror and suppression." In contrast, Judith (chaps. 9 and 16) discusses God's power as that which stops wars and associates this power with God's defense of the weak and the poor.[37] In its comparisons between God and Nebuchadnezzar, the book of Judith is making an argument that God is the only true divine being; it is also making an argument about the proper use of violence.

Judith next describes the threat to Jerusalem. The language of pollution and defilement Judith used earlier in reference to Dinah she now uses with reference to the temple—in this way, she equates the rape of Dinah with the threatened Assyrian assault on Israel's most holy place.[38] The Assyrians will, according to Judith, "cut down the horns of your altar with the sword" (9:8b). Unlike in the Hebrew text where the horns of the altar are always plural (for example, Exod 29:12 and 1 Kgs 1:5), the Greek phrase in Judith (κέρας θυσιαστηρίου σου) actually has the singular "horn." Horns are multivalent metaphors in the Bible that represent glory, power, divinity, light, and strength. In ancient Near Eastern iconography, sometimes

37. Judith Lang, "The Lord Who Crushes Wars: A Study of Judith 9:7; 16:2 and Exodus 15:3," in *A Pious Seductress*, 180–81.

38. Xeravits, "The Supplication of Judith," 165–66.

they are associated with male virility and sometimes with female fertility (for example, horns can be found on the heads of Egyptian deities Osiris and Hathor). With the unusual reference to the altar's horn, the rhetorical play of masculinity, femininity, and sexual violence continues. The Assyrians seek to cut down the virility of the Israelites through this war against their temple. Cutting off the horn is also the temple equivalent to breaking Dinah's womb. Together with the reference to the sword at the end of 9:8, it is also a foreshadowing of Judith's eventual decapitation of Holofernes. Continuing the foreshadowing, she immediately follows this vision of Assyrian desecration with a call to God to send his anger down "upon their heads" by giving her a "strong hand" to carry out her plan (9:9). References to horns and heads also resonate with phallic imagery and connect Judith's decapitation of Holofernes with castration.

Neither Judith nor God will match Assyrian military strength with their own army. They do not "outman" the Assyrians; rather, Judith wields words. She prays for the weapon of deception: "by the deceit of my lips strike down the slave with the prince and the prince with his servant: crush their arrogance by the hand of a woman" (9:10). Judith's language here echoes her description of the deaths of the princes and slaves of Shechem earlier in her prayer (9:3), again reinforcing her identification with Simeon. In both verses (9:3 and 9:10), the identity of the slave is subsumed under the identity of the master; the slave suffers the same fate, punished for their owner's sins. The lack of distinction that Judith makes between the prince and the slave, in the middle of a prayer where she lauds God for protecting the weak and the vulnerable, is further indication of how the text takes the institution of slavery for granted. Judith lacks class-consciousness, at least any that would include slaves. In this entreaty, she again references her "hand," and the phrase "hand of a woman" calls to mind Deborah's prediction of Jael's victory in Judges 4:9 ("the Lord will sell Sisera into the hand of a woman"). A soldier killed on the battlefield dies an honorable death; a soldier killed in bed by a woman dies a shameful death. Judith relies on the system of honor and shame in order to humiliate the Assyrians even more.

The final part of the prayer emphasizes again the difference between Nebuchadnezzar's power and the power of the God of Israel: "For your strength does not depend on numbers, nor your might on the powerful. But you are the God of the lowly, helper of the oppressed, upholder of the weak, protector of the forsaken, savior of those without hope" (9:11). Her final plea is ferocious in its appeal—repeatedly, Judith names God's power, using ten titles in two verses (9:11 and 12), and repeatedly, she appeals to this power to aid herself and all Israel.

She continues to pray for the ability to deceive (9:13), a most unorthodox request and one that has raised ethical concerns for some interpreters.[39] Discomfort with the prayer for dishonesty even emerges in biblical textual tradition itself since the Vulgate softens the language here: in Jerome's version, Judith does not pray for lying lips either in verse 10 or in verse 13. In 9:13, she asks instead for "gracious lips" (*labiis caritatis meae*). None of the characters in Judith, however, is the slightest bit concerned about her deception, nor do they think that it impugns her pious character, which is still lauded at the end of the book.

Judith is not the Bible's only celebrated deceiver, and subterfuge is not only a tactic for women. Jacob lies to Isaac in order to secure the blessing that was Esau's by right (Gen 27–28); the midwives Shiphrah and Puah lie to Pharaoh when he asks them why they are not killing Hebrew babies (Exod 1:18-21); Esther is deceitful concerning her Jewish identity (Esth 2:10). What makes Judith's lies stand out is that she is the only biblical figure who prays to God to make her a good liar.[40] Otherwise, Judith's duplicity fits the biblical pattern of the trickster, where those with less power tell lies to those with more power, often to save Israel.[41] The reception of Judith's deception is shaped, however, by gender expectations and anxieties. As we will see, Judith will become associated with the figure of the femme fatale—beautiful, untrustworthy, dangerous. In this way, feminist commentators sometimes worry that Judith does little more than confirm sexist stereotypes about women. Feminist commentators are also sometimes wary of Judith's methods. When faced with an existential threat, can one fight back against that threat by any means necessary? Does violence always beget more violence? Are feminists called upon to use other tools since, in the immortal words of Audre Lorde (also referenced in Athalya Brenner-Idan's foreword to this series), "The master's tools will never dismantle the master's house"?[42] This pronouncement is particularly pertinent to Judith who will quite literally pick up her oppressor's tool to strike him dead. The contributions

39. See Michael Wojciechowski, "Moral Teaching of the Book of Judith," in *A Pious Seductress*, 86; Moore, *Judith*, 197; Gera, *Judith*, 319–20.

40. Craven, *Artistry and Faith*, 45.

41. Ora Horn Prouser, "The Truth about Women and Lying," *JSOT* 61 (1994): 15–28. See also Susan Niditch's analysis of Esther as trickster, which notes similarities to Judith in *A Prelude to Biblical Folklore: Underdogs and Tricksters* (Champaign: University of Illinois Press, 2000), 126–45.

42. Audre Lorde, "The Master's Tools Will Never Dismantle the Master's House," in *Sister Outsider: Essays and Speeches* (Berkeley: Crossing Press, 1984, repr. 2007), 110.

of Barbara K. Peronteau, below, and Melissa Stewart and Linda Learman in the conclusion to this volume explore Judith as a model for activism.

Judith—a woman, a widow, a Jew—holds a position of informal power in her community but has no power (informal or otherwise) to face down an empire's army. No power, that is, except the strength of her faith and the lies of her lips.

Time to End the Siege

When I first heard about Judith, I was expecting more of a Joan of Arc kind of character who would sort of regender their presentation in order to accomplish a mission. Instead of a woman who changed her gender expression, I found a woman who embraced her femininity, becoming an irresistibly attractive femme fatale who was, indeed, dressed to kill. When asked how I pictured what she was wearing I imagined Judith going into her closet where she meticulously considered each dress, choosing her most alluring. Judith then moved to her dressing table where she accessorized herself with rings, necklaces, and bracelets with just the right amount of bling. Not too much sparkle; she wanted to draw attention to herself, not her jewelry. Her makeup was perfect. Her shoes were also a strategic choice. Judith is empowering herself with all that is available to her.

The other thing that surprised me about the book of Judith was the long introduction and description of the socio-political and military situation in which the city of Bethulia found itself. Half of the sixteen chapters are devoted to the lead-up of how the people of Bethulia were under siege by the Assyrian army under the command of General Holofernes. A siege, different from an attack, is when the opposing nation, through military and sometimes naval pressure, stops all supplies from coming in and out of the city. No water, no food, no medicine. Nothing.

The siege is working. The people of Bethulia are hungry, sick, and dying. Figuring it's better to be enslaved than dead, the people approach the leaders of the city to ask that the city surrender. Taking this request into consideration and without any imagination, the leaders decide to postpone the inevitable for five days. At the end of five days, the city would surrender to General Holofernes. As if five days would make a difference.

Enter Judith. What is striking about this story is that the author gives her a genealogy. When women had few rights, this genealogy tells us that Judith is a person in her own right.

As the widow of Manasseh, Judith has wealth, property, and political connections: she is well respected by the male political leaders. Her Jewish roots go all the way back to Jacob, whose name was changed to Israel after wrestling with God all night. Judith was going to have nothing to do with capitulation. Judith figures her people, as people of God who continue wrestling with their deity, have come too far to fade away into slavery with a whimper.

Judith is about to approach General Holofernes to do what the powerful, privileged, male dominated system was unable to do. Empowered by her own agency Judith approached the enemy and did what she needed to do in order to free her people. Judith was getting involved by claiming her own power. Freedom was her goal. Enslavement was never an option for Judith.

The siege of Bethulia and the genealogy of Judith are where I connect as a transwoman. When I give my talks about being a transwoman, I share my story. I do that so people can understand and know that I am a person in my own right. All transgender people, no matter how they express themselves, are real, live people. When sharing my story I tell people I was born in Latrobe, Pennsylvania; Dad was a Marine in World War II and Mom grew up in Greenville, Pennsylvania. I talk about places we've lived. Recently, I've been weaving my grandparents into my story too. By doing that, I believe I am perceived as a person, no longer an object to be scorned, hated, and sexualized. I am a feeling, thinking human being, and, like Judith, I am also faithful, having a strong faith in the same God in whom she believed.

Like Judith's people, transgender people are under siege right now. The so-called bathroom bills and other oppressive and restrictive laws that are being passed by ultra-conservative state legislatures have nothing to do with keeping other people safe and everything to do with keeping transgender people out of the public sphere. The laws designed to keep us out of bathrooms are based on the lie and false premise that transgender people attack other people. Never, not once, has this occurred. The people proposing and passing these laws know it's all based on lies. Their goal is to keep transgender people from participating in public life. If they prevent us from going to the bathroom while in public, at the restaurant, at the movies, at the ball game, or at school, then there is no place we can be. Just like the siege of Bethulia, this siege against transgender people is designed to eliminate us. These antitransgender laws based on intentional ignorance and prejudice are designed to put us in harm's way.

This is where Judith comes in. As in Judith's time, now is

the time to end the siege. It's time to shake off our depression, our mourning, our sadness, any hopelessness we might be feeling, and the dark shroud we have allowed others to put us under and claim who we are. As a feminine transwoman I like the idea of getting dressed to the nines, putting my best face forward, and going out there to better the lives of transgender people and society as a whole. Dressing in a feminine manner is not the point; rather, it is making space for who we are as individuals and expressing that personal identity through clothes and grooming. Unlike Judith, I do not advocate violence. The way we end this siege is to go out there and be who we are. Sometimes simply being transgender in the workplace or at school will change the world around us. Sometimes we need to go farther and advocate for trans rights. Other times the opportunity to run for public office is how we end this oppressive siege.

One other thing about Judith: she didn't tell anyone what she was up to. That would have sounded like asking for permission. As a transwoman attempting to come out, transition, and emerge into the charming and lovely woman I am now, I used to fumble around saying something like, "If it's okay with you I would like to transition now." No. Uh-uh. Like Judith we need to give ourselves permission to be who we are.

What's my takeaway and lesson learned from Judith? The way we end this siege is to go out there and live life boldly, courageously, and fearlessly, because each and every person who identifies as transgender is a human being worthy of praise, adulation, and celebration.

Barbara K. Peronteau

Judith 10:1–11:23

High Femme Warrior

After two long speeches, practically monologues, the loquacious Judith is now ready to begin the action of the book's final third. Until this time, she has been within her private and domestic spaces, even as she speaks to the town elders. In this section, Judith will move out into public spaces, first by leaving her roof, then her house, then her town, and finally by entering into the Assyrians' camp and then Holofernes's tent. Her movement from private to public space is accompanied by a change of dress, recounted in detail. Throughout it all, Judith continues to speak profusely, wisely, persuasively. These two chapters have received extensive attention as feminists struggle with how to assess Judith's character and methods. Judith is a shape-shifter in more ways than one.

Judith Begins the Execution of Her Plan (10:1-19)

Chapter 10 begins and ends with Judith prostrate, first before God and last before Holofernes. Much ground is covered to move her between the first prostration and the next. The narrative lingers on the scene where Judith prepares to leave Bethulia. Her disrobing and dressing are reminiscent of Greek warriors preparing for battle; Greek and ancient Near Eastern goddesses preparing for difficult journeys, seductions, or battles; and biblical figures preparing for the same. Judith emerges as

Jdt 10:1-19

10:1When Judith had stopped crying out
to the God of Israel, and had ended
all these words, 2she rose from where
she lay prostrate. She called her maid
and went down into the house where
she lived on sabbaths and on her festal
days. 3She removed the sackcloth she
had been wearing, took off her widow's
garments, bathed her body with water,
and anointed herself with precious oint-
ment. She combed her hair, put on a
tiara, and dressed herself in the fes-
tive attire that she used to wear while
her husband Manasseh was living.
4She put sandals on her feet, and put
on her anklets, bracelets, rings, ear-
rings, and all her other jewelry. Thus
she made herself very beautiful, to en-
tice the eyes of all the men who might
see her. 5She gave her maid a skin of
wine and a flask of oil, and filled a bag
with roasted grain, dried fig cakes, and
fine bread; then she wrapped up all her
dishes and gave them to her to carry.

6Then they went out to the town
gate of Bethulia and found Uzziah
standing there with the elders of the
town, Chabris and Charmis. 7When
they saw her transformed in appear-
ance and dressed differently, they were

a kind of culmination and capstone of the many gods, goddesses, heroes, and heroines that preceded her.[1] The narrative will linger again at Judith's departure as she orders the elders to open the gates: they open, she moves through, and they watch her walk away.

Preparations and Provisions (10:1-5)

This chapter opens with a variation on the classical motif of the arming of the hero. For example, as Achilles prepares for his decisive confrontation with Hector, the fraught pace of *The Iliad* slows to describe, in detail, the demi-magical shield and armor the god Hephaestus makes for Achilles (book 18). The otherwise action-packed narrative, which annotates the gruesome deaths of over three hundred men in its twenty-four books, slows again for yet another lengthy description of Achilles putting on his armor, taking up his weapons, and getting ready for the climactic confrontation.

1. See Deborah Levine Gera, *Judith*, CEJL (Berlin: de Gruyter, 2014), 328–30, for an extensive survey of ANE, Greek, and biblical adornment scenes. Caryn Tamber-Rosenau also reviews ANE and Greco-Roman goddesses in comparison to Judith (and Jael) in her *Women in Drag: Gender and Performance in the Hebrew Bible and Early Jewish Literature*, Biblical Intersections 16 (Piscataway, NJ: Gorgias Press, 2018), 29–89.

very greatly astounded at her beauty and said to her, [8]"May the God of our ancestors grant you favor and fulfill your plans, so that the people of Israel may glory and Jerusalem may be exalted." She bowed down to God.

[9]Then she said to them, "Order the gate of the town to be opened for me so that I may go out and accomplish the things you have just said to me." So they ordered the young men to open the gate for her, as she requested. [10]When they had done this, Judith went out, accompanied by her maid. The men of the town watched her until she had gone down the mountain and passed through the valley, where they lost sight of her.

[11]As the women were going straight on through the valley, an Assyrian patrol met her [12]and took her into custody. They asked her, "To what people do you belong, and where are you coming from, and where are you going?" She replied, "I am a daughter of the Hebrews, but I am fleeing from them, for they are about to be handed over to you to be devoured. [13]I am on my way to see Holofernes the commander of your army, to give him a true report; I will show him a way by which he can

For modern readers, such interludes interrupt the narrative flow. For ancient audiences, however, they were conventional and appreciated. The audience knew the outcome of the plot, of Judith's victory over Holofernes and of Achilles's victory over Hector. "Arming the hero" scenes contribute to the appreciation of the characters, allow the audience to develop an image of the figures, and increase the audience's anticipation by delaying the battle.

As with Achilles, so with Judith. Rather than moving to decisive action on the field, the author invites us into Judith's bedroom. The scene recounted in verses 1-5 is intimate. We watch as Judith rises from the ground, calls her slave, and descends from her roof into her house (10:2), the first of a series of descents that will bring her, downward step by downward step, into the Assyrian camp. Because Judith lives in her house instead of her roof on Shabbat and other festive days, this descent also has the aura of liturgical performance.

Once inside her house, Judith strips off her sackcloth and widow's dress, garments that have long marked her as both grieving and sexually unavailable. We watch her, naked, turning away from her life as pious widow. She bathes (10:3). That Judith has enough water in which to bathe is curious, given the lack of water that has driven the townspeople's desperation. Such a personal water supply may again underscore Judith's wealth and her separation from her people. The presence of water may

Jdt 10:1-19 (cont.)

go and capture all the hill country without losing one of his men, captured or slain."

[14]When the men heard her words, and observed her face—she was in their eyes marvelously beautiful—they said to her, [15]"You have saved your life by hurrying down to see our lord. Go at once to his tent; some of us will escort you and hand you over to him. [16]When you stand before him, have no fear in your heart, but tell him what you have just said, and he will treat you well."

[17]They chose from their number a hundred men to accompany her and her maid, and they brought them to the tent of Holofernes. [18]There was great excitement in the whole camp, for her arrival was reported from tent to tent. They came and gathered around her as she stood outside the tent of Holofernes, waiting until they told him about her. [19]They marveled at her beauty and admired the Israelites, judging them by her. They said to one another, "Who can despise these people, who have women like this among them? It is not wise to leave one of their men alive, for if we let them go they will be able to beguile the whole world!"

also underscore the sacred import of what Judith is about to do. As Eve Levavi Feinstein writes, "To us, bathing may seem like a mundane activity. But in biblical Israel, where water was scarce, bathing was often a momentous event, fraught with religious significance."[2] Women like Ruth (Ruth 3:3) and an unnamed woman in Ezekiel (Ezek 23:40) bathe in preparation for assignations; Bathsheba (2 Sam 11:4) and Susanna (Dan 13:15) take baths that ignite erotic attraction. For Bathsheba, an adulterous sexual encounter follows; for Susanna, an accusation of adultery. Bathsheba's bath was not just washing. It was a ritual bath after her menstrual period, a way of marking the transition from ritual impurity (and therefore a time of refraining from sexual relations with one's husband) to ritual purity (and therefore sex). Women bathe to prepare.

Thus, Judith's bathing is an act of symbolic and practical import. When Judith bathes, she emphasizes her liminality, her place between two worlds. It is as if she were washing away her widowhood, moving through the waters, being reborn an eligible woman. When she descends from her roof to prepare for her confrontation with Holofernes, she bathes as part of her process of moving from death to life, from cloister to public, from asceticism to decadence, from chaste widow to sexual

2. Eve Levavi Feinstein, "Bathing in the Hebrew Bible," Bible Odyssey, https://www.bibleodyssey.org/en/people/related-articles/bathing-in-the-hebrew-bible.

warrior.[3] This is only the first of Judith's baths. She will continue to immerse in water daily when she resides in the enemy's encampment. Her washings are markers of her separation and difference, of her moving from one state to another, and ultimately, as we will see, of the source of her salvation.

Judith bathes, and then she anoints herself with perfume. The Greek word for "anoint" used here is a verbal form of the more familiar term χριστός, whence "Christ" or "anointed one." Within the Hebrew Bible, anointing is a sign of consecration and dedication to God and those receiving anointing include kings, prophets, and priests. The sequence of bathing, anointing, and dressing also recapitulates Ruth's actions before she goes to the threshing floor to seduce Boaz (Ruth 3:3). Although in the immediate context of Ruth's story, she is just trying to save herself and her mother-in-law from poverty (Ruth 3:1), the ultimate outcome of her actions is that she becomes the foremother of David (Ruth 4:22) and Jesus (Matt 1:5). Judith is the "anointed" savior of her people, although, given the weaknesses of the Bethulian leaders, she has to anoint herself. That she anoints not with consecrated oil but with myrrh, with perfume, provides another ironic twist.

Once the bathing and anointing rituals are finished, Judith turns to her hair and dress. The specter of her dead husband graces the description of her clothes as she dons "the festive attire that she used to wear while her husband Manasseh was living" (10:3). The heroine is armed, but not with traditional weapons of shield, armor, and spear. She is armed with jewels, fine clothing, braids, ribbons, and perfume. Judith's transition in dress and appearance moves her from interiority and isolation to public life, dressed well and subject to the (approving) male gaze. She intends to use her beauty to attract and (as we will see) distract men: "Thus she made herself very beautiful, to entice the eyes of all the men who might see her" (10:4).

Judith's beautifying has been subject to feminist critique as well as feminist approval. On the one hand, Pamela Milne notes that Judith's combination of beauty and deceit "has serious consequences for the image of women it projects, and, hence, for the impact it has on women. . . . Through the propaganda of the femme fatale/female warrior character, men are taught, above all, to fear women. The otherness of

3. To use the phrase of Margarita Stocker, *Judith: Sexual Warrior; Women and Power in Western Culture* (New Haven: Yale University Press, 1998).

women is thereby emphasized and women become objects to be viewed suspiciously and trusted not at all."[4] Milne unequivocally rejects any notion that Judith could be a feminist hero.[5] On the other hand, explicitly countering the idea that Judith is presented as a femme fatale, Ora Brison understands her washing, anointing, and dressing as an indication of Judith's status as divine intermediary—these are the preparations of someone about to engage in cultic activities.[6] Hence, for Brison, Judith is a multifaceted figure who does provide a strong female model.

Rather than settling on one assessment of Judith's character or the other, we see merit in both approaches; in addition, we also seek other appraisals. Queer analysis provides another way to assess Judith's character by troubling binary distinctions of all kinds, whether of gender or of interpretation.[7] We can see Judith's character as seizing both masculine and feminine qualities and bending them to her own purpose. She combines violence with desirability, intelligence with exceptional beauty, wise speech with sexual availability. She presents whatever image will advance her purpose, and she will perform any role that will achieve her ends. Her success actually depends on her creating in Holofernes certain gendered expectations and then not conforming to them. This queering makes it difficult for modern readers to decide whether she is masculine or feminine, a positive or negative model, even calling those very categories into question.

This duality is demonstrated in her robing scene. The narrative adopts a traditional hypermasculine, heroic trope in the "arming of the hero" but queers this trope by changing the taking up of shields and spears to the putting on of tiaras and bracelets. The excessiveness of these external markers of femininity draws attention to the performative nature of

4. Pamela J. Milne, "What Shall We Do with Judith? A Feminist Assessment of a Biblical 'Heroine,'" in *A Feminist Companion to Tobit and Judith*, ed. Athalya Brenner-Idan and Helen Efthimiadis-Keith, FCB 20, 2nd ser. (London: Bloomsbury T&T Clark, 2015), 128. Milne is building on Betsy Merideth, "Desire and Danger: The Drama of Betrayal in Judges and Judith," in *Anti-Covenant: Counter-Reading Women's Lives in the Hebrew Bible*, ed. Mieke Bal (Sheffield: Almond, 1989), 63–78.

5. Milne, "What Shall We Do with Judith?," 136.

6. Brison, "Judith: A Pious Widow Turned *Femme Fatale*, or More?," in *A Feminist Companion to Tobit and Judith*, 190. Brison does not deny the femme fatale interpretation but sees it as secondary (199).

7. Tamber-Rosenau, *Women in Drag*, also uses a queer hermeneutic in her analysis of Judith. See her methodological section for a succinct review of queer criticism and its connections to feminist and gender criticism (9–23).

Judith's actions. In the same way that Holofernes's rage is a particular kind of masculine performance, Judith's dress is a particular kind of feminine performance. Nine verbs describe Judith's actions in fewer than two verses (Jdt 10:3-4a). Judith puts on not only clothes but also "anklets, bracelets, rings, earrings, and all her other jewelry" (10:4). As Caryn Tamber-Rosenau points out,

> The way the Greek is phrased gives the sense that Judith is piling one thing on top of another on top of another, as if she puts on a bracelet, then adds another, then perhaps an anklet, then a pair of earrings, then decides to go for broke and put on everything she owns. . . . It's just as the femme burlesque performer Sugar L'Amour . . . describes: "You think you're overly decorated, and then put 10,000 more things on it."[8]

Judith even seems to put on a device to make her steps smaller, thus not only wearing femininity but also shaping her bodily movements so that they are amplifying femininity. The anklet (literally "chain") may actually be a "step-chain" that links her ankles together to result in a mincing, and therefore more feminine, step (see Isa 3:16).[9]

Contemporary audiences may call to mind any number of literary and cinematic scenes of transformation through dress. Through fixing her hair (the NRSV says "combing" but the precise meaning of the verb διέξαν is uncertain), putting on the festive dress, jewelry, and mannerisms of "woman," Judith is becoming a high femme. Whereas such performance of dress is more obvious when people who identify as men dress as women, and when people who identify as women dress as men—in other words, what we call "drag"—all dress participates in gender performance, all dress is an aspect of how we express and communicate our gender identity. Identity is not just dual (masculine or feminine) but includes a wide range of positionalities. Judith may be putting on clothing appropriate to a woman of her time, but as readers watch her bathe and anoint and adorn in such an excessive manner, we can see something of a drag show.

Judith opens possibilities for gender experimentation and reexamination because she highlights how gender is a play we all act every day. Judith's identity is unstable, as demonstrated by how seamlessly she moves from pious widow to beautiful seductress with little more than a

8. Tamber-Rosenau, *Women in Drag*, 140–41. Sugar L'Amour is featured in the documentary *FtF: Female to Femme* (Kami Chisholm and Elizabeth Stark, 2006).

9. Carey A. Moore, *Judith*, AB 40 (Garden City, NY: Doubleday, 1985), 200.

change of hairstyle and clothes. We imagine her opening her wardrobe, surveying a range of possible outfits, considering a range of possible selves. Who will Judith be today? She is also foreshadowing the ways in which she will be an actor in the Assyrian camp when she plays the Israelite traitor entranced by Holofernes. Judith performs in more ways than one.

Judith gathers her wine, oil, grain, fig cakes, bread, and plates for her slave to carry (10:5). The Greek expression ἐπέθηκεν αὐτῇ, which the NRSV translates "gave them to her to carry," means literally "placed upon her," which conjures the image of a pack animal. Judith never asks her slave if she is willing to accompany her; the reader never hears the slave's voice to know if she goes willingly or under coercion (even presuming that we can untangle "willingness" from "coercion" in the mistress-slave dynamic). The reader does not even know if the slave is a Jew or a Gentile, which further complicates our understanding of the slave's participation in Judith's plans.[10] If she were Jewish, perhaps she would be equally invested in saving her people. If not, does she care? By nature of their status, slaves have few choices about where they go and what they do. Underneath the identity "slave" that is stamped upon them, however, they do have thoughts and ideas and desires of their own. They do have agency, no matter how constrained. The reader does see Judith's slave faithfully performing her duties, but the text gives no access to how deep her act might go.

The provisions that the slave carries are crucial for maintaining kosher dietary regulations in the Assyrian camp. These provisions are, however, also a part of Judith's act, even a kind of pious performance; feminine seduction is not the only show Judith must perform. As we discover in the next few chapters, the provisions are the props she will need to accomplish her plan. What a lot of weight the slave must carry.

Leaving Bethulia (10:6-19)

Prepared for battle, Judith with her slave leaves her house and meets the elders at the town gates (10:6). Judith's beauty invites amazement (10:7; cf. 10:14, 23). The elders marvel at her transformation in clothing and appearance. Beauty also seems like something Judith can put on and take off, like her festive garments and jewelry.

10. Jennifer Glancy, "Judith the Slaveholder," in *A Feminist Companion to Tobit and Judith*, 206–8.

The elders offer her nothing more than generic words of prayer (10:8). Perhaps as another indication of their lack of authority over her, Judith bows down to God rather than acknowledging the elders (10:8). She then commands them to order the gates open; they follow her directives and open the gates (10:9). They do not once express any doubt or misgiving about sending the two women out into a countryside filled with well-armed enemy soldiers with little more than kitchen accoutrements, even though what victorious soldiers do to women has been at the forefront of their conversations. Such an attitude may bespeak the confidence they have in Judith; it may also speak to their weakness as leaders. They are unable to protect "their" women in this time of crisis. All they can do is stand and stare after Judith until she disappears over the horizon (10:10).

Although two women leave Bethulia, here in the valley and throughout their adventure together, Judith's slave will variously appear and disappear. Plural verbs and pronouns are sometimes used but most of the time not. Verses 11 and 12 are emblematic: "As *they* [for clarity, the NRSV adds "the women"] were going straight on through the valley, an Assyrian patrol met *her* and took *her* into custody" (emphasis ours). The slave master's perspective is ingrained even in the grammar. Not only is the slave silent, she is ignored.

Although the slave gives Judith the support see needs to accomplish her plan, and although she too risks rape and murder equally with Judith, the text treats her as little more than a prop (both stage object and support). Perhaps the author, too, is dazzled by Judith's beauty, repeatedly stressed in this chapter, to see another woman.

When the Assyrian patrol meets Judith and her slave, they ask Judith (ignoring the slave) who her people are, from where is she coming, and to where is she going (10:12). In the last chapter, Judith prayed for deceit, and when she first opens her mouth to the Assyrians, the lies pour forth. She begins her lies, served with a generous dose of flattery, with her first words: "I am a daughter of the Hebrews, but I am fleeing from them, for they are about to be handed over to you to be devoured" (10:12). She then promises a "true report" to Holofernes and even some insider information to strengthen his hand against the small hill town. She holds out the prospect of a deathless battle, where he will be victorious "without losing one of his men, captured or slain" (10:13). An attractive proposition that repeats the promises already given by commanders of the Edomites, Moabites, and coastal areas (9:8-9).

The Assyrian patrol is so moved by Judith's loveliness (and her clever words) that they assemble one hundred men to escort her into the camp and straight to the general's tent, so that she arrives more like a special envoy than a captured prisoner of war. They assure her that she has saved her own life by seeking an audience with Holofernes (10:15), a true pronouncement but, ironically, not in the way that they mean. They even offer her advice on speaking with the general: "have no fear in your heart, but tell him what you have just said, and he will treat you well" (10:16). Ironically, they advise her to continue to lie.

Judith's beauty is such that on her arrival in the enemy camp, she causes a "great excitement" among the troops, and masses of armed men gather around her to see. They too "marveled at her beauty" (10:19). They are awestruck, and this awe (a corollary of fear) holds in check what we imagine a soldier's first impulse might be at seeing a captured foreign woman. The irony is that they may think that they have captured her, but in truth, she has captured them. As Carey Moore puts it, "Captive Judith captured her captors."[11]

She is so beautiful that the soldiers muse, "Who can despise these people, who have women like this among them? It is not wise to leave one of their men alive, for if we let them go they will be able to beguile the whole world!" (10:19). Judith's beauty may be saving her from harm at the moment, but it is now an additional threat to the survival of her people. Whatever her plan is (and the reader is still ignorant of it), it had better work or the Assyrian conquest may become a genocide.

Meeting Holofernes (10:20–11:23)

The narrative, which took so long to get to its heroine, who then spent so long talking to first the elders and then to God, suddenly starts moving at a rapid pace, which it will sustain though the next few chapters. Once Judith's plan has been put into motion, she moves quickly in and out (and in and out and in and out) of the camp before her final run back to the safety of Bethulia's walls.

Holofernes Greets Judith (10:20–11:4)

The real threat to Holofernes and his soldiers is not the men outside the camp but the women whom they have within. Holofernes in his tent is resplendent, "resting on his bed under a canopy that was woven with purple and gold, emeralds and other precious stones" (10:21). Judith,

11. Moore, *Judith*, 204.

Jdt 10:20–11:23

[20]Then the guards of Holofernes and all his servants came out and led her into the tent. [21]Holofernes was resting on his bed under a canopy that was woven with purple and gold, emeralds and other precious stones. [22]When they told him of her, he came to the front of the tent, with silver lamps carried before him. [23]When Judith came into the presence of Holofernes and his servants, they all marveled at the beauty of her face. She prostrated herself and did obeisance to him, but his slaves raised her up.

[11:1]Then Holofernes said to her, "Take courage, woman, and do not be afraid in your heart, for I have never hurt anyone who chose to serve Nebuchadnezzar, king of all the earth. [2]Even now, if your people who live in the hill country had not slighted me, I would never have lifted my spear against them. They have brought this on themselves. [3]But now tell me why you have fled from them and have come over to us. In any event, you have come to safety. Take courage! You will live tonight and ever after. [4]No one will hurt you. Rather, all will treat you well, as they do the servants of my lord King Nebuchadnezzar."

[5]Judith answered him, "Accept the words of your slave, and let your servant speak in your presence. I will say nothing false to my lord this night. [6]If you follow out the words of your servant, God will accomplish something through you, and my lord will not fail to achieve his purposes. [7]By the life of Nebuchadnezzar, king of the whole earth, and by the power of him who has sent you to direct every living being! Not only do human beings serve him because of you, but also the animals of the field and the cattle and the birds of the air will live, because of your power, under Nebuchadnezzar and all his house. [8]For we have heard of your wisdom and skill, and it is reported throughout the whole world that you alone are the best in the

who has moved out of her own protected space, encounters Holofernes in his protected space, the interior rooms of his private tent.[12] It is night time, so perhaps the most appropriate place for the general is in bed, and the canopy is a useful deterrent against insects; however, there is still something decadent about the reclining general among his jewels. The hypermasculine warrior who wreaks vengeance for his king and erupts in rage whenever he is questioned is now lolling in sumptuous comfort and covered in precious jewels. His role-reversal is as startling as hers is. But while Judith appears as hyperfeminine, Holofernes appears to be losing his signs of masculinity.

12. Barbara Schmitz, "Holofernes's Canopy in the Septuagint," in *The Sword of Judith: Judith Studies across the Disciplines*, ed. Kevin R. Brine, Elena Ciletti, and Henrike Lähnemann (Cambridge: Open Book Publishers, 2010), 73–74.

Jdt 10:20–11:23 (cont.)

whole kingdom, the most informed and the most astounding in military strategy.
[9]"Now as for Achior's speech in your council, we have heard his words, for the people of Bethulia spared him and he told them all he had said to you. [10]Therefore, lord and master, do not disregard what he said, but keep it in your mind, for it is true. Indeed our nation cannot be punished, nor can the sword prevail against them, unless they sin against their God.
[11]"But now, in order that my lord may not be defeated and his purpose frustrated, death will fall upon them, for a sin has overtaken them by which they are about to provoke their God to anger when they do what is wrong. [12]Since their food supply is exhausted and their water has almost given out, they will have planned to kill their livestock and have determined to use all that God by his laws has forbidden them to eat. [13]They have decided to consume the first fruits of the grain and the tithes of the wine and oil, which they had consecrated and set aside for the priests who minister in the presence of our God in Jerusalem—things it is not lawful for any of the people even to touch with their hands. [14]Since even the people in Jerusalem have been doing this, they have sent messengers there in order to bring back permission from the council of the elders. [15]When the response reaches them and they act upon it, on that very day they will be handed over to you to be destroyed.

The detail of the canopy contributes to this changing characterization. As Barbara Schmitz documents, references to canopies emerge in the classical literature of Rome during the first century BCE. In the writings of Horace, Propertius, and Varro, these canopies are associated with women, luxury, and an elevated class status, and they are described as disgusting and disgraceful. The women who own them also have some kind of power over men, and this is negatively regarded.[13] In Judith, however, the canopy belongs to a man,

> which serves to make Holofernes appear as a far more effeminate, weakened figure than at the beginning, and opens up an interesting gender perspective in the portrayal of Holofernes in two respects. Firstly, he is a man who surrenders himself to the beautiful Judith; although she says that she is his slave (Jdt 11:5, 16, 17), she in fact makes him her victim. Secondly, as he lies under the κωνώπιον he is characterized, in very strong terms that are suggestive of cross-gendering, as feminine. Holofernes is portrayed as womanlike and as having deficient masculinity.[14]

13. Ibid., 75–77.
14. Ibid., 77.

[16]"So when I, your slave, learned all this, I fled from them. God has sent me to accomplish with you things that will astonish the whole world wherever people shall hear about them. [17]Your servant is indeed God-fearing and serves the God of heaven night and day. So, my lord, I will remain with you; but every night your servant will go out into the valley and pray to God. He will tell me when they have committed their sins. [18]Then I will come and tell you, so that you may go out with your whole army, and not one of them will be able to withstand you. [19]Then I will lead you through Judea, until you come to Jerusalem; there I will set your throne. You will drive them like sheep that have no shepherd, and no dog will so much as growl at you. For this was told me to give me foreknowledge; it was announced to me, and I was sent to tell you."

[20]Her words pleased Holofernes and all his servants. They marveled at her wisdom and said, [21]"No other woman from one end of the earth to the other looks so beautiful or speaks so wisely!" [22]Then Holofernes said to her, "God has done well to send you ahead of the people, to strengthen our hands and bring destruction on those who have despised my lord. [23]You are not only beautiful in appearance, but wise in speech. If you do as you have said, your God shall be my God, and you shall live in the palace of King Nebuchadnezzar and be renowned throughout the whole world."

Holofernes lies on his bed in the back of the tent as Judith enters and stands in the front. In just a few days, he will again be lying on his bed while Judith stands. This will be his deathbed; the beautiful canopy will conceal his severed head as Judith escapes with it in her bag.

Reading Holofernes Queerly I

From the moment the bombshell Judith sashays into the Assyrian camp, Holofernes plays right into her seduction-and-destruction plan. Though Holofernes is sometimes portrayed as an uncomplicated paragon of lust, I argue that there is more to his character. Though scholars have begun to deconstruct issues of gender, sexuality, and power in the book of Judith as they relate to Judith herself, little has been done along these lines with Holofernes. Here, employing methodologies derived from queer theory, I reread Holofernes with an eye toward detailing the construction of his hypermasculine persona and detecting fissures in that portrayal.

To paraphrase a few methodological questions

proposed by Ken Stone in his essay on queer biblical criticism,[15] I ask regarding the book of Judith and the character of Holofernes: What conventions of masculinity does the book of Judith presuppose? How are assumptions about maleness manipulated in service of plot or characterization? Might Holofernes's success or failure at embodying norms of masculinity result from a strategy to cast him in a particular light? Does the text or Holofernes fail to "cite" conventions of masculinity in expected ways? What can these questions contribute to an understanding of both masculinity and the book of Judith?

From the beginning of the book of Judith, Holofernes is characterized as a highly effective military strongman. Holofernes is ordered by Nebuchadnezzar to command 120,000 foot soldiers and twelve thousand cavalry against the peoples of the Levant (2:5). Later on, in chapter 7, Holofernes is reported to have 170,000 foot soldiers, his ranks swelled with people who have joined up throughout his campaign (7:2). It is an absurd number of troops and serves to emphasize Holofernes's manly power: he is so tough that he can lead a city's worth of soldiers. Holofernes also expands on the king's orders by taking with him many beasts of burden to carry the supplies and, the Greek text tells us, "innumerable sheep, oxen, and goats" to feed the troops. Holofernes also takes plenty of rations, as well as a great quantity of gold and silver from the royal treasury (2:17-18). Then, Holofernes leads his army and an uncountable mass of followers across the land. In every element of the description of what Holofernes takes on his campaign, the words convey unimaginable magnitude. The point is clear: this is a major military campaign, and Holofernes is a major military leader. The book also spends eight verses detailing the army's march across the land, sacking and ravaging everything they come across, and the peoples' terrified reactions (2:21-28). Again, these verses serve to emphasize Holofernes's great prowess as a warrior and a leader and, by extension, his superlative virility.

Further reinforcing this portrayal of Holofernes is his reaction in chapter 3 to the peoples who want to surrender: he conquers them anyway. Holofernes's reaction in chapter 5 to the Ammonite Achior's description of the history and theology of the Israelites also

15. Ken Stone, "Gender Criticism: The Un-Manning of Abimelech," in *Judges and Method: New Approaches in Biblical Studies*, ed. Gale A. Yee (Minneapolis: Fortress, 2007), 192.

reinforces his characterization as a tougher-than-tough warrior. Holofernes declares that the Israelites' God is irrelevant because only Nebuchadnezzar is a god and that he will send his troops against Israel. In its exaggerated description of Holofernes's military might and the implication that this bears on his manliness, the book of Judith evinces what Cynthia Chapman calls the "understanding of battle as a masculine contest wherein masculinity and femininity function as metaphors for military victory and defeat respectively."[16]

Of course, there is a long history of describing war in hyperbolic terms, and the biblical texts do this frequently. In the context of the book of Judith, the over-the-top descriptions of Holofernes, his army, and their campaign serve to establish the Assyrians as particularly formidable enemies for Israel, which increases dramatic tension and makes Judith's triumph even more impressive. Reading these descriptions through the lens of gender criticism, however, shows how they also set up Holofernes as a paragon of masculinity.

When Judith walks into the Assyrian camp in chapter 10, she is escorted to the general's tent. This tent both epitomizes Holofernes's performance of military masculinity and undermines it. Holofernes's tent is decked out in a parody of the pomp that should surround a top commander's accommodations. It makes sense that his tent would be nicer than other tents, but perhaps not that a battlefield bed has a canopy woven with purple, gold, emeralds, and other jewels or that Holofernes's movements are preceded by attendants carrying silver lamps (10:21-22). The tent speaks to Holofernes's performance as a powerful man: he has all the trappings that should accompany his exalted station, even in battlefield conditions. Yet, while perhaps meant to signify Holofernes's powerful brand of manhood, it is ironic that the overdecoration of his tent bears more than a passing resemblance to the overdecoration of Judith herself.

Caryn Tamber-Rosenau

When Holofernes gets up and appears before her, Judith prostrates herself and rises again only when his slaves pull her up (10:23). Throughout their interactions, Judith will be excessively deferential both in speech and in act, showing an obsequiousness designed to feed his ego and thus

16. Cynthia R. Chapman, *The Gendered Language of Warfare in the Israelite-Assyrian Encounter* (Winona Lake, IN: Eisenbrauns, 2004), 141.

disarm him. She will position herself below him until the fateful moment when she will rise up above him, his head in her hands.

Both Holofernes and Judith engage in a war of words. Their dialogues may be full of reassurances and compliments, but they are martial contests nevertheless. Were Holofernes to win (over) this beautiful Hebrew woman (and he is convinced that he already has), then his victory over her people is assured and he will have a prize worthy of his rank and status; were Judith to win (over) this Assyrian general, he will die and her people will be saved. His first words to her can be construed as either soothing someone who is afraid or inspiring someone to battle: "Take courage," he says (11:1). He may mean his words to soothe and calm, but Judith will take these words to gird herself for the battle that has already begun.

Holofernes's words are also full of deceit, and Judith's response to him will be as well. He insists that he has never hurt anyone who has surrendered to Nebuchadnezzar, vows no one will hurt Judith, and finally suggests that the Israelites' current distress is of their own making. Even now, he asserts, he had no intention of harming anyone; had the hill people not slighted him first, he would not be threatening violence (11:2). Holofernes, mimicking the rhetoric of abusers and rapists, blames the victim for having excited and enraged the assailant. His masculinity is diminished and his emasculating fate foreshadowed as he stretches out under his canopy, but violence still simmers and attack is ever imminent.

After detailing his own identity, as he wants to present it to Judith, only then does he ask her to explain her presence in the Assyrian camp. He presumes she has "fled" from Bethulia, which he characterizes as a place of danger. In contrast to the Israelite city, his camp is a place of "safety." His words are all wrong, but for ironic reasons he does not yet realize. His tent will be the true place of danger. He also again advises her, "Take courage" (11:3). Judith has shown no sign of trepidation behind enemy lines. (Compare, for example, Esther in the LXX as she approaches Xerxes, leaning on the arm of a slave for support: "She was radiant with perfect beauty, and she looked happy, as if beloved, but her heart was frozen with fear" [Esth 15:5; Add D].)

In words full of unintended irony, Holofernes predicts both Judith's present safety and her long life (11:3-4). Judith is safe—but, as the reader knows, Holofernes is not. Finally, he vows that no one will harm her. His assurance is that she will be treated as well as the "slaves" (δοῦλοι; NRSV "servants") in the house of Nebuchadnezzar. He reduces her to the role of slave, and in so doing, we are reminded that her slave is present, silent and waiting. The language of being "like" a slave when there are actual slaves present shows how metaphors can sometimes deny actuality. When he ends his promise with the reference to the slaves of his lord (κύριος) Nebuchadnezzar, we are reminded of Judith's "lord," who will prove victorious through her hand.

Judith Responds (11:5-19)

Judith continues to be excessively deferential and cunningly deceptive. She begins her response to Holofernes by calling herself his "slave" (δοῦλος), here echoing his term but suggesting she is in service to Holofernes and not Nebuchadnezzar. She then asks for permission to speak even though he has just asked her a question. Amy-Jill Levine argues that Judith's "words subvert the metaphoric understanding of language in the public sphere—the sharing of a common code."[17] This subversion is seen most strikingly in her conversation with Holofernes, where she repeatedly interjects the address "my lord" (κύριος μου). Holofernes and his retinue assume that she is referring to Holofernes himself, but "my lord" is also a title for God. In her opening words to the Assyrian general, she vows, "I will say nothing false to my lord this night" (11:5)—but what does she mean? If she is promising Holofernes that she will tell the truth, then she is lying, but if she is swearing to God, then her words carry a truthful, albeit double meaning. She continues: "If you follow out the words of your servant, God will accomplish something through you, and my lord will not fail to achieve his purposes" (11:6). If Holofernes follows Judith's advice, God will work through him, but to achieve *God's* purposes, not Holofernes's. Double entendre, continuing throughout the encounter between our heroine and her enemy, contributes to the narrative's multifaceted ironies. Judith is clever and verbally adroit, as is the author of her book. Holofernes's own vanity is also underscored: from his perspective, who else could be Judith's "lord" but himself?

Judith continues to play on his vanity when she avers that Holofernes is the prime reason so many people serve and worship Nebuchadnezzar—not only the people of the earth but the animals and the birds as well (11:7-8). As aforementioned, Holofernes's mirroring of Nebuchadnezzar

17. Amy-Jill Levine, "Sacrifice and Salvation: Otherness and Domestication in the Book of Judith," in *A Feminist Companion to Esther, Judith and Susanna*, ed. Athalya Brenner, FCB 7 (Sheffield: Sheffield Academic, 1995), 217.

in chapters 2 and 3 results in his appropriating language of divinity for himself; Judith's words affirm this appropriation and even augment it. She is laying it on thick, so to speak. His vanity knows no bounds, so her exaggerations appear to him statements of fact, and her hinting that he is equal if not superior to his king seems to please him.

This praise becomes ominous as we turn from Holofernes's perspective to the biblical perspective and recall the prophetic oracles against human kings who presume to receive worship. Judith implicates Holofernes in this idolatry, and based on biblical precedent, we know that all will not go well for him. According to Judith, Holofernes alone is "the best," "the most informed," and even "the most astounding" (11:8; the book uses θαυμαστός ["astounding"] only one other time, in 16:3 to describe God).[18]

Once she has sufficiently flattered Holofernes, Judith reveals that God is about to deliver Bethulia to the Assyrians. She reminds the general of Achior's speech to the council (11:9). With the reference to Achior, we can see the ways in which Judith's and Achior's speeches to Holofernes share a number of features. Both Achior and Judith use deferential language when addressing Holofernes, repeatedly calling him "master" and "lord" (compare, for example, 5:20 with 11:10). Both use the language of truth in promising to tell no falsehoods (compare 5:5 with 11:5). Achior's speech also establishes Judith's excuse for leaving Bethulia: Achior has told Holofernes that the Jews will be defeated only if they sin against God; Judith arrives in Holofernes's camp by reporting their sin and therefore imminent defeat. Judith and Achior are paired figures, each speaking to Holofernes, each crossing between Bethulia and the Assyrian camp. Achior provides Judith her "cover story" in the Assyrian camp, and, as if to underscore how pivotal Achior is to the plot, the verse where Judith invokes Achior is the only verse in Judith's entire speech that is transparently and completely true (11:9). And yet, her truth-telling contains a warning: the people of Bethulia spared Achior; that is, they did not do what Holofernes expected them to do. They are a people who, represented by Judith, continue to surprise him.

According to Judith, the Bethulians are about to do the very thing that will lead to their defeat—they are about to sin against God. Their crime, she says, will be to consume forbidden foods: the first fruits of the grains, the wine and the oil that have been consecrated to the priests in Jerusalem (11:11-13). She adds that even the people in Jerusalem have been eating this sacred food (11:14), and therefore, she implies, God will hand

18. Gera, *Judith*, 355.

over not only Bethulia but all of Israel. Even when predicting victory for Holofernes, she is conforming to the worldview Achior outlined earlier. God will be the one who ensures the defeat of the Jews, and God will do so because the Jews have proven unfaithful to the covenant bond(s) and worship obligations. She couches her words in praise to the power of Holofernes and the worthiness of Nebuchadnezzar, but ultimately she is still affirming her God's supremacy.

In another layer of irony, Judith is essentially saying that she has left her city and entered the pagan army camp *so that* she can keep Jewish law (11:16-17). Since those in Bethulia, she says, are about to consume foods set aside for God, she has left in order not to consume or be implicated in their consumption. Judith's story about the people's sinful dining choices is fabricated from beginning to end, even including a couple of halakhic flourishes otherwise unknown from biblical or rabbinic law. For example, there is no law forbidding the touching of tithed offerings (11:13). Although some commentators attempt to glean information about actual Jewish practices,[19] it is best to remember that Judith is making up a story and telling it to a non-Jew who is wholly ignorant of Jewish law. She just needs to be convincing, not truthful. Even if the situation Judith describes were legally accurate and the people really did touch the tithed food, the principle of what the rabbinic sources call *pekuaḥ nefesh*, "saving a life," would apply. According to this principle, Jews are permitted (even required) to break every commandment except for the ones prohibiting murder, sexual immorality, and idolatry in order to "preserve life" (b. Sanh. 74a). One is to live by the Torah, not die by it (Yoma 85b). A people starving under siege would be expected, not forbidden, to eat otherwise forbidden foods. The extent of this principle seems to have been a matter of debate in the Second Temple period (see Josephus's Jewish Wars 5.562–66; Matt 12:3-4; and 1 Macc 2:39-41),[20] as it sometimes still is today,[21] but this debate suggests that the general idea would have been known at the time of Judith's writing. For an original

19. See for example, André Barucq, *Judith, Esther*, 2nd ed. (Paris: Cerf, 1959), 56.

20. Gera, *Judith*, 360–61.

21. As Jewish congregations face the challenges of the COVID-19 pandemic, rabbis have issued teshuvot (official halakhic rulings), including changes to the rules around communal worship, using technology on Shabbat, and rituals of burial and mourning. Different rabbis have reached different conclusions about these matters and different congregations are following different practices.

audience, Holofernes may look even more foolish for believing Judith's account of practices that are not actual or accurate.[22]

Judith continues to appear simultaneously deeply devoted to God and sincerely deferential to Holofernes. With her typical double entendre, she says, "God has sent me to accomplish with you things that will astonish the whole world" (11:16). Judith further capitalizes on her show of piety to lay the groundwork for her escape. Her ritual devotion sets the pattern that will later allow her to walk, unquestioned and unchallenged, out of the pagan camp. She claims that, to serve both God and Holofernes, she must leave the camp every evening for prayer. It will be during one of these nocturnal prayer sessions that God will tell her when the people of Bethulia have succumbed to sin and eaten the consecrated foods (11:17). Judith, in turn, will report to Holofernes the most opportune time to strike.

Although the text does not use this term, Judith is indeed playing the prophet (the charge Holofernes levels against Achior in 6:2). She is acting as a spokesperson for God and an intermediary between God and the general. She also plays the prophet in terms of announcing her commission ("I was sent to tell you" [11:19]) and predicting the outcome of the contest: "For this was told me to give me foreknowledge; it was announced to me, and I was sent to tell you" (Jdt 11:19). The double entendre of the prophetic voice is a trope that is, again, resonant in Greek literature and tradition, particularly Herodotus (1:46-51). Herodotus records the story of Croesus's ill-thought campaign against the Persians. Croesus carefully seeks out a strong oracle and discovers the Pythia at Delphi. He inquires whether he should wage war and is told, "If you attack, a great army will be destroyed." Buoyed by his own hubris, Croesus interprets this as a fine omen and attacks. His armies are routed. In a similar way, Holofernes interprets (the female) Judith's prophecies, again led by his arrogance, as promising victory instead of foretelling his humiliating defeat. Judith has subtly suggested that in his military victory, he will replace his own king Nebuchadnezzar. Judith also uses language that echoes Exodus 11:7 ("no dog will so much as growl at you" [11:19]), thereby both making Holofernes's triumphant march to Jerusalem a twisted likeness of the Hebrew's escape from Egyptian slavery and placing herself in the divine position or at least in the role of Moses. Her continual self-designation of "slave" reinforces the allusion, even as it yet again overlooks the real slaves, including Judith's slave, who

22. Gera, *Judith*, 359.

are in attendance. Ironically (again), here in 11:20 the narrator mentions as in attendance Holofernes's servants (θεραπόντων, lit. "healers," whence "therapy"); their services will go unused.

Whereas the Assyrians are imagining a triumphant procession with Judith and Holofernes at the head, the Israelites scattering in confusion and fear, Judith means that she will lead Holofernes to Jerusalem, and she will be carrying his head in a bag. *His* armies will be like sheep with no shepherd; no one will threaten or oppose him, no dog will bark, because he will be quite dead. An additional level of irony is present in this passage since Judith is not, as far as we know, in direct communication with God, and the words she promises to bring Holofernes are lies.

Holofernes Praises Judith (11:20-23)

Well pleased, Holofernes marvels at Judith's wisdom (11:20). It is easy to believe that someone who flatters you and tells you what you want to hear is exceedingly wise. His amazement and that of his servants at her intellect becomes yet another moment of irony. Holofernes does not realize how smart Judith really is. He has no idea of her plans, let alone that she has just hinted what she will do. Completely outplayed by her, Holofernes predicts his own ruin: "God has done well to send you ahead of [literally "at the head of," which may be a pun foreshadowing his decapitation] the people, to strengthen your hands, and to bring destruction on all those who have despised my lord" (11:22). His reference to her "hands" adds an even greater ironic touch. Judith is going to bring destruction down on all who have despised her lord, the God of Israel.

Holofernes also, rhetorically, seeks to establish his own glory, and masculinity, by proclaiming, "No other woman from one end of the earth to the other looks so beautiful or speaks so wisely!" (11:21). It appears, from his perspective, that he has the most beautiful woman in the world at his command. He should have remembered, as the book's original readers likely did, that the most beautiful woman in the world was Helen of Troy, and she brought destruction when she left her home for the bed of another. It will turn out that Judith is both Helen, albeit one faithful to her "Lord," and the proverbial Trojan horse.[23]

Holofernes continues, "If you do as you have said, your God shall be my God, and you shall live in the palace of King Nebuchadnezzar and

23. See the contribution below, pp. 111–12, for Steed Vernyl Davidson's complementary reading of Judith and Helen of Troy.

be renowned throughout the whole world" (11:23). The comment about the Jewish woman living in the Gentile king's palace should remind us of Sarah in Pharaoh's household (Gen 12) and Esther in the Persian court. In both cases, the women are placed in the position of the king's sexual object. Sarah receives her rescue from God by means of a plague; in the Septuagint's version of Esther, the heroine despises her Gentile husband. These allusions suggest it would not go well were Judith to go where Holofernes promises to take her.

The ironies continue. In words reminiscent of Ruth's promise to Naomi (Ruth 1:16), Holofernes sounds as if he is promising conversion if he is victorious. His worship of Nebuchadnezzar would seem to preclude even the acknowledgment of other gods, let alone their worship. Perhaps he is swept away by Judith's extraordinary beauty and pervasive speech. Perhaps he is vowing to raise her God to the level of Nebuchadnezzar's greatness. Perhaps he is implying that Judith will worship Nebuchadnezzar in the end as she lives out the rest of her days amid his wealth and glory (so, Holofernes's god will become Judith's god). All of these meanings are possible, but they all ignore the primary theological point of the text: there is no God but God, so Judith's God is already Holofernes's God. No matter what Holofernes believes, this God—his God—has already pronounced judgment on him, and this judgment is to be executed by the hand of Judith. She *will* be renowned, although not for the reasons Holofernes thinks.

Judith's beauty and wisdom are linked and foregrounded in this passage. We find the earliest readings of Judith in patristic sources, a time "when religious persecutions were not so much a threat to the Church Fathers as sexual temptations to a celibate priesthood."[24] The church fathers read all of Judith's attributes and actions through the lens of her chastity. For example, Jerome writes in the preface to his translation, "Receive the widow Judith, a paradigm of chastity, and with triumphant laud make her known in perpetual praise."[25] Her victory over Holofernes, for Jerome, is a reward for this chastity. The lens of "chaste widow" brings Judith's virtues into sharper focus while simultaneously diminishing her more ambivalent characteristics (deception, sexual attractiveness,

24. Moore, *Judith*, 64.

25. As cited in Elena Ciletti and Henrike Lähnemann, "Judith in the Christian Tradition," in *The Sword of Judith*, 43.

violence).[26] As we move into the Middle Ages, the emphasis on her chastity continues, and Judith becomes a personification of both the church (see, for example, Rabanus's commentaries) and the Virgin Mary herself. In striking illustrations, the medieval allegorical Bibles *Biblia Pauperum* and *Speculum Humanae Salvationis* both link Judith's beheading of Holofernes to Mary's conquering of the devil. In this way, Judith becomes a symbol of Fortitude, Justice, Wisdom, Magnanimity, and Eloquence,[27] her physical beauty an outward sign of her moral strength and grace. In these patristic and medieval readings, Judith's beauty is akin to God's own glory as it shines through the church and Mary.

Later, cultural appropriation of Judith becomes unmoored from early patristic emphases. Without the strong organizational lens of chastity, Judith's striking looks take on other meanings, ones associated with carnality and sensuality, not inner beauty. Her beauty, when linked to deception and sexually tempting behavior designed to get Holofernes into a compromising position, establishes her as a femme fatale, a dangerous sexual temptress bent on the destruction of men.

Feminist criticism challenges us to reconsider the ways in which we readers are invested in the process of interpretation. Alongside a number of other contemporary reading strategies, feminist criticism reveals that who we are influences how we read. Cultural context, social location, and even personal taste can shape readings in ways that are often invisible to us.

Judith foregrounds desire: Nebuchadnezzar's and Holofernes's desires for absolute mastery and control, the Bethulians' desire for water, Holofernes's sexual desire for Judith. We read Judith with desires of our own: desires to validate our own choice of chastity, or to see the powerless given power, or to see the strength of a woman, or to affirm our own prejudices against women and against any disruption of traditional gender roles. These desires, even the competing desires, are satiated or frustrated in various ways within the text, producing for us an ambivalence with respect to Judith's character. She is beautiful and we are drawn to beauty—but for what purpose and to what end?

26. Ibid., 44–45. See also Nicole Tilford, "Judith and Her Interpreters," in *Women's Bible Commentary*, ed. Carol A. Newsom, Sharon H. Ringe, and Jacqueline E. Lapsley, 3rd ed. (Louisville: Westminster John Knox, 2012), 391.

27. Ciletti and Lähnemann, "Judith in the Christian Tradition," 46, 50, 52–53.

Judith 12:1–13:10a

Wielding the Master's Tool

Judith's ruse, thus far, has succeeded. She has been accepted into the Assyrian camp, and she has won over the Assyrian general. Now she must lay the groundwork for her final triumph: the assassination of the enemy Holofernes. In this section, the story reaches its violent climax.

As Robin Gallaher Branch has noted in her contribution above, the scene where Judith beheads Holofernes is frequently depicted, especially by baroque and Renaissance painters. Biblical imprimatur gave them permission to combine sexuality with the beheading in all of its gruesome details. Many prominent male artists, such as Caravaggio and Donatello, took Judith as their subject, but women artists seem to be particularly drawn to this scene. Each canvas is like a freeze-frame. Giulia Lama captured the moment of Judith's prayer, right before the decapitation. Holofernes lies stretched out, suggestively naked except for a sheet thrown over his genitals (*Judith and Holofernes*, 1730). Artemisia Gentileschi takes us to the edge of the bed to see the slaughter in process, blood flowing in all directions (1612–1613, 1620). The decapitation is complete in Lavinia Fontana's picture, with Judith holding Holofernes's head in one hand, his sword in the other. Both she and her slave behind her calmly look at the viewer (*Judith with the Head of Holofernes*, 1600). Fontana painted Judith again, looking behind her shoulder while putting the severed head in the bag (*Judith and Holofernes*). Elisabetta Sirani also painted, several times, the moment immediately following the assassination. In *Judith and Holofernes* (mid-seventeenth century), Sirani's Judith towers over the other figures while she slides the general's head into her bag. In another, she is gripping his hair in both hands while turning her head at an almost coquettish angle (*Judith with the Head of Holofernes*, 1660). Fede Galizia paints this scene with Holofernes's head displayed on a platter (*Judith with the Head of Holofernes*, 1596). Gentileschi paints Judith a third time, pausing and listening with her slave just as she is about to escape (*Judith and Her Maidservant*, c. 1623–1625), a painting that another contributor, Jessica Jernigan, will address below.

These paintings and others explore the general ambivalence about Judith: Is she a warrior and a hero, a chaste exemplar, a femme fatal? Is her act that of a savior or a terrorist? More recently, Diane Goodpasture (2010) created a stained-glass window of Judith holding Holofernes's decollated head. The sword, which looks more like a giant machete, dominates the scene. Judith's arms are bare, her dress bespattered with blood. Holofernes's face still has a look of surprised horror. Judith's face, though, is blank. No eyes, no nose, no mouth, no expression; her face reveals nothing about who she is or what she is feeling.

Judith Establishes Her Routine (12:1-9)

Holofernes invites Judith to dine with him on "delicacies" and wine, at a table set with silver. Judith demurs. To eat at his table would be "an offense" (Greek: σκάνδαλον, whence "scandal" [12:2]), but she assures him that she has brought her own food and drink so she can still sit with him. Meals are heavy with cultural import, and like Judith's words, her meals carry double meanings. On the one hand, they demonstrate her piety. She is determined to keep kosher no matter where she is or what she is doing; thus, the centrality of keeping kosher for establishing Jewish identity is underscored, much like it is in other Second Temple texts.[1] It is likely that her food is not only kosher but also simple, the kind of items one can place in a bag and carry into a camp. Holofernes, on the other hand, sets his table with markers of his power and wealth: fine food served on silver, fit more for royalty in the palace than for a soldier in the field. Again, we can imagine those slaves forced to carry not only

1. See Deborah Levine Gera, *Judith*, CEJL (Berlin: de Gruyter, 2014), 368–70, for other examples.

Jdt 12:1-9

12:1Then he commanded them to bring her in where his silver dinnerware was kept, and ordered them to set a table for her with some of his own delicacies, and with some of his own wine to drink. 2But Judith said, "I cannot partake of them, or it will be an offense; but I will have enough with the things I brought with me." 3Holofernes said to her, "If your supply runs out, where can we get you more of the same? For none of your people are here with us." 4Judith replied, "As surely as you live, my lord, your servant will not use up the supplies I have with me before the Lord carries out by my hand what he has determined."

5Then the servants of Holofernes brought her into the tent, and she slept until midnight. Toward the morning watch she got up 6and sent this message to Holofernes: "Let my lord now give orders to allow your servant to go out and pray." 7So Holofernes commanded his guards not to hinder her. She remained in the camp three days. She went out each night to the valley of Bethulia, and bathed at the spring in the camp. 8After bathing, she prayed the Lord God of Israel to direct her way for the triumph of his people. 9Then she returned purified and stayed in the tent until she ate her food toward evening.

weapons of war but also plates of luxury. These markers also indicate an underlying (effeminate) decadence. Biblically literate readers may be reminded of other decadent meals that do not end well, in particular the death of King Belshazzar and so the end of Nebuchadnezzar's empire in Daniel 5.

Judith's eating practices are not just about piety. Judith is particularly punctilious with her food. In the Hellenistic period, a time known for the development of the symposium and so of meals as identity markers, food regulations were becoming increasingly more important for binding Jewish communities together and distinguishing them from the surrounding pagan cultures. Judith has already lied about dietary laws, however, by claiming that touching consecrated grain, wine, and oil would be violations of the law and call down God's wrath (11:13). Is her bag of kosher ware and fare evidence of Judith's extreme piety or just another performance, or is it both? A performance can be false, or sincere. Fastidious keeping of food proscriptions (whether real or not) also buttresses her story about needing to leave Bethulia to maintain proper eating.[2]

2. Both Moore (*Judith*, AB 40 [Garden City, NY: Doubleday, 1985], 218) and Gera (*Judith*, 371) make this last point.

Judith's meal practices in the Assyrian camp convey a "mixed message."[3] Having a meal with someone is a way to build community; if the person is a newcomer, the meal welcomes them into the community. Achior is treated in a similar fashion (invited to a πότος, a drinking fest) when he enters Bethulia, and this festive, communal meal signals his acceptance among the Israelites. Holofernes intends the meal he prepares for Judith to mean the same. Judith accepts, but with the caveat that she will use her own plates and food. He does not realize that her presence at his table is a feint. She resists incorporation into the Assyrian community by maintaining her ethnic/religious difference through what she allows to enter her mouth. As Holofernes's table, so his bed: since eating is often associated with sexuality, the separation that Judith maintains in her dining is a subtle indication that she will later resist other attempts he makes to penetrate her body.

When Judith explains the conditions for accepting his dinner invitation, Holofernes expresses concern about her supply: what will she do in the camp when she runs out of food? The man who would starve an entire population through siege is now concerned about a single woman's rations. Holofernes also remarks, "none of your people are here with us" (12:3). How we read this verse in relation to the slave, who is likely present, is our choice. Is that slave actually one of Judith's people? Has the general simply ignored her? Has the slave herself made her presence unobtrusive, as a "good slave" should?

As if turning to her readers and winking, Judith replies: "As surely as you live, my lord, your servant will not use up the supplies I have with me before the Lord carries out by my hand what he has determined" (12:4). Despite the NRSV's decision to capitalize the second occurrence of the word κύριος and thus indicate that Judith first addresses Holofernes and second references God, this verse continues the double use of the word "lord." Readers can "see" the distinction in intent; hearers, such as Holofernes, cannot. Unable to "hear" a capital letter, he understands himself as the referent to both of Judith's "lords." With this wink, Judith retires for the night.

It is difficult to determine exact time. According to 9:1, Judith begins her prayers and preparation for confronting Holofernes when the priests offer the evening incense at the temple. Since then, she has left Bethulia, been captured by the Assyrians, been taken to Holofernes, had an audience with the general, eaten a late night snack, been taken to her own

3. Gera, *Judith*, 369.

tent, and slept for a period—a lot to accomplish in only a few hours. The text itself also seems somewhat confused about how long she slept. We read that she sleeps until midnight, but then gets up toward morning (12:5). Does Judith arise at midnight or at the morning watch? Does she wake up at midnight and then lie awake until the first light filters through the tent? If the latter, what is she doing? Does she have a bout of insomnia? Is she formulating her plan? Is she praying? The long hours of the night slip by, silent about what Judith is doing.

At dawn, Judith sends a message (the messengers themselves remain unidentified) to Holofernes to ask him to command the guards to let her leave the camp; he obeys her (12:6-7). For three days, she leaves to bathe and pray. Commentators have questioned exactly what Judith is accomplishing in her bathing rituals. Because the text notes that she is "purified" (12:9) by these baths, some have suggested that her nightly dips are more than just removing the dirt and grime of the day. Within Judaism, the tradition of ritual washing has biblical origins. Certain actions, bodily processes, or diseases rendered a person ritually impure and thus unable to perform certain sacrifices. The process for removing impurity entailed waiting a period of time, bringing a sacrifice, and/or ritual washing. For example, after healing from a diagnosis of leprosy, an elaborate sacrificial ritual is performed, after which the healed man washes his clothes, shaves his beard, and bathes in water. He then must live outside the camp for seven days (Lev 14:1-9). According to archaeological evidence, ritual washing was practiced widely during the Hellenistic and early Herodian periods in specially constructed tubs (*mikvot*). Ritual baths are found among diaspora Jewish communities, in the homes of Jerusalem elites, throughout the lower Galilee, at Qumran, lining the roads into Jerusalem, even at Masada. Ritual immersion becomes integral for rituals of conversion into Judaism, although we are not certain of the origins of this rabbinic practice. John the Baptist immersed people in preparation for the eschaton, not to cleanse them from sin, but as a public testimony that they had repented, and Jesus and his early followers immersed people as an initiation rite for their entry into the movement.

Some have suggested that Judith is cleansing herself "from the uncleanliness" of either menstruation or contact with Gentiles.[4] Neither explanation suffices since marking the end of menstruation necessitates

4. See Moore, *Judith*, 219, and Gera, *Judith*, 372, for a review. Both Moore and Gera conclude that Judith is simply purifying herself for prayer, not cleansing from an impurity.

only one bath, not three, and simple contact with Gentiles is never a source of impurity (certainly the elders in Bethulia did not go and wash after they prayed with Achior [6:20-21]). Like her bath in chapter 9, Judith's bathing here is also a method of preparation as she moves from one state to another. She is in a liminal space: she has left permanent dwellings for temporary ones; she has left city for countryside; she has left her people to dwell with foreigners invading her homeland. She acknowledges her liminality in her first encounter with the Assyrians when she calls herself a Hebrew (10:12)—"Hebrew" means "one who crosses over." Rather than washing away uncleanliness (whatever the origin), her nightly bathing is best understood as marking her movement from the camp into prayer, death to life, profane to sacred space. She may also be, at this moment as she was in her earlier bath, her most true self, minus the trappings of luxury or the mourning clothes of the widow. But it is dark, and we cannot see her clearly.

Most immediate, her bath is preparing her for her nightly prayer; more broadly, she is preparing to save her people. The murder of Holofernes is a kind of ritual sacrifice, which she approaches in a state of ritual purity.

Judith's eating and her bathing practices also fulfill several narrative needs. Like her food restrictions, these actions evidence her deep and abiding piety. Like her food practices, they are also her means of establishing the routine that will provide her a safe escape route. These actions are also sites of ambiguity, if not outright deception. She may, indeed, be pious, but she is also not above using sacred rituals to deceive her enemies. We are reminded here of her ancestor Simeon, who used the ritual of circumcision not to welcome the Shechemites into Israel but to punish them for the rape of Dinah and weaken them for the slaughter to come. For Judith's scheme to be successful, she must beguile with her beauty, disarm with her deference, and misdirect with her religiosity.

Holofernes's Party (12:10-20)

On the fourth day, Holofernes makes his move. He plans a banquet (a drinking party) for his closest attendants, and he sends his eunuch Bagoas to invite Judith. His intentions are clear: "For it would be a disgrace if we let such a woman go without having intercourse with her. If we do not seduce her, she will laugh at us" (12:12). Holofernes's masculinity is at stake. The type of masculinity that the book of Judith locates in Nebuchadnezzar and Holofernes is in constant need of affirmation. It is linked to rage and excessive violence; in this verse, it is linked to

Jdt 12:10-20

[10]On the fourth day Holofernes held a banquet for his personal attendants only, and did not invite any of his officers. [11]He said to Bagoas, the eunuch who had charge of his personal affairs, "Go and persuade the Hebrew woman who is in your care to join us and to eat and drink with us. [12]For it would be a disgrace if we let such a woman go without having intercourse with her. If we do not seduce her, she will laugh at us."

[13]So Bagoas left the presence of Holofernes, and approached her and said, "Let this pretty girl not hesitate to come to my lord to be honored in his presence, and to enjoy drinking wine with us, and to become today like one of the Assyrian women who serve in the palace of Nebuchadnezzar." [14]Judith replied, "Who am I to refuse my lord? Whatever pleases him I will do at once, and it will be a joy to me until the day of my death." [15]So she proceeded to dress herself in all her woman's finery. Her maid went ahead and spread for her on the ground before Holofernes the lambskins she had received from Bagoas for her daily use in reclining.

[16]Then Judith came in and lay down. Holofernes' heart was ravished with her and his passion was aroused, for he had been waiting for an opportunity to seduce her from the day he first saw her. [17]So Holofernes said to her, "Have a drink and be merry with us!" [18]Judith said, "I will gladly drink, my lord, because today is the greatest day in my whole life." [19]Then she took what her maid had prepared and ate and drank before him. [20]Holofernes was greatly pleased with her, and drank a great quantity of wine, much more than he had ever drunk in any one day since he was born.

heterosexual prowess. Although Holofernes has remarked on Judith's beauty and wisdom (11:23), he does not attribute his wanting sex with her to these characteristics. Rather, to feel like a man, the man must bed a woman, not because of any inherent desire but because that is simply what men do. This type of masculinity, then, is entirely dependent on women and thus leads to a paradoxical gender dynamic where women are essential to the verification of a man's masculinity. This dynamic will be Holofernes's undoing.

The Greek word ὁμιλήσαντες, translated by the NRSV as "having intercourse with" (12:12), has a wider range of meaning than that clinical phrase indicates. The verb ὁμιλέω is often used in the context of illicit sex (Prov 5:19 and Susanna [Dan 13:37, 57, 58]) but also means "to associate with" and is sometimes found in nonsexual contexts (examples include Prov 23:31 and Dan 1:19). The next verb Holofernes uses to describe what he wants to do with Judith, ἐπισπάομαι, means "to draw upon or after" and signifies seduction; some commentators have argued that it has an even rougher valence, indicating rape.[5] Although the line separating seduction and rape may blur in a late-night drunken encounter between a general and his quarry, no force is explicitly implied in Holofernes's words here.[6] One of the only other places where we find the verb in a sexual context is in the Septuagint translation of Genesis 39:12. Potiphar's wife uses this word when she grabs hold of Joseph's coat and demands that he have sex with her. Both Joseph's and Judith's situations are fraught, and certainly either of them could have been subjected to forced intercourse, since Joseph is a slave and Judith is encamped among enemy soldiers, but Holofernes speaks of seduction, not rape, when he discusses his plans for the evening.

Ideologies and expectations of masculinity and femininity (the man must penetrate, the woman must be penetrated) shape the narrative and set up the final confrontation. For Holofernes not to penetrate Judith (her body if not her false identity) would impugn his masculinity and make him a laughingstock to her (or perhaps he is thinking of how his men will regard him). His worry about being laughed at reminds the reader of Achior's warning—that the Assyrians as a whole will become laughingstocks if they are defeated by the Israelites (5:21). Ironically, in his attempt *not* to be laughed at by Judith, he will fulfill Achior's words: his banquet will be the occasion of the Assyrian defeat. Israel will have the last laugh.

In the middle of this masculine show, the presence of Bagoas complicates the matter of Assyrian masculinity. As Sean D. Burke avers, "Ancient eunuchs can be read as queering figures—that is, as figures in and through whom the constructedness and instability of ancient identity categories can be made visible. Eunuchs can be read as queering figures because they trouble and destabilize the intersecting discourses of gender, sexuality, class, and race that produced the ancient constructions of masculinity."[7] Although the term was also applied to people born with atypical genitalia, the label generally pertains to men who have had their testicles removed, sometimes before and sometimes after puberty. The book of Judith gives us no access to the exact configuration of Bagoas's body, nor do we hear when and under what circumstance he became a eunuch. We can only surmise his condition based on what we know about eunuchs in the ancient

5. For this reason, Moore uses the word "make" to capture the meanings of both seduction and rape (*Judith*, 223–24).

6. In her contribution below, pp. 107–9, Tamber-Roseneu examines the possible translations of these verbs in more detail.

7. Sean D. Burke, *Queering the Ethiopian Eunuch: Strategies of Ambiguity in Acts* (Minneapolis: Fortress, 2013), 95.

Near East and Greco-Roman worlds.[8] Most eunuchs were castrated as a condition of their enslavement. Castration demonstrated the power the slave owner or trader had over the body of the enslaved. Sometimes slave boys were castrated to enhance their sexual attractiveness. Often eunuchs were employed in female spaces because they could not reproduce and therefore presented no threat to the lineage of the head of the household. As their bodies inhabit a fluid space between typical male and female bodies, many stories also employ eunuchs as messengers who move back and forth between male and female spaces within the house, as well as intermediaries between areas inside and outside the house (in the biblical corpus, see especially the book of Esther, where eunuchs oversee the harems and also carry messages between the main characters [Esth 2:8, 14; 4:4-17]). Because of their unique ability to move through different spaces, they sometimes rose through the ranks to become the most trusted slaves of their owner. Especially in royal contexts, the eunuch could become "an extension of the ruler's person in spaces into which the ruler could not, or would not, enter."[9] This appears to be the status of Bagoas. We cannot be certain of all the affairs to which Bagoas attended, nor all of the needs that Bagoas fulfilled, but we see him here moving from male to female space, bearing the message of sexual desire.

Bagoas invites Judith not only to the special drinking festival prepared just for her and Holofernes but also "to become today like one of the Assyrian women who serve in the palace of Nebuchadnezzar" (12:13). The invitation reminds us that Holofernes had earlier suggested that Judith would live in Nebuchadnezzar's palace (11:23); like general, like eunuch. He also invites her to make her transformation—her crossing-over from the Israelite to the Assyrian side—complete. Bagoas's request is polite but pointed. He calls her "pretty girl," a complimentary appellation in English. The Greek παιδίσκη, however, also implies subordination; hence, the phrase may be more accurately translated as "pretty maid" in order to capture the dual valence. This is the same term the NRSV translates as "servant" in parallel to "slave" (δούλη) in 11:5. In Greek, the word can also means "prostitute."[10] Bagoas addresses Judith in the third person, which is deferential; yet, there is no doubt about the kind of service Bagoas is inviting her to perform. Judith has been performing throughout the narrative, playing "woman," "pious," and "defector." Now another level of performance comes to the fore. She is ready to

8. What follows relies on the extensive research of Burke (ibid., 95–122).

9. Ibid., 102.

10. Moore, *Judith*, 224.

"service" in her plan to save the Israelites. Judith is a shape-shifter in word and deed. Appropriately, she accepts Holofernes's invitation by first saying, "Who am I . . . ?" (12:14a).

Judith accepts Holofernes's invitation with her now typical double entendre by pledging to do whatever pleases her "lord" (12:14b). Judith is a character of many words; her speech dominates the book. Yet, it is rare to hear her inner voice. What is Judith thinking? Deborah Levine Gera notes a parallel in Chariton's Greek novel *Chaereas and Callirhoe*, set in the Persian court. The king's most trusted eunuch is sent to persuade Callirhoe to have sex with the king. Chariton writes, "Callirhoe's first impulse was to dig her nails into the eyes of this would-be pimp and tear his eyes out, but being a well-brought up and sensible woman, she quickly remembered where she was, who she was, and who it was who was talking to her."[11] She instead responds with manipulative words. Perhaps Judith thinks much the same when she hears Bagoas presenting Holofernes's invitation. Then again, this is the moment she herself has planned. We can imagine that Judith feels nervous, thrilled, relieved, satisfied; we can also imagine feelings of revulsion and the desire to tear Bagoas's eyes out. No matter her interior emotions, her response is calm and calculated; she expresses "joy" at pleasing her lord (12:14). She prepares for the feast by dressing again in all of her "woman's finery," her final and most deadly performance. Her slave takes the lambskins (another luxury item) Holofernes had given Judith and goes ahead of her to prepare for her to recline in Holofernes's tent (12:15). In many ways, at many levels, Judith is a wolf in sheep's clothing.

As soon as Judith appears in his tent and lies down, Holofernes's "heart was ravished" and his "passion was aroused" (12:16). Reclining on the floor while eating was not unusual in the cultural context of Judith; yet, the image of a woman, beautiful and adorned, lying down on a lambskin rug is an erotic one. Accordingly, Holofernes is overwhelmed with desire. He sees his seduction plans coming to climax, and he invites her to drink. In our current age, it is difficult to read this scene without thinking of the ways in which men ply women with drugs and alcohol in order to make them vulnerable to sexual assault. The number of high-profile cases, as well as the increasing publicity about the role of alcohol in sexual assaults on college campuses, gives this scene an even more ominous nuance. Drinking parties often end badly in ancient stories as well—Ahasuerus's banquet ends with Vashti's expulsion (Esth 1:10-17), and Esther's banquet

11. As cited in Gera, *Judith*, 382–83.

ends with Haman's hanging (Esth 6:14–7:10). In later biblical literature, the banquet given by Herod Antipas ends in the beheading of John the Baptist (Matt 14:6-11). Similar themes linking banquets, drinking, and death are found in Herodotus.[12] When the setting is a banquet, we anticipate that something will go awry, and someone will probably die.

The general invites Judith to "Have a drink and be merry with us!" (12:17), which is "an implicit sexual invitation."[13] Holofernes is not subtle. He wants Judith to drink away her inhibitions in order to pave the way for his seduction (at best) or assault (at worst). As in her early repasts with Holofernes, she reclines with him but eats only her own food and drinks only her own wine. In contrast to his overt eagerness, Judith only feigns a similar eagerness: she uses hyperbolic language in stating that she will agree to drink with him. She declares, "today is the greatest day in my whole life" (12:18).

Holofernes is so pleased, so sure of his success, so disarmed by her beauty and distracted by her demeanor that he drinks too much, "more than he had ever drunk in any one day since he was born" (12:20). Sexual excitement fueled by alcohol consumption is causing him to lose his head.

Reading Holofernes Queerly II

In Holofernes's initial interactions with Judith, he plays into stereotypes of masculinity that are distinct from the character of the mighty soldier that he performed previously. Like the simple man of Proverbs 9, seduced to his ultimate doom by an alluring woman, in chapters 10–12 Holofernes is comically entranced by the beautiful and seductive Judith. He responds to Judith's beauty, her obsequious bowing before him, and her flattering words (many of which are double entendres that he completely misses) by granting her sanctuary in his camp and even allowing her to leave and return nightly. He should know better than to let an unknown woman come and go freely in his camp, but not for the last time, his masculine lust for her means that he does not have his head on straight.

When, on Judith's fourth day in the camp, Holofernes orders his eunuch servant Bagoas to bring her to him, his phrasing troubles these conventions of lustful masculinity. Holofernes

12. Herodotus chronicles many banquets that involve the deaths of people in attendance, including ones where the victims are deliberately made drunk. See Gera, *Judith*, 384, for a full list of references.

13. Ibid., 387.

says, "Go and persuade the Hebrew woman who is in your charge to come to us and eat and drink with us. For look, it would be shameful to us if we let such a woman go without consorting with[14] her, because if we do not entice[15] her, she will laugh at us."[16] To Holofernes, Judith is the very epitome of womanhood, a seductive siren come sashaying right to his doorstep. He is afraid that failing to have sex with such a woman would call into question his efficacy as a powerful man. For three days now, as Holofernes must see it, Judith has practically been wearing a neon "seduce me" sign; between the clothes, the ornaments, the obsequious language, the physically lowering herself before him, and her nightly baths inside or just beyond the camp's borders, she is sending him all the right signals. If he does not respond to these signals, what does it mean about him? His statement can also be read from a Butlerian point of view, as a performance of the gender "man." Holofernes knows the script, and he knows what his role is supposed to be: a beautiful woman throws herself on his mercy, so he is supposed to be intimate with her, whether by consent or by rape. Holofernes does not say to Bagoas, "For look, I am overcome with lust and must have her now." He says, in effect, "This is what I am supposed to do in this situation, so I should probably do it now, because otherwise, she might

14. The verb ὁμιλέω can mean "to be in company with," "to consort with," "to converse with," and a range of other meanings. Moore is correct when he observes that its use in Susanna (1:37, 57, and 58) can only connote sexual intercourse (*Judith*, 223). It is also sexual in meaning in Prov 5:19. Moore consequently translates "without having her." The verb is used, however, in several nonsexual contexts as well: Prov 23:31; Sir 11:20; Dan 1:19; Luke 24:14-15; Acts 20:11; and Acts 24:26. I translate it as "consort with," since this English verb can mean either "associate with" or something more intimate, the latter clearly being what Holofernes has in mind.

15. The verb ἐπισπάομαι is problematic, as evidenced by the wide variety of translations, from NRSV's "seduce" to Moore's "make" to Enslin and Zeitlin's "force." While I agree with Moore's observation that "genteel" translations can "sanitize" the Greek or Hebrew of the Bible, I do not see enough linguistic evidence to translate as he does here, even though, as he points out, to "make" a woman could encompass both seduction and rape (*Judith*, 223–24). Likewise, Enslin and Zeitlin are true to the sense of the story but not to the literal meaning of the word when they observe, "To read in the thought of 'enticing' or 'coaxing' is as false to the Greek as it would have been to Holofernes. Force here is surely more accurate than 'allure' or 'persuade.'" Morton S. Enslin and Solomon Zeitlin, *The Book of Judith* (Leiden: Brill, 1972), 148.

16. Author's translation. Although it is not out of the question that Holofernes uses the first-person plural here because he intends to allow others to have intercourse with Judith after he does, we can also read this as the "royal we."

question my masculinity." I am not suggesting that Holofernes does not want to have sex with Judith; it is obvious that he does. To wit, 12:16 says that, when Judith enters his tent and reclines for their banquet, "the heart of Holofernes was amazed by her and his soul was shaken. He was exceedingly eager to have intercourse with her; he had been looking for a time to deceive her since he had first seen her."[17] Holofernes's desire for Judith is not, however, the reason he gives his servant for summoning her. In this story, Judith embodies over-the-top femininity, and Holofernes responds with the compulsory display of masculinity.

Caryn Tamber-Rosenau

Judith Beheads Holofernes (13:1-10a)

Decapitation is a uniquely human act, the rise of culture and the development of decapitation being nearly simultaneous.[18] When Judith takes Holofernes's head, much is being accomplished. She is killing him and bringing back incontrovertible evidence of her deed. She is also making a statement: his head is both trophy and political proclamation.

> Beheading is the body's catachresis: a violation of the rules of the body's grammar that generates a sensation of dismay, horror, delight, or absurdity. "Catachresis" names the shocking literary figure that goes "against use": *kata chresthai*. Abusing the order of meaning, catachresis wrenches words form their proper contexts and puts them where they do not belong. Wrenched from its body, a head no longer performs its usual acts and is no longer available for self-confirming, assertive, or responsive uses. Its open eyes no longer move. Selves know themselves only through the body of the other . . . and such catachreses undo the claims of community, founded on sympathetic identification with others who define us.[19]

Holofernes's severed head says it all.

As Judith predicts (12:18), the greatest day of her life is about to be realized. Holofernes's slaves are well aware of their master's plans. When

17. As Craven points out, Judith and Holofernes engage in a contest to see who can deceive the best. Judith wants to deceive the Assyrians and thus foil their attack plans, and Holofernes wants to deceive (beguile) Judith into becoming intimate with him. See Toni Craven, *Artistry and Faith in the Book of Judith* (Chico, CA: Scholars Press, 1983), 96.

18. Regina Janes, *Losing Our Heads: Beheadings in Literature and Culture* (New York: New York University Press, 2005), 13–14.

19. Ibid., 12.

Jdt 13:1-10a

13:1When evening came, his slaves quickly withdrew. Bagoas closed the tent from outside and shut out the attendants from his master's presence. They went to bed, for they all were weary because the banquet had lasted so long. 2But Judith was left alone in the tent, with Holofernes stretched out on his bed, for he was dead drunk.

3Now Judith had told her maid to stand outside the bedchamber and to wait for her to come out, as she did on the other days; for she said she would be going out for her prayers. She had said the same thing to Bagoas. 4So everyone went out, and no one, either small or great, was left in the bedchamber. Then Judith, standing beside his bed, said in her heart, "O Lord God of all might, look in this hour on the work of my hands for the exaltation of Jerusalem. 5Now indeed is the time to help your heritage and to carry out my design to destroy the enemies who have risen up against us."

6She went up to the bedpost near Holofernes' head, and took down his sword that hung there. 7She came close to his bed, took hold of the hair of his head, and said, "Give me strength today, O Lord God of Israel!" 8Then she struck his neck twice with all her might, and cut off his head. 9Next she rolled his body off the bed and pulled down the canopy from the posts. Soon afterward she went out and gave Holofernes' head to her maid, 10who placed it in her food bag.

evening comes, they hurriedly withdraw and Bagoas himself closes the tent from the outside. Judith and Holofernes are alone. In fact, it had been such a long day of drinking that everyone goes to bed; no one bothers to wait outside or stand guard (13:1). Judith's slave is also outside of the bedchamber, but, unlike her male counterparts, her owner has instructed her to wait, and wait she does. Judith uses the pretense of her nightly prayers to explain her slave's attendance outside the door (13:3). Does the slave know for what she really waits?

No one remains to see what takes place between Judith and Holofernes, no one except the reader. That Holofernes and Judith are alone is repeated several times. The presence of two people alone behind closed doors echoes other biblical scenes of erotic violence. Jael and Sisera are alone in her tent (Judg 4–5); Ehud and Eglon withdraw into the king's inner chamber (Judg 3); Amnon has his sister come into his room alone (2 Sam 13); Susanna and the elders are alone in an enclosed garden (Dan 13:18). While Holofernes and his men may anticipate a pleasurable sexual encounter, we readers, given these intertexts, anticipate something more hostile.

Inside Holofernes's bedchamber, there is a reversal of Assyrian expectations even as there is a confirmation of the expectations of biblically literate readers. Instead of a compliant Judith, Holofernes is stretched out "dead drunk" on his bed (Jdt 13:2); instead of Holofernes above her in a posture of sexual conquest, Judith stands, clear-headed and resolved, beside him. His prone body is completely within her power.

Judith silently prays to God (13:4-5). Unlike her prayer in chapter 9, this one is succinct. She asks God to give her the strength she needs to carry out the work of her hands. She also emphasizes her own power and planning—God may provide support but Judith has devised and executed. Judith may attribute her success to God's providence, but she is no passive conduit for God's work. It is *her design* (13:5) that she is about to execute.

The narrative recounts each detail of Judith's movement in the dark and quiet bedroom. She goes to the top of the bed; she takes down Holofernes's sword; she comes closer to the bed; she grabs hold of his hair (13:6-7). Each movement builds tension. The work of her hands, literally and figuratively, is about to be completed. She says one last prayer, "Give me strength today, O Lord God of Israel!" (13:7). Does she whisper it? Does she shout? With all of her might, she strikes his neck twice. Prayers are on her lips; blood is on her hands.[20] It takes some effort to remove a head from a body. Stabbing or poisoning would have been easier. Yet, this easier path is not the one that Judith chooses. With a man's sword and showing masculine strength, Judith severs Holofernes's head from his body.

Judith and Caribbean Tourism

In his epic poem *Omeros*, Derek Walcott gathers multiple referents from Greek and biblical texts. The confluence and conflict of these different textual traditions provide Walcott the space to reflect on the legacies of European colonialism on his native St. Lucia. The construction of the colonial-era mythology of St. Lucia as the "Helen of the West" perpetuated in the contemporary tourism discourse provides one of the motivations to make Helen a central character of the poem. Desired by local suitors, an expatriate general, and other leering tourists, Helen is joined by biblical women: Eve, Judith, and Susannah. Through an internal reflection in the mind of Major Plunkett, whose growing

20. Gera remarks, "This combination of prayer and murder is quite notable" (*Judith*, 391). Craven points out the similarities between Judith's prayer while killing Israel's enemy and the figures in Ps 149:5-7 who praise God with their mouths as they hold two-edged swords in their hands (*Artistry and Faith*, 114).

attraction to Helen generates notions of the disasters of male sexual desire, Walcott at first contrasts Eve and Judith. He positions Eve as the potential attraction that leads to divine judgment and leaves a haunting legacy. Judith, on the other hand, is invoked to point to more serious consequences.

> Lies in this Judith from a
> different people
> whose long arm is a sword,
> who has turned your head
> back to her past, her tribe;
> you live in the terror
> of age before beauty.[21]

While Eve's weapon was a "golden apple," Judith's "long arm is a sword." Walcott here pulls on artist depictions of Judith's killing of Holofernes where she holds his hair in one hand while cutting his head off with the other. The text (13:7-8) at best appears ambiguous as to whether this is the precise physical stance since the move from verse 7 to verse 8 may not involve her holding on to his hair while cutting his head off. In any event, Walcott's imagery shows how the sword lengthens Judith's arm and in fact her arm becomes a sword. The menace of the sword stands out in Walcott's read of Judith. Although Walcott does not completely ignore the risible obsession of the men with Judith, he complicates the role feminine beauty plays in the multiple texts that he invokes in the verse. The threat of the sword and Judith's difference—presumably her difference compared with Eve but certainly the racial differences that Walcott points to in his poem—set the stage for the potential destruction of European maleness. This difference threatens the sword but its potency lies in the power of the past and the reliance on tribal identity in the way that Judith adheres to dietary and sabbath regulations. Walcott uses Judith as a fulcrum to turn toward biblical/apocryphal Susanna lusted over by old men to caricature Major Plunkett's clumsy attention for Helen. The subtle move pays deference to Judith's beauty but uses it as the fear factor that old men and perhaps decaying empires face as they live into the terrifying reality of their powerlessness and abject needs. Like most interpreters, Walcott centers Judith's heroism, but his praise for Judith lies not in the fact that she saves her people's future but rather that she draws attention to the past. Judith's head-turning capacities are not about her beauty but rather point to the uniqueness of the heritage and history of her people.

Steed Vernyl Davidson

21. Derek Walcott, *Omeros* (New York: Farrar, Straus and Giroux, 1990), 97.

Holofernes has lost his head—to Judith's beauty, to excessive drinking, and now to the work of his own sword. Despite some artistic depictions, the sword that Judith uses is a short, straight sword and not some kind of large, curved scimitar. A man's sword, straight and hard and worn at the hip, is associated with his phallic power. Its very presence whispers violence, and its use exerts brutal mastery over others. Judith appropriates this power when she takes Holofernes's sword. She penetrates him with it, striking off his head in what Sigmund Freud sees as a symbolic castration.[22] Although Freud bases his understanding of Judith more on certain artistic afterlives of the story (especially Friedrich Hebbel's 1840 play *Judith*),[23] Judith's self-identification with Simeon does invite comparisons between what she does to Holofernes and what Simeon does to the Shechemites, killing them as they recuperate from circumcision. Circumcision is not castration, yet the rite is still a cut to the genitals, and thus associations between the cutting off of Holofernes's head and the mutilation of Holofernes's penis are evoked. Because the Shechemites are killed to avenge a rape and because of the resonances with Jael's assassination of Sisera (another enemy general, another bed, another blow to the head), it is also possible to read Judith's use of the sword as vengeance for anticipated rape and even as a reverse rape.[24] Just as Sisera would have overseen, even participated in, the rape of the conquered Israelite women, so would Holofernes. The rape of the women of Bethulia is a threat that hangs over the entire narrative. Judith violently penetrates him before he can do the same to her and her compatriots.

Viewing Judith's deed as revenge for rape is likely present in the most famous artistic depiction of the scene: Artemisia Gentileschi's two paintings titled *Judith Slaying Holofernes* (c. 1612–1613 and c. 1620). Gentileschi was born in Rome in 1593, oldest child of Prudentia Montone and the well-known painter Orazio Gentileschi. Orazio Gentileschi mentored his daughter, whose early artistic gifts were apparent, and hired another artist and family friend, Agostino Tassi, to supplement her training. After repeated attempts to get her alone, Tassi finally cornered her in

22. Sigmund Freud, "The Taboo of Virginity," in *The Standard Edition of the Complete Psychological Works of Sigmund Freud*, vol. 11, ed. James Strachey (London: Hogarth Press, 1957), 207–8. See also Freud, "Notes on Medusa's Head," in *The Standard Edition* for more of his equating of castration and decapitation.

23. Margarita Stocker, *Judith: Sexual Warrior; Women and Power in Western Culture* (New Haven: Yale University Press, 1998), 179; Janes, *Losing Our Heads*, 138.

24. See Susan Niditch, "Eroticism and Death in the Tale of Jael," in *Gender and Difference in Ancient Israel*, ed. Peggy L. Day (Minneapolis: Fortress, 1989), 52 for the interpretation of Jael's actions as a reverse rape.

her bedroom, with the aid of Gentileschi's housekeeper, Donna Tuzia, and raped her in May 1611. He then promised to marry her in order to gain sexual access for several more months before it became clear that he had no intention of following through. The Gentileschi family pressed charges in 1612, and there followed a highly public, dramatic, and salacious trial for which the court transcripts still exist.[25]

The defense, in a move eerily familiar to twenty-first-century ears, called Artemisia's reputation into question. Tassi testified that she was not a virgin when they met, she was a flirt and a "whore," and he never had sex with her.[26] He also accused her dead mother (whom he had never met) and her aunts of being "whores," and he marshalled several witnesses to testify to Artemisia's promiscuity. Despite the fact that Artemisia had fought back and wounded Tassi with a knife, despite her detailed and consistent testimony, the presiding judge ordered her to submit to a gynecological examination and to thumbscrews to test her honesty. The examiners confirmed that her hymen had been broken but added that she had not recently lost her virginity.

The prosecution countered with their own witnesses. Apparently, Tassi had sent spies to inquire about Artemisia's virtue when he first developed designs upon her. A number of people also testified that Tassi had bragged about his sexual conquest. Giovanni Battista Stiatessi, a close friend of Tassi's, testified on Gentileschi's behalf. Such testimony revealed that Tassi had spent time in prison for sex crimes (incest with his sister-in-law), had fathered children with his sister-in-law, and was suspected of having his wife murdered. In the end, he was convicted but spent just eight months in exile. Orazio Gentileschi subsequently sued him and several of his witnesses for perjury.

Artemisia Gentileschi began painting her first work depicting Judith in the middle of disarticulating Holofernes's head during her trial and finished shortly after it ended. Ever since the critical reevaluation of Gentileschi in the twentieth century, the rape and trial have become the "axis of interpretation of the painter's work."[27] Several feminist revision-

25. Mary D. Garrard, *Artemisia Gentileschi: The Image of the Female Hero in Italian Baroque Art* (Princeton: Princeton University Press, 1989), 20–22. Garrard reprints an English translation of the entire transcript (403–87).

26. See especially Tassi's testimony on April 6, 1612, and May 11, 1612, in ibid., 442–50, 458–59.

27. Griselda Pollock, "Feminist Dilemmas with the Art/Life Problem," in *The Artemisia Files: Artemisia Gentileschi for Feminists and Other Thinking People*, ed. Mieke Bal (Chicago: University of Chicago Press, 2005), 174.

ist critics offer a near conflation of Judith with Gentileschi and Holofernes with Tassi; however, other feminist art critics have offered more complex and nuanced interpretations of the relationship between the artist and her life.[28] Gentileschi was a great artist whose work transcends any particular experience or personal intention she may have had. We do not want to reduce her paintings to an expression of proto-feminist rage. At the same time, there is a reason why her paintings of Judith, especially infused with the knowledge of her story, resonate so strongly with people today.

Gentileschi's renditions of Judith (at least five of which are documented) demonstrate a marked break with other baroque depictions of Judith. Compare Gentileschi's 1612 work with the other most famous depiction of the same scene, Caravaggio's *Judith Beheading Holofernes* (1598–1599). According to Mary Garrard, Caravaggio introduced a number of novel elements in the representation of Judith and Holofernes, in particular, a focus on the dramatic human conflict between the two protagonists. Judith and Holofernes are a study in contrasts, yet Caravaggio better imagines Holofernes's feelings of pain and surprise than Judith's feelings; whereas his face and body are realistic and emotive, Judith's are static and emotionless.[29] Caravaggio's Judith stands at arm's length from Holofernes, her slave behind her; she seems tentative, even demure. Jessica Jernigan, in her contribution below, describes her as a "sleepwalker." In distinction, Gentileschi's determined Judith stands close, and her slave is actually on top of the drunk general, pinning down one of his arms against his chest. His eyes are open, his face is flushed, and he is trying to push away the slave with his other arm. His hand looks massive compared to the slave's face—a perspective "error" designed to highlight his strength, now overcome by the weaker woman. Garrard speculates, "Out of a manifest need to exorcise her own demon, the man who sexually exploited her and against whom her expressed anger is recorded, Artemisia depicted the killing of Holofernes in an unprecedented way, as a bloody murder carried out with clinical precision by two women whose cold determination is almost vengeful."[30] In every rendering of Judith, Gentileschi portrays her as active, self-determining,

28. Garrard's scholarship is the most comprehensive of this critical reevaluation. For different critiques of conflating Gentileschi with Judith, see Garrard, *Artemisia Gentileschi*, 278–80; Laura Benedetti, "Reconstructing Artemisia: Twentieth-Century Images of a Woman Artist," *Comparative Literature* 51 (1999): 43–61; Pollock, "Feminist Dilemmas," 201–5.

29. Garrard, *Artemisia Gentileschi*, 290–91.

30. Ibid., 312.

complex. Garrard also argues that Judith is the artist's portrait of her own independence and autonomy, "possibly the freest of masculine stereotype in the entire genre of Judiths."[31]

Judith and Her Maidservant

Most Holy Father,
Orazio Gentileschi, painter, most humble servant of Your Holiness, respectfully reports to You how, through Madame Tuzia his tenant, and as a result of her complicity, a daughter of the plaintiff has been deflowered by force and carnally known many, many times by Agostino Tassi, painter and close friend and associate of the plaintiff; also taking part in this obscene business was Cosimo Quorli, your orderly. By this I mean that besides the rape, the same orderly Cosimo, through his intrigues, took from the hands of the same young woman some paintings of her father's, and in particular a *Judith* large in size.

—Excerpt from the petition of Orazio Gentileschi to His Holiness Pope Paul V, Rome, 1612

Judith and Her Maidservant takes the viewer by surprise. It's visible from the entrance of the gallery where it hangs in the Detroit Institute of Art, but it's only when we get close that we begin to understand what's happening in this picture. It's a large canvas—six feet high and a little more than four-and-a-half feet wide—dominated by the figures of two women. The eye is immediately drawn to the left hand—raised as if to say "Be still! Be quiet!"—of the woman standing in the middle distance. It takes a moment to notice the sword in her right hand. It's almost easy to miss that the second female figure, crouching in the foreground, is holding a severed male head.

Artemisia Gentileschi painted it in or around 1625. This is not her only treatment of the Apocryphal story of Judith, nor is it her most famous. A *Judith and Holofernes* that hangs in the Uffizi Gallery in Florence is perhaps her best-known work. There is a similar painting in the National Museum of Capodimonte in Naples. These works are earlier by a few years than *Judith and Her Maidservant*. They're also more violent.

Judith's story was popular with European writers and artists from the medieval period onward, although approaches to this narrative varied. Some

31. Ibid., 305. See also her summary of the Judith paintings, 336.

playwrights and painters saw Judith as prefiguring Mary, the Mother of God. Some saw her as a reincarnated Eve or Mary Magdalene—or a Hebrew Venus. Visual depictions of Judith vary, but it's safe to assume that Gentileschi had Caravaggio's in mind when she was painting.

Caravaggio's *Judith Beheading Holofernes* is just as gory as Gentileschi's more graphic paintings. Blood shoots from the Assyrian general's neck as Judith slices through it, but Judith herself looks like a passive participant in this act of violence. She's holding Holofernes's hair in her left hand while she wields a sword with her right, but her face looks like that of a sleepwalker who is only just beginning to understand what she's doing. Except for her slightly furrowed brow and her parted lips, this Judith could be any Renaissance beauty. Caravaggio's maidservant, Abra, is also worth considering. Here, we see a hag eagerly awaiting the head of Holofernes. During the Renaissance and baroque periods, Abra was often an old woman or a woman with African features. Either makes her suspect. It's not hard to see Caravaggio's Abra as the instigator here, the malign force behind Judith's act of violence. It's as if, hampered by the classical view that youthful, fragile beauty and passivity are synonymous with feminine virtue, Caravaggio doesn't quite know what to do with this heroine.

He's not alone in this. Although Judith was a popular subject for premodern artists, there was no fixed imagery or iconography. Some artists used the models of David and Goliath or Perseus and Medusa as inspiration. Some, like Caravaggio, rendered this brave Jewish widow as an Italian princess. Botticelli's Judith could pass for one of his nymphs. There are bare-breasted Judiths and naked Judiths. Peter Paul Rubens's Judith looks like a sorceress.

Gentileschi's Judiths participate in this tradition while being entirely her own. If we look at her Uffizi picture and Caravaggio's Judith and Holofernes, we get a sense of the conversation she was having with her influential predecessor. Both artists use dramatic lighting and drapery to create a claustrophobic interior scene. Both offer graphic depictions of bloodshed. But only Gentileschi suggests the physical force needed to cut a man's head from his body. Her Judith is not a willowy girl. She's a powerfully built, mature woman who has pushed up her sleeves to prepare for the hard work of hacking through skin, muscle, and bone. Her Abra is not a crone whispering from the shadows; instead, she's Judith's equal and partner, holding down Holofernes while Judith does her strenuous and gruesome work.

People in the past were no less drawn to the sensational

than we are now. Biblical and classical themes dominated centuries of Western art not just because patrons wanted their art to be edifying but also because Christianity and Greek and Roman myth gave a patina of culture to nudes and depictions of incredible violence. The story of Judith was popular because it was so adaptable for allegorical purposes and also because it featured a beautiful woman committing an outrageous act of violence.

Gentileschi was, herself, a sensational woman. It's always a dubious strategy to analyze art—written, musical, visual—through the biography of the artist. This is especially fraught when the woman is an artist, since creative genius has so often been seen as a purely male attribute. But the fact remains that Artemisia Gentileschi was the subject—not the plaintiff, since the wronged party was not her, but her father—of a well-documented and widely publicized rape trial. It's also the case that, in his petition to the pope, Orazio Gentileschi also complained about an accomplice of the accused rapist stealing a Judith Orazio had painted.

Agostino Tassi was eventually found guilty and banished from Rome, but not before Artemisia was compelled to appear in court—a process that included two midwives assuring the court, after physical inspection, that Artemisia was not a virgin. Justice, of a kind, was served, but it did not restore Artemisia's lost honor. Some art critics have interpreted her earlier Judiths as revenge fantasies, and that's certainly a seductive reading. Artemisia's own testimony includes her recounting that she threatened Tassi—"I'd like to kill you with this knife"—and her assertion that she merely nicked him when she threw the blade at him. It's easy to see the gouts of blood spurting from Holofernes's neck as the blood she wanted to draw from the man who sexually assaulted her. Similarly, it's difficult to ignore the fact that her father seemed to equate the rape of his daughter with the theft of a Judith painting. One doesn't have to get deep into psychoanalytic criticism to sense that Judith might have been a powerful—and powerfully ambivalent—subject for Artemisia.

I keep all of this in mind when I look at *Judith and Her Maidservant*. This is the Judith best-known to me. The Detroit Institute of Art is the major museum closest to my home, and I spend some time with this picture whenever I visit. Even though I know about Tassi and the trial, I only see lingering echoes of that experience in this painting, not a phantasm of vengeance denied. What I see, more than anything, is that the male antagonist is falling out of the frame. He is reduced to nothing more than a nose, a brow, and one closed eye engulfed in darkness. The contrast between Holofernes's green complexion and Abra's ruddy fingers emphasizes the fact that this military leader is quickly passing from authority into dissolution. Whatever power he possessed, it's gone now.

What I see, when I look at this painting, is two women acting in concert. They are working together, supporting each other in a perilous situation. As in Artemisia's earlier works, the artist presents Judith as a grown woman, full-bodied, not a frail child. Her beauty—usually an integral part of her legend—is inconsequential here. Her body is not on display, and her face is obscured by shadow. And Abra could be her sister rather than her subordinate. The maid wears a blue gown over fine white linens, a sheer fichu visible at her neckline. Judith wears a coronet—barely visible in the darkness—while Abra wears a white veil. This is the only obvious mark of their difference. Class distinction is flattened; lady and servant are equal.

I also think about Madame Tuzia, the female tenant who was expected to act as chaperone to the motherless Artemisia. In her indispensable study of the artist, Mary D. Garrard notes that, in Renaissance and baroque art, old women often suggested procuresses. This is obviously an available interpretation in Caravaggio's picture, among others. It's also one that Artemisia clearly rejects. Whatever part Madame Tuzia played in Tassi's crime, Artemisia is giving this woman no place in her art.

Judith and Her Maidservant is not, to my mind, a story of revenge. This is, I think, Artemisia Gentileschi's masterpiece not just because of its technical sophistication but also because of its dramatic subtlety. In this picture, the sensational act is over. We are poised between righteous murder and the gory display that causes an army to lose heart. What we see here is two strong, determined women, working together to save themselves and their people. And I can't think of another painting—premodern or otherwise—that shows that.

Jessica Jernigan

David cutting off the head of Goliath, another subject of heroic art in the baroque era, finds connections to Judith's act, particularly as both David and Judith sever their enemy's head with his own sword (1 Sam 17:50-51). Artists sometimes reproduce this connection. For example, Michelangelo's Sistine Chapel positions Judith and her slave in one corner, walking with Holofernes's head on a platter; across the room in the adjacent corner, David beheads Goliath.

Rita Dolce notes that, in the ancient Near East, "cutting off someone's head was a unique act, not comparable to other types of mutilation, and therefore charged with a special symbolic and communicative significance."[32] Even though Dolce's focus is narrow—pictorial depictions of heads in Mesopotamian and Syrian cultures between the third and first millennia BCE—she begins by analyzing a sixteenth-century tapestry depicting the story of Judith. Dolce notes that the primary elements of the representation of decapitation in the cultures she is examining also appear in the Renaissance tableau—the killer holds up the head by its hair, transports it from one place to another, and then displays it on the city walls, gate, or tower.[33] The only deviation from this ancient Near Eastern pattern is that in the story of Judith, the person who decapitates and displays is a woman.[34] We will return to Dolce's analysis in the next chapter after Judith carries the head back to Bethulia.

After Judith severs the head, the narrative pace accelerates—just three verses later, Judith will be yelling for the sentries of Bethulia to open the gates. The pace underscores the urgency of the situation. Judith must smuggle the head out and return safely to her hometown before the murder is discovered. She quickly rolls Holofernes's body off of his bed and then takes down his sumptuous canopy (Jdt 10:21); she decapitates the bed along with the general. Leaving the tent, she hands the head to her slave who puts it in the food bag. The slave never reacts. If she was not aware of Judith's plan, she responds with remarkable equanimity to Judith's handing her the bloody head.

By focusing on the objects of the bed and the canopy, the narrative connects Judith's meeting of Holofernes with their last moments together. There are also narrative connections between this final scene with Holofernes and the death of Judith's husband Manasseh. As Amy-Jill Levine explains:

> The circumstances of his [Manasseh's] death, heatstroke while watching the binding of barley sheaves, graphically anticipate the decapitation of Holofernes. The phallic imagery of the bound sheaves prefigures the general's dismembered head; both symbolize castration. The psychosexual suggestiveness of this imagery is complemented by barley meal's ritual function: it is the offering required of a man who suspects his wife of infidelity even "though she has not defiled herself" (Num. 5.15). Linguistic parallels make the ties between Manasseh and Holofernes

32. Rita Dolce, *"Losing One's Head" in the Ancient Near East: Interpretation and Meaning of Decapitation* (New York: Routledge, 2018), 1–2.

33. Ibid., 4–5.

34. Ibid., 3.

> even more pronounced. While the general is decapitated by Judith, Manasseh is cut down when the burning fever attacks his head. . . . Each man takes to his bed . . . , and each dies.[35]

Judith did not kill her husband. By all accounts, she was a good and faithful wife; even if she had not been, she certainly could not have caused his sunstroke. Still, the connections drawn between the death of her husband and her beheading of Holofernes hint at a greater danger that Judith may prove to all men. The text subtly casts suspicion over Judith even as it explicitly celebrates her heroism. The anxiety that Judith's power provokes does not end at the edge of the page; it continues to emerge in the cultural appropriations of the biblical story.

As we have previously discussed, in the first centuries of interpretation, Judith and her story had largely positive meanings for Christian communities. In her piety and chastity, she was a model for both men and women; in her bravery and strength, she symbolized the church's victory over sin and Satan. These associations continued to obtain through the Middle Ages.[36] In addition, perhaps influenced by her presence in Christian texts and iconography, Judith reemerges in the Jewish tradition through a series of medieval midrashim, liturgical poems, and commentaries.[37] In these Jewish rereadings, some details are altered, especially around the character of Judith. For example, in some stories Judith is an unmarried virgin; most stories omit her long speeches, even her prayers. Nevertheless, the framework of the plot remains: Judith's town is threatened; she decides to intervene and meets with the Assyrian general, who wants to seduce (or marry) her; there is a banquet; he gets drunk; she kills him.[38] Several of these readings compare Judith to Esther and celebrate her for her piety, courage, and loyalty to her people. Her

35. Amy-Jill Levine, "Sacrifice and Salvation: Otherness and Domestication in the Book of Judith," in *A Feminist Companion to Esther, Judith and Susanna*, ed. Athalya Brenner, FCB 7 (Sheffield: Sheffield Academic, 1995), 212.

36. Nicole Tilford, "Judith and Her Interpreters," in *Women's Bible Commentary*, ed. Carol A. Newsom, Sharon H. Ringe, and Jacqueline E. Lapsley, 3rd ed. (Louisville: Westminster John Knox, 2012), 391. Elena Ciletti and Henrike Lähnemann, "Judith in the Christian Tradition," in *The Sword of Judith: Judith Studies across the Disciplines*, ed. Kevin R. Brine, Elena Ciletti, and Henrike Lähnemann (Cambridge: Open Book, 2010), 48–55, 60.

37. Gera, *Judith*, 19–25; and "The Jewish Textual Traditions," in *The Sword of Judith*, 30–36.

38. Gera, "Shorter Medieval Hebrew Tales of Judith," in *The Sword of Judith*, 81–82. See pages 83–87 for details of the innovations introduced by the midrashim.

story is also connected to the Maccabean revolt and thus she becomes associated with the holiday of Hanukkah, as Esther is the heroine of the holiday of Purim.[39] Even today, certain Hanukkah traditions are rooted in Judith's story. In one midrash, Judith feeds Holofernes salty cheese to encourage his drinking. For this reason, it is traditional to eat cheese dishes on Hanukkah.[40]

Judith's reputation begins to tarnish as we move into the early modern period, both in biblical commentaries and in popular renditions. Her ornamentation and her beauty open up interpretations to more carnal understandings of her actions and so strip them of their earlier spiritual sanction. There is even a foreshadowing of this shift in some of the medieval midrashim. In these Jewish interpretations, her purifying bath before prayer is transformed into a cleansing after menstruation. As Deborah Levine Gera suggests, it was easier "for these storytellers to depict an impure, menstruating woman than to envision a holy woman of God, who immerses herself in water in a near-spiritual act of purification, common to men and women alike."[41] She is frequently challenged and doubted by the guards and the townspeople after she accomplishes her deed; their interrogations bespeak a distrust not present in the biblical text.[42] In one midrash, she is compared to Delilah.[43] We have already mentioned the inflection point represented by Joseph Swetman's indictment of Judith in his work *The Arraignment of Lewd, Idle, Forward, and Unconstant Women* (1615).[44] These trends do not replace the others in this period—Judith is still sometimes depicted in moral terms. Yet, what was ignored or suppressed in patristic readings, what begins to rumble in some midrash, erupts in the seventeenth century. Judith begins to be associated with biblical villains like Eve and Delilah, with Holofernes recast as a hero like Adam and Samson.[45]

By the eighteenth and nineteenth centuries, Judith as femme fatale gains traction and outpaces the other images. The beautiful woman who cuts off her aspiring lover's head while he lies prone on a bed covered in a bejeweled canopy even becomes a central sexual fantasy in Leopold

39. Gera, "Shorter Medieval Hebrew Tales of Judith," 87–91.

40. Gera, "The Jewish Textual Traditions," 35–36. See also Susan Weingarten, "Food, Sex, and Redemption in *Megillat Yehudit* (the 'Scroll of Judith')," in *The Sword of Judith*, 97–125.

41. Gera, "Shorter Medieval Hebrew Tales of Judith," 87.

42. Ibid., 85.

43. Ibid., 94–95.

44. Tilford, "Judith and Her Interpreters," 393.

45. Ciletti and Lähnemann, "Judith in the Christian Tradition," 59.

Sacher-Masoch's novel *Venus in Furs* (1870).[46] In just a few centuries, Judith has transformed from a champion of God to a sexual dominatrix. Gustav Klimt's paintings of Judith, completed at the beginning of the twentieth century, exemplify this trend.

In "Judith I" (1901), Judith looks out of the frame, straight at the viewer. Her face is magnetic, even perverse; her breasts are partially exposed. Her face is so alluring that viewers may miss the severed head she holds, only partially visible because it is cut off by the frame. The fact that it is Holofernes's head, an enemy general leading a war against Judith and her people, barely (if at all) registers. The focus is on the dangerously seductive figure who looks like she might devour the viewers. In "Judith II" (1909), her face is turned as if she is in motion; her breasts are exposed; the head is only partially visible in the bag, like an incidental prop.

Vastly different from Gentileschi's Judith, Klimt's Judith (and the head she carries) is bloodless, her breasts are exposed instead of her arms, and her face beckons all to come hither. The femme fatale expresses a common sexist fear about women, that they (that we) will use their (our) sexual appeal for nefarious purposes, that they (that we) are beautiful and dangerous in equal measure. Men are vulnerable, even defenseless, before a woman's charms. Men are always already her victim.[47]

Reading Judith with Jael as Horror Heroine

Judith is a pious and largely demure figure; the drama of Holofernes's beheading is counterbalanced by the unimpeachable reserve and modesty of the story's heroine. As many commentators have noted, behind Judith lurks a much less polite, though equally lethal, heroine: Jael. Judith's carefully planned execution of Holofernes is modeled on the exuberantly violent story of Jael (also spelled Yael), told in prose in Judges 4:17-22 and poetry in Judges 5:24-30 (the second version, likely the older account, is part of the "Song of Deborah," a poem placed in the mouth of the female prophet Deborah). Approaching Judith through Jael opens new ways of thinking about violence, gender, and pleasure in the text.

The two iterations of the Jael story in Judges are not identical; each account contains details that the other lacks. A complete

46. Stocker, *Judith*, 176–77.

47. For an art-historical perspective on the transformation of Judith from a paragon of chastity to a dangerous femme fatale, see Garrard, *Artemisia Gentileschi*, 282–302.

account emerges, however, when they are read together:[48] Jael is the "wife of Heber, the Kenite" (Judg 4:17; 5:24), and she is living among the Israelites at the time when they are at war with the Canaanites. The Canaanite general, Sisera, seeks to hide in her tent; she invites him in (4:18) and covers him with a rug (4:19). Sisera asks for water and Jael gives him milk (4:19; 5:25), a gesture that signals hospitality but also carries with it maternal and sexual overtones. This hospitality is short-lived, as Jael proceeds to murder Sisera by hammering a tent peg through his head. The prose version in chapter 4 includes a detail that he is asleep (perhaps following sex); the poetic version is unconcerned with his sleeping or waking state. Instead, it offers a gleeful escalation of violence as Jael strikes Sisera, crushes his head, and shatters his temple, killing him (Judg 5:26-27). As in the story of Judith's murder of Holofernes, this act of female violence is the cause of great celebration; Jael is lauded as the "most-blessed of women" (5:24).

In analyzing Jael, I have argued that the story can be productively read in conversation with the category of horror.[49] In particular, the Jael accounts in Judges 4 and 5 resemble two modern horror genres: the slasher film and the rape-revenge film. Jael specifically resembles the "Final Girl," the female sole survivor of the classic slasher film. The name "Final Girl" and the most famous description of the type come from Carol Clover's *Men, Women, and Chain Saws: Gender and the Horror Film* and will be familiar to even casual horror viewers. As Clover describes, the Final Girl is androgynous; she has a masculine name (like Sidney or Chris) and is less feminine—and less sexual—than her friends. She is unattached to a husband or boyfriend. She has technical and practical skills. And in the climax of the film, she kills the killer using a phallic weapon in a location with heavy uterine coding.[50] All this applies to Jael. Her name is a masculine grammatical form (a *yiqtol*).[51] More telling, when Sisera speaks directly to her, he at one point uses a masculine second-person verb, as if she is male (4:20). Jael is the "wife of Heber," and yet her husband never appears in

48. On this approach, and for more on the history of reading Jael, see Conway, *Sex and Slaughter in the Tent of Jael: A Cultural History of a Biblical Story* (Oxford: Oxford University Press, 2017).

49. Rhiannon Graybill, "Day of the Woman: Judges 4–5 as Slasher and Rape Revenge Narrative," *Journal of Religion and Popular Culture* 30 (2018): 193–205.

50. This description is summarized from Carol J. Clover, *Men, Women, and Chain Saws: Gender and the Horror Film* (Princeton: Princeton University Press, 1993), 21–64.

51. Ellen van Wolde, "Yaʿel in Judges 4," *ZAW* 107 (1995): 240–46.

the text; she is for all practical purposes a single woman, like the Final Girl. Jael is certainly handy with a tent peg and able to take down what Barak, the Israelite general, cannot. Of course, the tent peg is a clear phallic weapon, wielded against Sisera in the uterine space of the tent.

There is, however, one major detail in which Jael deviates from the Final Girl pattern. It is a rule of the slasher—even a punchline—that characters who have sex must die. And yet the Jael story contains strong insinuations of either sex or rape between Jael and Sisera.[52] I would argue that reading a consensual sex scene between Jael and Sisera, a lone and vulnerable woman and a powerful military general notorious for his abuse of women (here it is also worth noting that the rape of women in warfare is also well known in the ancient world), is at best disingenuously naïve and at worst rape-apologism. Instead, if we take seriously the implications of sex and rape, then Jael becomes an avenging figure of female violence, and the Jael story becomes a rape-revenge narrative along the lines of such anticlassics as *I Spit on Your Grave*.

If Judith is inspired by Jael, and Jael is a horror-worthy heroine, then what of Judith? The text is careful to veil Judith in respectability; while Jael is a foreign woman, seemingly living alone, who invites a strange man into her tent (cue the rape-apologists, *what did you think would happen?*), Judith is a virtuous Judean widow, with both class privilege (she can afford a maid, along with other luxuries) and much admired piety. Even as the text teases her beauty, it is careful to insist on her good morals: she acts only in accordance with her prayer. She is never raped by Holofernes, who is too drunk. The motivations for her actions are thus theological and political, not personal.

The narrative of Judith is thus less a "sequel" or a "reboot" of the Jael story than it is its sublimation. It is *The Accused* to Jael's *I Spit on Your Grave*, the presentable version that resolves all the uncomfortable moments and excesses of the original (the reveling in violence, the lack of concern for Jael's morals, the phallic spectacle of hammering a tent peg into a man's face, often read by critics as "reverse rape" in its visuals). Still, I would suggest that reading Judith

52. The evidence is reviewed in detail in Graybill, "Day of the Woman." On rape, see also Danna Nolan Fewell and David M. Gunn, *Gender, Power, and Promise: The Subject of the Bible's First Story* (Nashville: Abingdon, 1993), 394; Nicole Duran, "Having Men for Dinner: Deadly Banquets and Biblical Women," *BTB* 35 (2005): 119. For sex, see Yair Zakovitch, "Sisseras Tod," *ZAW* 93 (1981): 364–74; Pamela Tamarkin Reis, "Uncovering Jael and Sisera: A New Reading," *SJOT* 19 (2005): 24–47.

with and through Jael-as-horror opens the text of Judith in at least three ways.

First, it allows us to discern the impulse of female violence unmoored from its careful ideological framing. Though Judges 4 and 5 contain accounts of the Israelites' military struggle against the Canaanites, Jael's actions are not justified by either political or theological reasons. Sisera takes shelter in Jael's tent precisely because she is *not* an Israelite and thus (falsely) he perceives that she is not a threat. Instead, her violent actions are personal—either rape-revenge or unmotivated violence against a male other. In either case, the Jael example allows us to think of Judith's action not as a heroic sacrifice for a larger Judean cause but as a gleeful female embrace of violence, either for vengeance or for pleasurable sadism (or perhaps both).

Second, approaching Judith through Jael-as-horror-story opens new perspectives in thinking about narrative deployments of respectability. Horror plots thrive on the politics of respectability: the villains are racialized others, religious curiosities (such as witches or pagan), sexual deviants, gender nonconformists, rural dimwits, or all of the above. The exercise of violence, particularly by an innocent female victim taking revenge on the villains, allows the viewer simultaneously to enjoy the buttressing of preexisting ideological claims. Judith fits this plot: she is a virtuous Jewish widow; her victory over the brutish, drunken Holofernes is the victory of "good Jewish values." Critical readings of the horror genre have, however, exposed and pushed back against its tacit ideological assumptions. Clover argues that the rape-revenge plot frequently assumes an urban-rural split that uses gender violence (the female victim) to justify class violence (the rural villains) and ethnic violence (Native Americans, who are represented in distorted form in the rural villains).[53] Queer readings of horror have likewise explored the ways the genre opens spaces, however, briefly, for nonnormative gender performance and queer sexualities, even as these characters reach hideous ends.[54] Bringing these questions into conversation with Judith summons us to be critical about what ideologies we are sustaining when we celebrate Judith's act of beheading.

53. Clover, *Men, Women, and Chain Saws*, 163.

54. Judith Halberstam, *Skin Shows: Gothic Horror and the Technology of Monsters* (Durham: Duke University Press, 1995); Harry M. Benshoff, *Monsters in the Closet: Homosexuality and the Horror Film* (Manchester: Manchester University Press, 1997); Darren Elliott-Smith, *Queer Horror Film and Television: Sexuality and Masculinity at the Margins* (London: I.B. Tauris, 2016).

Third, and finally, reading Judith with and through Jael suggests an alternative economy of female friendship that the Jael narrative, for all its "strong female character"-ness, is lacking. The poetic praise of Jael in Judges 5 is part of a longer unit of text known as the "Song of Deborah" and attributed to Deborah, one of the five female prophets in the Hebrew Bible. Deborah and Jael, however, never meet in the text (*pace* Deryn Guest's book title, *When Deborah Met Jael*[55]). Only Barak, the hapless male general, interacts with both (Judg 4:6-9, 14, 22). Jael never even interacts with the other woman in the Jael story, Sisera's mother, who remains at her window, awaiting her son's return. In the narrative of Judith, in contrast, Judith has a female companion in the figure of her maid. While there are, of course, questions of social class to consider here, the text does offer a moment of female solidarity. The maid assists her in the murder, providing a bag to hide the head of Holofernes, which they plan to bring with them as a ghastly souvenir. Of course, the maid vanishes later in the text, as Judith alone is lauded for the murder. Still, the scene in the bedroom, with two women working together to dispose of a man, suggests the possibility, however fleeting, of the "Final Girl" maturing into a woman with (living) friends.

Rhiannon Graybill

Sympathy for Holofernes rooted in an implicit sexist attitude toward Judith continues through the twentieth century, not just in popular culture but in biblical scholarship as well. Such sexism can be seen most clearly in Carey Moore's venerable Anchor Bible commentary from 1985, particularly in the more informal sections that preserve part of a personal correspondence between Moore and David Noel Freedman. Writing to Moore, Freedman compares Judith to Jael, a common coupling. Instead of focusing on the ways in which these two women assassinate an enemy general in the middle of a war, thus saving the Israelites, however, Freedman highlights instead an apparent violation of the ethic of hospitality:

> In some ways, Jael is worse because she invites the man to enter her home, which signifies both hospitality and protection, and then cold-bloodedly kills him when he is helpless. In Judith, the hospitality is extended by Holofernes, but Judith certainly violates the law of guests

55. Deryn Guest, *When Deborah Met Jael: Lesbian Biblical Hermeneutics* (London: SCM, 2005).

> in a stranger's home. Certainly there is no sympathy for Sisera in the poem or the prose account, but he is an oddly appealing figure: a beaten warrior, but a warrior nevertheless, and one whose mother is concerned about him.[56]

Freedman omits the threat of rape that hangs over both accounts. The text of Judith alludes to the threat over and over again; Sisera's mother's lament is assuaged by the court women (and she even answers her own worries herself) that Sisera will return after he has divvied up the Israelite women as spoils of war (Jdg 5:30).

Freedman continues by preserving very candidly the sorts of views toward women entertained by many biblical scholars of his generation:

> Holofernes has some admirable characteristics in terms of his generalship and his devotion to his master, as well as less ingratiating traits. That he succumbed to the temptations of Judith is hardly surprising; how many others would have resisted (like Joseph who certainly is unusual in the Bible)? One can chiefly criticize his gullibility and stupidity in failing to take ordinary precautions with a foreigner. But that is the basic paradox. Everyone, even Holofernes, knows Judith's reputation for piety and devotion to the God of Israel. As a woman of honor, her word should be true, so Holofernes should believe her. At the same time, her devotion to the Law of Moses would rule out the possibility of any kind of contact with a foreigner like Holofernes, so the question of deception has to be raised from the beginning. Her showing up in the Assyrian camp violates so many rules that Holofernes should have been on guard. But then his head was turned by her beauty.[57]

Apart from a tendentious misreading of Jewish regulation—there is no blanket prohibition against contact with foreign peoples—the sympathy for a martial aggressor, murderer, and (at least) potential rapist is disturbing. He even suggests that the author of Judith has an "obvious and blatant prejudice" against Holofernes.[58]

To be fair, such explicit sympathy for Holofernes is rare in modern biblical scholarship; Moore himself argues that Holofernes "got exactly what he deserved."[59] Freedman, however, attests to attitudes about women that run deep. We are reminded of cases in the recent news where male perpetrators of violent crimes receive sympathy they did not de-

56. Quoted in Moore, *Judith*, 84.
57. Quoted in ibid., 84–85.
58. Quoted in ibid., 85.
59. Ibid.

serve while the women who accused them were silenced and shamed.[60] There is concern for the man's "ruined life," with little to no interest in the woman's suffering. Such perspectives could come only through the solidarity of male privilege and the protection of male power. One need look no further for reasons to read Judith in light of feminist issues and women's experiences.

Judith acted to avert the murder, rape, pillage, and desecration threatened by the Assyrian army. Her methods were underhanded, as befits the asymmetrical power relations between the two peoples at war and as are also manifest in the asymmetrical relations between a man trained in combat and an unarmed woman. Beheading is a very gruesome form of execution, precisely orchestrated to produce certain effects and affects. There is no other form of death as psychologically troubling to a person—a disarticulated head arouses emotions that no other mutilation will cause. The head is the place of both the face, the premier bodily site of identification and connection, and the brain, the control center for the body. To take the head is to confound identification, connection, and control; to take the head is to dehumanize. The Assyrians were known for their deployment of beheading to strike terror and fear in their subject peoples.[61] The act shows absolute power over the victim of the beheading. Judith will use this power to her people's advantage in the next chapter.

We have asked before and we will ask again. Who is Judith—chaste paradigm, triumphant savior, sexual warrior, national hero, sadomasochistic fantasy, femme fatale? Victim, perpetrator, or avenger? Judith is what Mieke Bal calls an "ideo-story": "a narrative whose structure lends itself to be the receptacle, or projection screen, of different, often opposing ideologies which the narrative appears to emblematize."[62] In the case of Judith, confusion is endemic to the story itself, gender confusion especially but also a kind of epistemological confusion, a confusion about how to understand her, that bifurcates her reception into mutually

60. For just one recent example, see Chanel Miller, *Know My Name: A Memoir* (New York: Random House, 2019), who recounts her own experience of sexual assault and the sympathetic sentencing of her assailant.

61. At least, that is the impression left by their art. The largest extant collection of visual images of decapitations (headless bodies as well as decapitated heads) is from the Assyrians dating from the ninth to the sixth century BCE. Dolce, *"Losing One's Head" in the Ancient Near East*, 7–8.

62. Mieke Bal, "Head Hunting: 'Judith' on the Cutting Edge of Knowledge," in *A Feminist Companion to Esther, Judith and Susanna*, 264.

exclusive trajectories. More than just the rules of the body's grammar have been violated as Judith's fingers lace through the damp hair of her enemy, wrench up his head to expose his neck, and saw the knife across skin and sinew. The rules of all sorts of grammars—ideologies of gender, sex, sexuality, hospitality, ethics, power, prayer—are all disrupted in her act of decollation. Is it any wonder, as Bal suggests, that Judith "scares many of us out of our wits"?[63]

63. Ibid., 266.

Judith 13:10b–16:25

Judith Triumphant

Judith's work is not yet done, for a severed head has no meaning if no one sees it. The display is just as important as the decollation, whether the head be held aloft by victorious soldiers (as in Assyrian reliefs[1]) or brought in on a silver plate (as Salome requests[2]). Judith and her slave must return to Bethulia to reveal their deed and prepare for the ensuing battle.

Before the beheading, Judith's power was still mediated through the town elders since they were still the ones to command the guards at the gates; after the beheading, Judith will directly lead the people. Her wisdom, bravery, and resourcefulness continue to manifest as she turns a single assassination into a full-scale military rout. In addition, the narrative threads of Achior and Judith will finally unite when they come face-to-face (or face-to-face-to-face, considering the role of Holofernes's head in their encounter). Achior will complete his crossing over as the two halves of the story of Judith meet and resolve. In the end, Judith returns to the solitude of her home, leaving interpreters to wrestle with her legacy.

1. See, for example, Panel 17, Room M of the North Palace at Nineveh, Neo-Assyrian Period, 645–635 BCE, currently in The British Museum, London.

2. Matt 14:8, 11; and Mark 6:25, 28.

Judith's Triumphant Return to Bethulia (13:10b-20)

After the climactic beheading, the story begins its dénouement. The narrative moves quickly to get Judith and her slave out of the Assyrian camp and into the Israelite town. The distance between Bethulia and the military camp took ten verses to traverse at 10:10-20; now, with Holofernes's head stuffed into a bag, the journey takes the women only half a verse (13:10b). We can imagine the fast-moving pair, in the dark of night, a breathless Judith calling out "from a distance" to "'Open, open the gate!'" (13:11), with the heavy bag swinging to and fro in the arms of the slave rushing beside her mistress. The repetition of the imperative "open" is accompanied by the particle δέ in Greek. The construction is unique in the LXX and has no Hebrew equivalent.[3] Such a repetition emphasizes the urgency of the situation; it does not convey fear or relief as much as it does triumph. We also see Judith's new power in this command; whereas she told the elders to have the gate opened for her when she left (10:9), now she issues the directives herself. There is a practical reason for this shift since the elders could not have known when the women were returning. Even so, Judith's double imperative, spoken directly to the gatekeepers, signals a change in the way Judith relates to her people. Before she left town, she spoke only to the elders; now she will speak directly to the inhabitants, both to the Israelites and to Achior. In fact, the townspeople will summon the elders when they hear Judith approaching (13:12), another indication that the elders' authority has faded into the background. In her return, Judith replaces them as the leader to her people.

The quick pace continues as the people, surprised at Judith's return, "hurried down" and "all ran together" to open the gate (13:12-13). The people welcome the two women and surround them. While Judith's slave sometimes disappears from the narrative as the Greek notes only Judith's presence (for example, after the two women leave Bethulia in 10:10, all subsequent pronouns are singular until the slave is again noted in 10:17), the townspeople acknowledge both women and gather around them both. They light a fire, and Judith tells the story of their daring adventure.

Judith speaks "with a loud voice," a descriptor used more often in the book of Judith than in any other LXX text,[4] twice with reference to Judith

3. Deborah Levine Gera, *Judith*, CEJL (Berlin: de Gruyter, 2014), 402.
4. Ibid., 404.

Jdt 13:10b-20

10bThen the two of them went out to-
gether, as they were accustomed to
do for prayer. They passed through the
camp, circled around the valley, and
went up the mountain to Bethulia, and
came to its gates. 11From a distance
Judith called out to the sentries at the
gates, "Open, open the gate! God, our
God, is with us, still showing his power
in Israel and his strength against our
enemies, as he has done today!"
12When the people of her town heard
her voice, they hurried down to the town
gate and summoned the elders of the
town. 13They all ran together, both small
and great, for it seemed unbelievable
that she had returned. They opened the
gate and welcomed them. 14Then she
said to them with a loud voice, "Praise
God, O praise him! Praise God, who
has not withdrawn his mercy from the
house of Israel, but has destroyed our
enemies by my hand this very night!"
15Then she pulled the head out of the
bag and showed it to them, and said,
"See here, the head of Holofernes,
the commander of the Assyrian army,
and here is the canopy beneath which
he lay in his drunken stupor. The Lord
has struck him down by the hand of a

(9:1 and 13:14). Judith is a woman who speaks authoritatively; she is loud. Later traditions arise in both Judaism and Christianity that seek to suppress women's voices: a rabbinic proscription called *kol isha* declares women's voices intrinsically sensual and forbids women's singing, especially in worship; using New Testament verses like 1 Corinthians 14:33, Christian women have been forbidden to teach and preach. Prohibitions that begin in religious contexts often extend outward, and there are still communities that react with suspicion to women with loud voices, in both the literal and figurative sense. Judith's voice cuts through those prejudices and proscriptions. In her loud voice, Judith again praises God (13:14) and then, dramatically, pulls Holofernes's head out of the bag for everyone to see. We can imagine the collective gasp from the townspeople, Judith's eyes bright with victory, the head looking even more gruesome in the flickering firelight. The head not only offers definitive proof of the truth of her story, but Judith's act of pulling it out of the bag for viewing establishes her relationship to Holofernes: she is now the owner of his head, this site "of all human energies and potentials." The once-mighty general has been reduced to a commodity, a "coveted object" in the possession of the enemy.[5]

5. Rita Dolce, *"Losing One's Head" in the Ancient Near East: Interpretation and Meaning of Decapitation* (New York: Routledge, 2018), 17, 23.

Jdt 13:10b-20 (cont.)

woman. [16]As the Lord lives, who has protected me in the way I went, I swear that it was my face that seduced him to his destruction, and that he committed no sin with me, to defile and shame me."

[17]All the people were greatly astonished. They bowed down and worshiped God, and said with one accord, "Blessed are you our God, who have this day humiliated the enemies of your people."

[18]Then Uzziah said to her, "O daughter, you are blessed by the Most High God above all other women on earth; and blessed be the Lord God, who created the heavens and the earth, who has guided you to cut off the head of the leader of our enemies. [19]Your praise will never depart from the hearts of those who remember the power of God. [20]May God grant this to be a perpetual honor to you, and may he reward you with blessings, because you risked your own life when our nation was brought low, and you averted our ruin, walking in the straight path before our God." And all the people said, "Amen. Amen."

And not just any enemy. For the third time since she returned, Judith attributes the victory over Holofernes to God but now emphasizes that it was her hand, "the hand of a woman" (13:15), that accomplished God's will. The Greek word θῆλυς, translated as "woman" by the NRSV, can also be translated "female" and refer more broadly to female animals. Consequently, Carey Moore suggests that she is making herself abject in order to heighten further the contrast between the general and his assassin.[6] The more lowly Judith, the more shame sticks to Holofernes as he is subjected to death, dismemberment, and display.

The gender ideologies in the book of Judith are not consistent. Whereas there is something subversive about a strong, smart, and beautiful woman who takes matters into her own hands and marshals forth to save her community from a foreign military threat, part of the reason Judith's act is so celebrated by Bethulia is that a woman murdering a man is so shameful for the man. Holofernes is not just dead; he is humiliated. Being killed by one's own sword while lying in a lustful and drunken stupor would be embarrassing no matter the sex of the assailant. This natural embarrassment is, however, augmented by a gender ideology that positions men and women in hierarchical relationship, embedded in an honor-shame framework where sexuality is a particularly fraught site of shame. Judith was alone with Holofernes in his bedroom. She needs

6. Carey A. Moore, *Judith*, AB 40 (Garden City, NY: Doubleday, 1985), 232.

to guarantee that none of the shame associated with this scene sticks to her; she swears: "it was my face that seduced him to his destruction, and . . . he committed no sin with me, to defile and shame me" (13:16). All shame adheres to Holofernes alone. And yet, Judith does need to explain herself. Her explanation necessarily hints at the doubts her audience, and we readers, might still hold.

Comparison to Jael is again instructive. The Hebrew text in Judges 4 and 5 (especially in Judges 5) is replete with sexual innuendo. Even though there is, strictly speaking, no sex scene between Jael and Sisera, it is difficult to argue definitively that there was no intimate engagement between the two. In Judges 5 especially, it almost seems as if Jael kills Sisera *in coitus interruptus*. Sisera is awake and standing when she strikes. Does he not notice the tent peg and mallet in Jael's hands because he is otherwise distracted? Once struck, he falls "at her feet" (Jdg 5:27) in a way that implies sexual congress.[7] As aforementioned, some commentators have read Judith as a "cleaned up" Jael.[8] Jael violates the laws of hospitality; Judith is offered hospitality but is careful never fully to accept. Jael's ethnicity is unmarked and her motives unknown; Judith is an Israelite woman who is intent on the salvation of her people. Jael may or may not have had sex with Sisera (either consensual or forced); Judith unequivocally, emphatically, did not.

Judith's sexual purity also functions symbolically as she represents the inviolable people of Israel with their sacred precincts. Deborah Levine Gera notes, "The language of defilement, dishonor, and shame is also used in our book in conjunction with the threat to Jerusalem and its temple (4:12; 9:8)."[9] As Judith successfully defends her chastity, she also defends her town Bethulia, the "Virgin"; as her body remains undefiled, so do the holy centers of Jerusalem and the temple. She represents not only these locales but also all the people within. No one will be violated; no one will be shamed. Israel's honor is preserved. Judith is triumphant as the defender of Israel, her people, and her God.

7. Susan Niditch, "Eroticism and Death in the Tale of Jael," in *Gender Difference in Ancient Israel*, ed. Peggy L. Day (Minneapolis: Fortress, 1989), 47–48; see also Colleen Conway, *Sex and Slaughter in the Tent of Jael: A Cultural History of a Biblical Story* (Oxford: Oxford University Press, 2017), 17.

8. Sidnie White Crawford, "In the Steps of Jael and Deborah: Judith as Heroine," in *"No One Spoke Ill of Her": Essays on Judith*, ed. James C. VanderKam, EJL (Atlanta: Scholars Press, 1992), 6; Conway, *Sex and Slaughter*, 27–31.

9. Gera, *Judith*, 406. See also Ellen Juhl Christiansen, "Judith: Defender of Israel—Preserver of the Temple," in *A Pious Seductress: Studies in the Book of Judith*, ed. Géza G. Xeravits (Berlin: de Gruyter, 2012), 81–83.

The people react by bowing down and praising God (13:17). Uzziah also blesses Judith, blessing her above all other women (13:18). His words are probably best recognized in their more archaic translation: "Blessed art thou. . . ." The scriptural link between Judith and Mary is forged through this phrase, spoken here by Uzziah to Judith, and then again by the angel Gabriel to Mary in the Gospel of Luke (Luke 1:28). Later the words "blessed are you among women" (and the connections between Judith and Mary) were enshrined in the prayer Hail Mary.[10] Uzziah's blessing, in conjunction with the words that Joakim will next speak to Judith (15:10), is also a part of Marian feast day liturgies.[11] Read typologically, Judith represents Mary in her chastity, humility, piety, and prayerfulness; her triumph over Holofernes represents the church's victory over sin, especially the sins of lust, blasphemy, and pride. As the second Eve, Mary crushes Satan's head, prefigured by Judith cutting off Holofernes's head. During the counter-Reformation, when Marian theology especially was under attack by Protestant reformers, Judith's role as warrior was particularly prominent in image and idea. Mary shared in this martial identity, fighting both heretics (i.e., Protestants) and infidels (i.e., Muslims).[12]

Uzziah ends with a remarkable paean: "May God grant this to be a perpetual honor to you, and may he reward you with blessings, because you risked your own life when our nation was brought low, and you averted our ruin, walking in the straight path before our God" (13:20). Uzziah's prayer for Judith to be given "perpetual honor" is comparable in the LXX only to Judas Maccabeus's eulogy where his memory is "blessed forever" as a reward for his military might (1 Macc 3:7). Judith's "straight path" again indicates that, no matter the qualms subsequent readers have about her deeds, the text regards her as exemplary. All the people affirm Uzziah's words with an enthusiastic "Amen. Amen."

Judith's Counsel and Achior's Conversion (14:1-10)

Despite the celebratory prayers and extravagant blessings, the war is not yet over. A well-armed Assyrian army is camped outside Bethulia's gates; the spring is still captured; the city is still under siege.

10. Elena Ciletti, "Judith Imagery as Catholic Orthodoxy in Counter-Reformation Italy," in *The Sword of Judith: Judith Studies across the Disciplines*, ed. Kevin R. Brine, Elena Ciletti, and Henrike Lähnemann (Cambridge: Open Book, 2010), 362.

11. Ibid., 358–59.

12. Ibid., 357–58.

Jdt 14:1-10

14:1Then Judith said to them, "Listen
to me, my friends. Take this head and
hang it upon the parapet of your wall.
2As soon as day breaks and the sun
rises on the earth, each of you take
up your weapons, and let every able-
bodied man go out of the town; set a
captain over them, as if you were going
down to the plain against the Assyrian
outpost; only do not go down. 3Then
they will seize their arms and go into
the camp and rouse the officers of the
Assyrian army. They will rush into the
tent of Holofernes and will not find him.
Then panic will come over them, and
they will flee before you. 4Then you and
all who live within the borders of Israel
will pursue them and cut them down
in their tracks. 5But before you do all
this, bring Achior the Ammonite to me
so that he may see and recognize the
man who despised the house of Israel
and sent him to us as if to his death."

6So they summoned Achior from
the house of Uzziah. When he came
and saw the head of Holofernes in the
hand of one of the men in the assembly
of the people, he fell down on his face

Thus far, Judith has played many roles: grieving widow, pious woman, seductress, assassin. Now she becomes the Israelite army's general as she gives tactical orders to the people of Bethulia. In this way, she combines Jael with Deborah (Judg 4–5): she assassinates the enemy general *and* devises military stratagems. Judith's first instruction is to hang the head of Holofernes on the parapet. The display of the decollated head is a process that begins with Judith's dramatic reveal as she pulls it from her bag and ends with its exhibition on the walls. Judith's speech to the Israelite men suggests the hanging head is not intended to alert the enemy to Holofernes's demise. Indeed, the Assyrian camp is too far away to notice, let alone accurately identify, a head on a parapet; they will know Holofernes is dead when they find his headless corpse (14:3 and 14:15). Rather, the head's display functions as a sign of God's favor and thus encouragement to the Israelites. Rita Dolce identifies two primary purposes of the head: definitive proof of the enemy's death and demonstration of the victor's glory.[13] Judith accomplishes the first purpose during her fireside report (and will repeat it when she meets Achior); she will accomplish the second purpose when the head is hung on the outer walls.

There are many possible places to display decapitated heads. In ancient Near East iconography, when hung in a public place "with a strong

13. Dolce, *Losing One's Head*, 28.

Jdt 14:1-10 (cont.)

in a faint. [7]When they raised him up he threw himself at Judith's feet, and did obeisance to her, and said, "Blessed are you in every tent of Judah! In every nation those who hear your name will be alarmed. [8]Now tell me what you have done during these days."

So Judith told him in the presence of the people all that she had done, from the day she left until the moment she began speaking to them. [9]When she had finished, the people raised a great shout and made a joyful noise in their town. [10]When Achior saw all that the God of Israel had done, he believed firmly in God. So he was circumcised, and joined the house of Israel, remaining so to this day.

ideological significance, such as city walls and gates," these heads not only provide "proof of the annihilation of the enemy and of the glory of the victor" but also "ostentatiously demonstrate control of an area that has been secured or recently conquered, of its borders and of the security of the kingdom."[14] Before the onslaught begins, Judith is confidently signaling Israel's imminent success.

Next, Judith instructs the able-bodied Israelite men by accurately anticipating the effect their movements will have on the Assyrian patrols. She describes how the Assyrians "will rush into the tent of Holofernes and will not find him. Then panic will come over them, and they will flee before you" (14:3). As Gera notes, "It is almost as if she is telling the Assyrian forces what to do."[15] Judith's directives reach a crescendo when she commands the Israelites—not just those in Bethulia but those in all of Israel—to pursue and strike the fleeing Assyrians down (14:4). Judith has taken Holofernes's head; in this act she has taken his power to command a nation's armies, not just Israel's but even Assyria's own.

She then summons Achior, ordering the people to go and bring him to her. Although the Israelites show no doubt that the head is indeed that of the Assyrian general, Achior is the only witness who can confirm his identity. Confirm he does. The very sight of Holofernes's severed head causes him to faint (14:6). In her role as assassin and general, Judith fully embraces masculinity and male roles. Achior, by contrast, has been safely sequestered in Uzziah's home, not even leaving it when the townspeople

14. Ibid., 29.

15. She bases this conclusion on the text's use of the future indicative, compared to the jussive futures in 14:2. Gera, *Judith*, 413.

run to meet Judith at the gates. Judith calls him out, through the townspeople, and he obeys. In their only meeting, Achior and Judith reverse gender roles.[16]

As discussed in chapter 3, when Achior is introduced into the narrative, he represents a masculinity that is in contrast to the one embodied by Holofernes. Holofernes's masculinity is then paired with Judith's feminine play, a gender dynamic that leads to his demise. Now, Judith and Achior finally come together, and again gender roles are highlighted. He is the only man in the narrative who is not overcome by her beauty; rather, he appears to be moved by her bravery. Her actions cause him to be amazed. Different models for masculinity, femininity, and male-female interactions unfold through Achior's story.

When Achior sees Holofernes's face, we recall Holofernes's threat that Achior would not see his face again until he had wreaked his vengeance upon the Israelites (6:5). Holofernes's prediction has come true but with a cruel twist. They have indeed come face-to-face again but on the day of *Israel's* vengeance.

Once Achior recovers from his initial shock, he throws himself down again (this time consciously) at Judith's feet and does "obeisance to her" (14:7; προσκυνέω). Achior bows down to Judith in an act that may acknowledge her superiority, as Judith does (albeit not in truth) before Holofernes when she first meets him (10:23). Achior's act also seems to be acknowledging Judith as a representation of God on earth, since this verb is also used in contexts of worshiping God (see Matt 4:10; Heb 11:21). Achior blesses and praises her, saying, "Blessed are you in every tent of Judah!" with language reminiscent of Deborah's praise of Jael ("Most blessed of women be Jael, the wife of Heber the Kenite, of tent-swelling women most blessed" [Judg 5:24]). He asks to hear all that she has done.

Judith recounts her exploits again, "from the day she left until the moment she began speaking to them" (14:8), not only to Achior, but to all the people who remain around her. Although not repeated for the reader, the narrative pace has slowed considerably as we pause between military order and military action for this now twice-told tale.

When she finishes, the people cheer. Achior has an even more profound reaction: "When Achior saw all that the God of Israel had done, he believed firmly in God. So he was circumcised, and joined the house

16. Such a gender role reversal is noted by many commentators. See, for example, Moore, *Judith*, 235.

of Israel, remaining so to this day" (14:10). Achior's conversion began when he was first introduced as a Gentile lauding the actions of the God of Israel (like other noteworthy biblical Gentiles, including Jethro in Exod 18:8-12 and Rahab in Josh 2:9-11). His incorporation into Israel began when he, like Ruth, entered Bethulia and accepted the elder's hospitality. His circumcision completes his crossing over. As Helen Efthimiadis-Keith notes in her Jungian reading, "Achior undergoes the most intense, permanent psychological changes" of any character in the book of Judith.[17] His religious conversion is made even more dramatic by the fact of his Ammonite ethnicity.

Achior is not just any Gentile: he is an Ammonite. Lest we forget, Judith specifically notes his ethnicity when she summons him (14:5). His character opens up a space to examine issues of ethnicity, religion, and nationalism in the book of Judith. Ammonites are the descendants of Ben-Ami, son of Lot and his unnamed youngest daughter (Gen 19:38). Products of the same drunken and incestuous rape as the Moabites, Ammonites are prohibited from joining Israel "even to the tenth generation" (Deut 23:3). We may understand Achior's conversion in the same way that many understand Ruth's inclusion (and possible conversion, although the term is anachronistic in Ruth's context). Achior provides a counter-testimony to any prohibition (de facto or de jure) against Ammonite incorporation.

Moreover, Achior's journey to conversion is central to the book's theological message. He steps forward in chapter 5 to recount the power of Israel's God; in doing so, he implies that Israel's God is superior to Nebuchadnezzar. Since this witness comes from an *Ammonite*, he is also establishing the universality of the God of Israel and the role of the people of Israel. One purpose of God's deliverance to the faithful covenant-keeping Israelites is to witness to the nations regarding God's fidelity and power. Achior is quite aware of Israelite history and he becomes prophet in his advice to Holofernes (5:5-21). He is also the goal of this history. Knowing God, speaking for God, and then responding to God's salvation by worship and conversion, Achior becomes the fulfillment of the theological logic he earlier describes. In Hebrew, Achior's name may mean, "brother of light," an image that reflects the idea that Israel will be a light to all nations (Isa 42:6; 49:6; 52:10; 60:3). Achior's

17. Helen Efthimiadis-Keith, *The Enemy Is Within: A Jungian Psychoanalytic Approach to the Book of Judith* (Leiden: Brill, 2004), 312.

conversion points toward the prophetic hope that Gentiles will join with Israelites to worship YHWH in Jerusalem (Isa 60:1-14; Zech 8:21-23).

Some commentators find that Judith's interview with Achior is out of sequence and recommend moving the scene so that it immediately follows her firelight speech to the Bethulians.[18] The intercalation of Achior's conversion, however, interrupting the flow from military orders to military action, demonstrates the interconnections between this conversion and the martial engagement. The victory is not one of military might alone; the victory is one of theological triumph. The victory is not just for the Israelites; the victory is for all peoples. All peoples, at least, who will join with the people of God.

Achior's Ammonite identity makes his affirmations of the superiority of Israel's God even more dramatic, paralleling how Judith's sex makes her victory over Holofernes more spectacular.[19] His act of conversion, accomplished through circumcision, is also his entrance into Israelite manhood. It is the mark of the covenant, a permanent and painful sign that one has submitted to the law of Moses. Cutting the penis signals a special relationship between the men of Israel and the (male) God of Israel. It sanctifies the reproductive and sexual powers of men, acts as a pledge to keep them properly focused (and in a religion that stresses progeny and inheritance this is particularly important), and is a mark of virility. Because of the psychoanalytical connections between penises and heads, Achior's circumcision may also be read as a counterpoint to Judith's decapitation of Holofernes, a way of matching her bravery with his own. At the same time, cutting this most tender organ is a kind of wounding, a kind of vulnerability. Although a much more complex story, Rhiannon Graybill notes that Moses's circumcision (Exod 4:25) "ushers in a new way of understanding masculinity and male embodiment, one that foregrounds openness and vulnerability over phallic domination of the other."[20] Achior's circumcision may have the same resonances. Unlike Moses, his circumcision is not performed by a woman, but it is prompted by a woman nevertheless. Achior thus consistently presents an alternative version of masculinity that also challenges phallic domination. On the one hand, Achior acts like a stereotypical weak woman (inhabiting private spaces, obedient, fragile, fainting); on the other hand,

18. For example, Moore, *Judith*, 234.

19. Gera, *Judith*, 420.

20. Rhiannon Graybill, *Are We Not Men? Unstable Masculinity in the Hebrew Prophets* (New York: Oxford University Press, 2016), 41.

his larger story reveals a man of many registers, capable of strength and resolve (confronting Holofernes, converting to Judaism). Together, Judith and Achior are people who queerly embody both "masculine" and "feminine" characteristics; together, they remake the very meaning of these categorizations.

The Assyrians Panic and the Israelites Attack (14:11–15:7)

As Judith said, so it is. As dawn breaks, the Bethulians hang the head of Holofernes on the city walls and the Israelite men arm themselves and exit the gates. Assyrian patrols send word that the Israelites are arrayed. Displaying their confidence and power, they call the Israelites "slaves" and predict their "utter destruction" (14:13). Their bravado will be short-lived.

The patrols instruct Bagoas to wake "our lord" (14:13). Bagoas knocks at Holofernes's entrance. Hears no answer. Opens. Enters. Each of his movements builds narrative tension as he comes closer and closer to the revelation within. He expects to find Holofernes "sleeping with Judith" (14:14). Instead of a sexually satisfied man, he finds his master's dead and headless body.

Bagoas's response is full of pathos: "He cried out with a loud voice and wept and groaned and shouted, and tore his clothes" (14:16). Bagoas appears genuinely aggrieved, although in Greek literature, eunuchs are often portrayed as histrionic, emotional, and emasculated.[21] The scene also seems influenced by Judges 3:25, the finding of Eglon's dead body after Ehud kills him. Eglon's servants too wait outside of the room in which he has been killed, then finally enter. Like Holofernes, Eglon is found in a shameful posture (he has shat himself). Both stories are replete with sexual innuendo. Given the sexual use of eunuchs by their owners in the Greco-Roman world,[22] this intertext may also be implying that Bagoas also served Holofernes in that capacity.

Bagoas then goes to Judith's tent and, finding it empty, surmises the cause of his master's death. He rushes out of Judith's tent to sound the alarm: "The slaves have tricked us! One Hebrew woman has brought

21. Gera, *Judith*, 73–74, 428. See Xenophon's account of Cyrus the Younger's eunuch committing suicide on the news of Cyrus's death, or Ctesias's story of a eunuch who sits at Darius's tomb for seven years before he too dies.

22. Sean D. Burke, *Queering the Ethiopian Eunuch: Strategies of Ambiguity in Acts* (Minneapolis: Fortress, 2013), 98–99.

Jdt 14:11–15:7

11As soon as it was dawn they hung the
head of Holofernes on the wall. Then
they all took their weapons, and they
went out in companies to the moun-
tain passes. 12When the Assyrians saw
them they sent word to their command-
ers, who then went to the generals and
the captains and to all their other offi-
cers. 13They came to Holofernes' tent
and said to the steward in charge of all
his personal affairs, "Wake up our lord,
for the slaves have been so bold as to
come down against us to give battle,
to their utter destruction."

14So Bagoas went in and knocked
at the entry of the tent, for he supposed
that he was sleeping with Judith. 15But
when no one answered, he opened
it and went into the bedchamber and
found him sprawled on the floor dead,
with his head missing. 16He cried out
with a loud voice and wept and groaned
and shouted, and tore his clothes.
17Then he went to the tent where Judith
had stayed, and when he did not find
her, he rushed out to the people and
shouted, 18"The slaves have tricked us!
One Hebrew woman has brought dis-
grace on the house of King Nebuchad-
nezzar. Look, Holofernes is lying on the
ground, and his head is missing!"

19When the leaders of the Assyrian
army heard this, they tore their tunics
and were greatly dismayed, and their

disgrace on the house of King Nebuchadnezzar. Look, Holofernes is lying on the ground, and his head is missing!" (14:18).

In a growl of contempt, Bagoas calls both women "slaves." Bagoas attributes the assassination to "one Hebrew woman," highlighting the three factors that make the beheading so humiliating: one single person, a despised Hebrew, an inferior woman. Compare this to Holofernes's boast that he could defeat the Israelites "as if they are one man" (Jdt 6:3) and the ironic reversal of expectations becomes particularly clear. He then draws attention to Holofernes's missing head. It is the beheading that is particularly shocking, both to Bagoas and to some contemporary readers. For some interpreters, the beheading, more than any other act of Judith's, invalidates the text's moral value. Pamela Milne notes that today beheadings draw international condemnation; they are called "barbaric" and considered "war crimes." She believes that readers of Judith should express similar outrage.[23] Judith is not any kind of hero,

23. Pamela J. Milne, "A Self-Response: What Would I Do with Judith Now?" in *A Feminist Companion to Tobit and Judith*, ed. Athalya Brenner-Idan and Helen Efthimiadis-Keith, FCB 20, 2nd ser. (London: Bloomsbury T&T Clark, 2015), 140. Michael Wojciechowski

Jdt 14:11–15:7 (cont.)

loud cries and shouts rose up throughout the camp.

15:1When the men in the tents heard it, they were amazed at what had happened.
2Overcome with fear and trembling, they did not wait for one another, but with one impulse all rushed out and fled by every path across the plain and through the hill country.
3Those who had camped in the hills around Bethulia also took to flight. Then the Israelites, everyone that was a soldier, rushed out upon them.
4Uzziah sent men to Betomasthaim and Choba and Kola, and to all the frontiers of Israel, to tell what had taken place and to urge all to rush out upon the enemy to destroy them.
5When the Israelites heard it, with one accord they fell upon the enemy, and cut them down as far as Choba. Those in Jerusalem and all the hill country also came, for they were told what had happened in the camp of the enemy. The men in Gilead and in Galilee outflanked them with great slaughter, even beyond Damascus and its borders.
6The rest of the people of Bethulia fell upon the Assyrian camp and plundered it, acquiring great riches.
7And the Israelites, when they returned from the slaughter, took possession of what remained. Even the villages and towns in the hill country and in the plain got a great amount of booty, since there was a vast quantity of it.

let alone a feminist hero, from her perspective.[24] Yet, violence cannot remain only in the purview of the oppressor. Certainly, some of the most revolutionary social movements have employed nonviolent resistance to great effect (Mahatma Gandhi and Martin Luther King Jr., for example). At the same time, few would fault Nat Turner for killing slave owners in Virginia, claiming that God had told him to kill his enemies with their own weapons, or Mordechai Anielewicz for shooting the Nazi soldiers sent to liquidate the Warsaw ghetto? Moreover, on closer review, neither the struggle for national liberation led by Gandhi nor the fight for civil rights led by King was bloodless. The riots and clashes and threats worked in concert with civil disobedience in the accomplishment of the movements' goals. For us, a better feminist approach to violence is one that neither sanctions all nor condemns all but rather regards each situation in its own particularity and assesses each act according to its need.

---

also calls Judith's act a "terrorist murder" ("Moral Teaching of the Book of Judith," in *A Pious Seductress*, 86).

24. Milne, "A Self-Response," 138. See also her earlier work "What Shall We Do With Judith?"

Bagoas

Bagoas, the eunuch in charge of the belongings of Holofernes, is a most significant secondary character in the book of Judith.[25] His textual introduction is probably intended for humor and emphasis.[26] His name in Persian is a title frequently given to eunuchs and therefore may mean *eunuch*.[27] So a translation could be, "He said to Eunuch the eunuch in charge of his personal affairs, 'Go . . .'" (12:11). As Holofernes's aide de camp, Bagoas holds a gatekeeper position; he controls access to the great general. The status, fortunes, and lives of the two entwine throughout the narrative and military campaign. It is entirely possible that even as their lives interlocked, so did their deaths. The text recounts Holofernes's death specifically (12:8) and seems to indicate Bagoas's death as among those of the scattered army (14:5).

Bagoas displays the following characteristics: arrogance, pride, power, condescension, and anger. It would seem that Holofernes picked someone of like disposition. Bagoas fulfills the folk tale role of villain because he seeks to disturb the happiness of many nations, Israel included, and seeks to do misfortune, damage, and harm to many.[28] Bagoas can also be read as a traitor. Mieke Bal argues that a traitor in appearance looks like a helper;[29] Bagoas appears to help Judith in the camp by giving her access to the great general himself, Holofernes. He clearly is a theological traitor, for he fails to worship the God of Israel.

He may be a secondary character, but Bagoas speaks (12:13; 14:18), is pivotal in significant plot twists, and proves a foil for two characters: his master Holofernes and Judith's silent unnamed maid. Let's consider Holofernes first.

Bagoas mirrors Holofernes's swagger and misplaced confidence. Numerous victories

25. This section takes material from Robin Gallaher Branch, "Joakim, Uzziah, and Bagoas: A Literary Analysis of Selected Secondary Characters in the Book of Judith," *OTE* 25 (2012): 71–78, 80–81.

26. Bagoas's function as eunuch/chamberlain in the folktale provides stability, what Vladimir Propp calls a constant element that is necessary and foundational for a story like the book of Judith to unfold. *Morphology of the Folktale* (Austin: University of Texas Press, 1968), 21.

27. Henry Snyder Gehman, ed., *The New Westminster Dictionary of the Bible* (Philadelphia: Westminster, 1970), 281.

28. Propp, *Morphology*, 27.

29. Mieke Bal, *Narratology: Introduction to the Theory of Narrative* (Toronto: University of Toronto Press, 1985), 35.

deaden both master and slave to present danger. Bagoas mirrors Holofernes's sloppiness. Losing self-control, Holofernes acts without discretion (or suspicion!) toward one who is an enemy Israelite, the beautiful Judith. Consequently, the text exposes both to ridicule; it portrays both general and eunuch as fools.

Taking his cue from Holofernes, Bagoas copies the general in his dealings with the people. He mirrors Holofernes's reaction to Judith: delight in her words and in her defection to the camp of the Assyrians (11:20-21). They agree on Judith's beauty, wisdom, eloquence (11:23). They also immediately see what the text refrains from mentioning specifically: Judith's desirability, availability, vulnerability, and lack of male protection.

All too sadly, Bagoas mirrors Holofernes in his stupidity. A good subordinate—whether a slave, servant, or paid employee—must at times question the one in charge. Tragically, for his army and himself, Holofernes asks no questions of Judith. He believes her gracious words, a speech filled with double meanings and wordplays (11:5-19). Thoroughly taken in by her beauty, brains, wisdom, and eloquence, Holofernes welcomes her into the camp (11:23). If Bagoas really had his master's best interests at heart, he would have asked questions. He would have been exceedingly suspicious of a beautiful woman in a tiara and her maid coming so surprisingly to the camp of the enemy at night. Bagoas is both lax and inept.

Bagoas is also a foil to the unnamed, silent maid of Judith. This maid is Judith's counterpart in every way, taking part with her mistress in this life-or-death adventure. The text introduces the maid as someone Judith trusts and has placed "in charge of all her property" (8:10). Bagoas likewise is a slave and in charge of Holofernes's property. Bagoas knows Holofernes likes to party (12:19-20; 13:1). The maid knows Judith enjoys a quiet life of prayer, fasting, seclusion, and restricted eating. They prepare the food of their masters. Bagoas knows Holofernes likes wine and rich food; the maid knows that Judith eats selected food only once a day in the evening (12:9, 19). Significantly, both know the sexual preferences of their masters. Judith prefers to stay a widow and remain chaste. Bagoas knows Holofernes enjoys a fresh conquest (8:4-8; 13:16; 16:21-22).

Holofernes wants Judith, so he charges Bagoas to arrange all the details and to "persuade" Judith to attend an intimate banquet (12:10-12). Bagoas goes as commanded. He displays a silver tongue. His condescending speech reveals his arrogance and pride; he is oblivious to his danger. Judith also displays a silver tongue and in her response means the opposite of what Bagoas believes she says.

Let's continue looking at this meeting, for it is textually quite rich. Bagoas insults Judith in several ways. First, he insults her by not using the pronoun *you*; he talks to her as if she is an object. Second, he insults her by his familiarity, by giving her a nickname, *lovely maid*. Third, he insults her through reference to her age. He knows Judith (presumably) is not a virgin but a widow—and is therefore (presumably) sexually experienced. Yet he seeks to flatter her by slicing years off her age and calling her a *maid* (12:13). Fourth, he insults her by letting her know that she is expected to be a courtesan like the Assyrian women; in modern parlance, the Assyrian court seems to be filled with sex groupies. His condescending manner indicates he views women as men's playthings, Assyrian women as alive to serve the sexual needs of Assyrian men. He equates Judith with these courtesans. In a way, however, Judith invites Bagoas's bad manners, for in front of an appreciative audience of men engaged in war, she earlier praised Holofernes as brave, experienced, and dazzling in the art of war (11:8). Her response to Bagoas seems to give Holofernes the chance to dazzle her in bed. No doubt Bagoas quickly relays her reply to the executive tent!

Arriving for the intimate banquet, Judith steps on lambskins spread by her maid and provided by Bagoas (12:15). Bagoas closes the tent from the outside and dismisses the weary servants (12:20; 13:1). Bagoas leaves Holofernes unprotected. Bagoas's discretion and absence allow Judith to behead Holofernes. Bagoas fails as a servant.

The text humorously depicts Bagoas as waiting patiently past sunrise for his master to emerge from his sexual conquest. Bagoas's hesitant stand outside the tent of Holofernes smacks of humor. One can see the perplexity on his face. If he intrudes, does he provoke *coitus interruptus*? Would he come upon a lady displaying sexual satisfaction? Finally, duty demands that Bagoas must interrupt the (presumed) lovers. Notice the verbs; they convey his quick actions (14:14-16). He shakes the tent curtain, draws it aside, goes into the bedroom, and finds his master on top of the bedstool, a headless corpse! Bagoas suddenly acts quickly. It is in his best interests to do so, and his actions show a distinct measure of self-protection. He lets out a yell, and successively adds wailing, groaning, and shouting to it; he rips his clothes. Overall, it's quite a convincing display of his surprise, outrage, and innocence. He immediately goes to Judith's tent, finds her and her maid missing, and rushes into the midst of the *people* (λαὸν, 14:17). The word "people" is significant: one expects the text to say "army." This textual putdown indicates, however, the disunity of what is trumped up to be the best fighting force in the world. This Assyrian fighting force cannot withstand a change of command at the top. Chaos prevails; the Israelites decimate the fleeing army. The story progresses quickly, verifying the veracity of the servant's insult.

Bagoas, the chamberlain/eunuch of Holofernes and by far the most interesting of the book's secondary characters, unknowingly serves an important narrative purpose. He affirms his own supervision of the tent of his master: he knows he left it secured; he knows none entered its confines for hours. Consequently, when he shouts Holofernes's death, he is quickly believed. In fact, such is his credibility that the ripple effect of his announcement is astonishing. Officers tear their clothes; enlisted men quiver with fear and on common impulse break rank, desert, and "escape along every path in the plain and the hill country" (14:19–15:2).

When he sees the headless corpse, Bagoas immediately realizes Judith and her maid have succeeded on several levels: Judith has humiliated Holofernes and the Assyrian army by killing Holofernes with his own sword, in his own tent, in his own bed, and surrounded by the Assyrian army. She and her maid have successfully escaped through the camp and carry the missing head as proof. In short, Judith and her maid successfully shame Holofernes; Bagoas, his chamberlain-eunuch; and the Assyrian army. The God of Israel wins over Nebuchadnezzar the god of the Assyrians. It is a stunning triumph.

Robin Gallaher Branch

The headless body compounds the shock and the grief among the Assyrian army. When confronted with the news of Holofernes's death, the other Assyrian leaders also cry, shout, and tear their clothing as a sign of grief and alarm (14:19). As everyone in Bethulia was amazed that Judith had returned alive (13:13), the Assyrian men are amazed that their general is dead (15:1). Whereas the amazement in Bethulia gives way to worship and praise, the amazement in the Assyrian camp leads to pandemonium and chaotic retreat (15:2). The army, in spasms, has lost its head, its leader, and its composure. Portraying the men in the army as weeping and running continues the gender reversals: once-mighty men are emasculated.

Uzziah, finally taking some useful action, sends word to other towns in Israel that Holofernes has been killed and the Assyrians are running; he calls them to rally and rout their enemies (15:3-4). Like all other geographic details in the book of Judith, the place names and locations that follow, documenting the battle sites, are not clear (14:4-5). As in those other instances, however, actual locations do not matter as much as the effect of naming them. All of Israel rises up and overwhelms the warriors of the Assyrian army.

The Bethulians take the lead in the plunder of the army camps, although the riches are so bounteous that the other Israelites get a share once their skirmishes subside (15:6-7). The plundering receives more emphasis than the killings. This emphasis is distinctive in biblical texts; in fact, the Jews refrain from looting at the end of the book of Esther (Est 9:10, 15, 16). The excessive amount of booty, enough to enrich all the towns in the hill country as well as the towns throughout Israel that had fought the Assyrians while they were in retreat, underscores both the vastness of the Assyrian military threat and the enormity of the Israelite victory. The focus on the booty may also be another indication of the decadence of the Assyrians, similar to the ways in which the narrative lingers on the richness of Holofernes's canopy. Such dissolution leaves an empire open to smaller but harder, more battle-ready foes, fiercer because they have little left to lose.

Celebration of Victory (15:8–16:20)

Victory belongs to the people of Israel! The national triumph may also be the triumph of alternative gender ideologies. The defeat of the Assyrian army demonstrates the instability of the type of masculinity the Assyrians represent, a masculinity based in rigid social hierarchies, domination, bravado, and violence. This masculinity is a mask that Judith removes when she kills the army's leader. The celebrations of the Israelites that follow are gynocentric, characterized by effusive praise of Judith and parades of women. The celebrations also establish definitively the theological question raised at the beginning of the story: who is God, Nebuchadnezzar or YHWH?

In the immediate aftermath of the military victory, the leaders of Jerusalem travel to Bethulia to "witness" all that God has done and to see Judith. When Joakim and the other leaders meet Judith, they praise her by calling her "the glory of Jerusalem" (15:9); they also emphasize her agency by stating how all has been accomplished with Judith's "own hand" (15:10). Joakim and the elders focus so exclusively on Judith that they "virtually assimilate" her to God.[30] In Catholic liturgy, the words

30. Gera, *Judith*, 441.

Jdt 15:8–16:20

[8]Then the high priest Joakim and the elders of the Israelites who lived in Jerusalem came to witness the good things that the Lord had done for Israel, and to see Judith and to wish her well. [9]When they met her, they all blessed her with one accord and said to her, "You are the glory of Jerusalem, you are the great boast of Israel, you are the great pride of our nation! [10]You have done all this with your own hand; you have done great good to Israel, and God is well pleased with it. May the Almighty Lord bless you forever!" And all the people said, "Amen."

[11]All the people plundered the camp for thirty days. They gave Judith the tent of Holofernes and all his silver dinnerware, his beds, his bowls, and all his furniture. She took them and loaded her mules and hitched up her carts and piled the things on them.

[12]All the women of Israel gathered to see her, and blessed her, and some of them performed a dance in her honor. She took ivy-wreathed wands in her hands and distributed them to the women who were with her; [13]and she and those who were with her crowned themselves with olive wreaths. She went before all the people in the dance, leading all the women, while all the men of Israel followed, bearing their arms and wearing garlands and singing hymns.

[14]Judith began this thanksgiving before all Israel, and all the people loudly sang this song of praise. [16:1]And Judith said,

Begin a song to my God with
tambourines,

of the priests here are applied to Mary, who is also called "the glory of Jerusalem . . . the joy of Israel."[31] Geoffrey D. Miller has analyzed this exceptional blessing, in conjunction with several other unusual elements in the narrative (including Achior's own prostration to Judith in 14:7), to propose that Judith is a hero not in her modeling of moral behavior but in her symbolizing God's saving power.[32] If so, her moral ambiguity and her contravention of the gender norms are not problems. Instead, it is another way that the text establishes the affinities between Judith and God; like Judith, God also "resists easy categorization and cannot be circumscribed by simplistic ideologies."[33] By embodying the Divine

31. Ciletti, "Judith Imagery as Catholic Orthodoxy in Counter-Reformation Italy," 358–59.

32. Geoffrey D. Miller, "A Femme Fatale of Whom 'No One Spoke Ill': Judith's Moral Muddle and Her Personification of Yahweh," *JSOT* 39 (2014): 224. Miller enumerates Judith's "questionable behavior" (224–27), as well as surveys some of the scholarly solutions for the dilemma posed by this behavior (228–32).

33. Ibid., 242. For the full catalog of correspondences between Judith and God, see 232–43.

sing to my Lord with cymbals;
Raise to him a new psalm;
exalt him, and call upon his name.
2For the Lord is a God who crushes wars;
he sets up his camp among his people;
he delivered me from the hands of my pursuers.
3The Assyrian came down from the mountains of the north;
he came with myriads of his warriors;
their numbers blocked up the wadis,
and their cavalry covered the hills.
4He boasted that he would burn up my territory,
and kill my young men with the sword,
and dash my infants to the ground,
and seize my children as booty,
and take my virgins as spoil.
5But the Lord Almighty has foiled them
by the hand of a woman.
6For their mighty one did not fall by the hands of the young men,
nor did the sons of the Titans strike him down,
nor did tall giants set upon him;
but Judith daughter of Merari
with the beauty of her countenance undid him.
7For she put away her widow's clothing
to exalt the oppressed in Israel.

Warrior in Judith, the text also offers a "creative solution" to the problem of God's apparent absence. Judith assumes the role of God and even becomes God's personification. "Judith is more than God's emissary or proxy; she becomes an expression of divine providence, concretizing the saving action of a seemingly absent God."[34] And all the people say, "Amen!" (15:10).

The excessiveness of the plundering spills over into this section as well. The people continue to plunder for thirty more days (15:11). In a kind of poetic justice, the people give Judith Holofernes's tent along with his furniture, beds, and all of the silver dinnerware. The very instruments intended to (im)press her into submission become the signs of her victory over him. His tent with its luxurious trappings represents his power (military, political, and even religious given the theological thrust of his campaign). This power is now disassembled and handed over to Judith, another indication that she has assumed Israelite leadership. Ever pious

34. Ibid., 244. See also Margarita Stocker, *Judith: Sexual Warrior; Women and Power in Western Cuture* (New Haven: Yale University Press, 1998), 11.

Jdt 15:8–16:20 (cont.)

She anointed her face with
perfume;
8she fastened her hair with a
tiara
and put on a linen gown to
beguile him.
9Her sandal ravished his eyes,
her beauty captivated his mind,
and the sword severed his
neck!
10The Persians trembled at her
boldness,
the Medes were daunted at
her daring.
11Then my oppressed people
shouted;
my weak people cried out, and
the enemy trembled;
they lifted up their voices, and
the enemy were turned
back.
12Sons of slave-girls pierced them
through
and wounded them like the
children of fugitives;
they perished before the army
of my Lord.
13I will sing to my God a new song:
O Lord, you are great and
glorious,
wonderful in strength,
invincible.
14Let all your creatures serve you,
for you spoke, and they were
made.
You sent forth your spirit, and it
formed them;
there is none that can resist
your voice.
15For the mountains shall be
shaken to their foundations
with the waters;

and humble, Judith loads all of these spoils onto her mules; she will take them to Jerusalem and dedicate them to God (16:19).

After Judith has been invested with Holofernes's treasures, a great public celebration commences led by "all the women of Israel." The women bless Judith and dance around her. Next, Judith distributes ivy-wreathed wands for the women to hold, and they all crown themselves with olive wreaths (15:12-13). Judith leads the people in a victory parade, the dancing women first, followed by the men "bearing their arms and wearing garlands and singing hymns" (15:13). It is not unusual for women to greet victorious warriors with song and dance (see Exod 15:20-21; Judg 11:34; 1 Sam 18:6-7). Such actions in Judith may be a variation of the rite and reflect an Israelite practice performed by women. This display of wands and wreaths is, however, otherwise unattested. The wand-waving, dancing women seem to be involved in something more wild, more spontaneous, than the ritual dances welcoming warriors. Amy-Jill Levine notes, "The combination of the *thvrsa* [ivy-wreathed wands] with

before your glance the rocks
shall melt like wax.
But to those who fear you
you show mercy.
[16]For every sacrifice as a fragrant
offering is a small thing,
and the fat of all whole burnt
offerings to you is a very
little thing;
but whoever fears the Lord is
great forever.
[17]Woe to the nations that rise up
against my people!
The Lord Almighty will take
vengeance on them in
the day of judgment;
he will send fire and worms into
their flesh;
they shall weep in pain forever.

[18]When they arrived at Jerusalem,
they worshiped God. As soon as the
people were purified, they offered their
burnt offerings, their freewill offerings,
and their gifts. [19]Judith also dedicated to
God all the possessions of Holofernes,
which the people had given her; and
the canopy that she had taken for her-
self from his bedchamber she gave as
a votive offering. [20]For three months
the people continued feasting in Jeru-
salem before the sanctuary, and Judith
remained with them.

the decapitated head and the women's celebration is strongly reminiscent of the *Bacchae*, another story in which gender roles are muddled and in which an 'other' is both dangerous and desirable."[35] She also points out that the wands held by the women are analogous to the weapons the men carry; thus, they represent phallic power in their shape and in their correspondences.[36] Judith's victory disrupts standard gender ideologies; the celebrations around her victory affirm such gender trouble.

All the people sing hymns during the procession, but we hear only Judith's special thanksgiving. In some ways, her song resembles other victory songs composed by women such as Miriam (Exod 15) and Deborah (Judg 5). Instead of recounting someone else's victory, like Miriam, Judith is singing about her own triumph, similar to Deborah's song, although Deborah is also praising Jael. Thus, she combines the roles of both the victor and the female singer who memorializes the courageous deeds.[37] Parallels between Judith's song and Moses's song

35. Amy-Jill Levine, "Sacrifice and Salvation: Otherness and Domestication in the Book of Judith," in *A Feminist Companion to Esther, Judith and Susanna*, ed. Athalya Brenner, FCB 7 (Sheffield: Sheffield Academic, 1995), 218 n. 1.

36. Ibid., 218.

37. Gera, *Judith*, 444.

in Exodus 15 are particularly noteworthy. Judith again proclaims that YHWH is a "God who crushes wars" (see also 9:7) and is almost quoting Exodus 15:3. More than a single citation, Judith's hymn references the exodus story by equating her victory with the paradigmatic story of God's saving power.[38] The song also positions Judith as the culmination of the leaders and saviors that had come before her: she embodies Moses, Miriam, Jael, Deborah, Barak, among others.

Judith's hymn is a lengthy seventeen verses. It begins and ends with generic words of praise and thanksgiving, but the body describes in detail the threat that Judith and the Bethulians faced. Judith's words focus especially on the threat of slavery and rape—the Assyrians were going to "seize my children as booty, and take my virgins as spoil" (16:4d). Using the first-person possessive, the childless Judith speaks metaphorically as a mother.[39] More so, she also embodies her city, her nation, and maybe even the voice of God. The song then shifts to the third person as Judith declares, "the Lord Almighty has foiled them by the hand of a woman" (16:5; literally "female"), Judith, daughter of Merari (16:6). This brief genealogical note sets Judith apart from many other women who are usually identified as the wives of their husbands. Even Deborah, whose husband is completely absent, is referred to as the wife of Lappidoth (Judg 4:4), and Jael, whose actions are so like Judith's, is repeatedly called the wife of Heber the Kennite (Judg 4:17; 5:1, 12, 24). Next, the prayer recounts Judith's actions—how she put away her widow's clothes and donned beautiful gowns, a tiara, and perfume in order to "beguile him" (16:8). The drama is heightened by lingering on her toilette, then turning and ending with a blunt and brief statement of her murderous deed: "Her sandal ravished his eyes, her beauty captivated his mind, and the sword severed his neck!" (16:9). The song explicitly connects her beauty with her deadliness, the very connection that will later lead readers to see her as a femme fatale.

While she is describing her own deeds, Judith speaks in the third person; then verse 11 switches back to first person as Judith describes the response of her people and the defeat of the Assyrians. She concludes her song praising God as both creator and redeemer, warrior and protector. These verses extol the virtues of fearing the Lord (Jdt 16:15, 16)

38. Judith Lang, "The Lord Who Crushes Wars: A Study of Judith 9:7; 16:2 and Exodus 15:3," in *A Pious Seductress*, 186.

39. Toni Craven, *Artistry and Faith in the Book of Judith* (Chico, CA: Scholars Press, 1983), 107.

even above ritual sacrifice. The last line is particularly vivid, perhaps influenced by the images in the final words of the book of Isaiah: "And they shall go out and look at the dead bodies of the people who have rebelled against me; for their worm shall not die, their fire shall not be quenched, and they shall be an abhorrence to all flesh" (Isa 66:24). Those who fight the Israelites will suffer the wrath of their God: "he will send fire and worms into their flesh; they shall weep in pain forever" (Jdt 16:17cd). To challenge this God through his people is to bring down God's fearsome wrath, a wrath experienced as a violation of the body, as God's weapons penetrate the flesh.

With that, the people arrive in Jerusalem. Here, the people ritually bathe before they enter the temple to give to God their gifts (16:18). Fear of the Lord is better than sacrifices (16:16), but sacrifices also have value. The Israelites have enriched themselves with Assyrian plunder; now they return to God what God has so generously enabled them to receive. Judith gives all of the booty she had taken or been given from the Assyrian camp, including the canopy that she had cut down from Holofernes's bed (16:19). Giving the canopy to the temple is a final humiliation as it represents Holofernes's complete subjugation to the Israelite God. After proper thanks through gift offerings, the people continue to celebrate with feasting in Jerusalem for another three months (16:20). An excessive party to commemorate a spectacular victory.

Reading Holofernes Queerly III

There is also the matter of what happens to Holofernes's canopy after his murder. In 13:9, we learn that Judith "pulled down the canopy from the posts." She takes it with her back to Bethulia, but no explicit reason is given for this curious action. Morton Scott Enslin and Solomon Zeitlin proposed that the canopy serves as a trophy of her kill, which seems likely.[40] There is, however, more: as Lawrence Wills proposes, we can draw an analogy between Holofernes's canopy and the בתולים of Deuteronomy 22, which relates to a husband's claims that his new bride was not a virgin when they married.[41] If she truly were a virgin, her father is to

40. Morton S. Enslin and Solomon Zeitlin, *The Book of Judith* (Leiden: Brill, 1972), 153.

41. Lawrence M. Wills, *The Jewish Novel in the Ancient World* (Ithaca, NY: Cornell University Press, 1995), 149.

bring evidence of her virginity, referred to as בתולים, and spread it out before the elders of the town. The proof here is presumably the bloody sheets from the wedding night, proving that the woman bled when her hymen broke and thus had been a virgin when she was married. The blood serves to show that intercourse between the bride and groom has occurred and that the bride had been pure. Wills argues that in Judith's case, the canopy serves a similar role as the bedsheet in Deuteronomy 22: Judith brings Holofernes's canopy to the elders of her town as proof that she has "done" him. In the canopy, we have a symbol of Holofernes's importance as a general and thus his masculinity—nonetheless problematic for his masculinity because of its ostentation—turned into a symbol of defeated, corrupted femininity.

It is no coincidence that the major fissures in Holofernes's performance of masculinity—his overly fussy canopy and surroundings, his ambiguous words concerning his desire for Judith, and the role of the canopy as a sexual trophy—appear once Judith enters the story. While the first half of the book builds up the Assyrians as fearsome enemies and Holofernes as their terrifyingly effective commander, the second half moves the story toward the triumph of Israel over these paragons of masculinity, by the hand of a woman. Questioning the masculinity of one's enemy is a classic strategy for shaming him. When Holofernes fails to cite accepted conventions of masculinity, it is because the author now wishes to cast him in an unflattering light. The fierce general who threatened to conquer Israel is showing some cracks in his portrayal of manhood. He is now ripe for the taking by a character doing a flawless portrayal of over-the-top womanhood. At the same time, the ways in which Holofernes continues to perform conventional masculinity in the second half of the book, such as the lust for Judith that overcomes his good judgment, contribute to his downfall.

When we examine the character of Holofernes through a queer-theoretical lens, we see that for Holofernes, as for Judith, gender is but a performance, a series of stylized acts repeated to produce the illusion of a defined, definable gender. Here and there, we can see cracks in the armor of Holofernes's masculinity, both because the over-the-top nature of his portrayal serves to expose it as constructed artifice and because some of his own words and surroundings highlight deviations from expected conventions of manhood. For Judith, her gender performance allows her to get in position to kill Holofernes and save the day. For Holofernes himself, however, his performance of the masculine sets him up to lose his head.

Caryn Tamber-Rosenau

They All Lived Happily Ever After (16:21-25)

The last section of the book of Judith constitutes an epilogue. Everyone returns home from Jerusalem. For Judith, returning home is also returning to the life she lived before the Assyrian threat, although with increased honor (ἔνδοξος, the same word used of God in 16:13) and renown. Many men are attracted to this fierce, beautiful, and wealthy woman. They want to marry her, but she refuses them all. She remains a widow until her death (16:22). A more literal rendering of the Greek than the one provided by the NRSV is "many men wanted her but no man knew her." Since "to know" is a common biblical euphemism for sexual intercourse, this line emphasizes her sexual status more than, strictly, her marital status. Her continued chastity is unusual, albeit not unique, in Scripture where marriage and motherhood are more typical routes to societal standing for women. By finding honor another way, Judith enters the ranks of other women like Miriam, Deborah, Jael, and Esther. Judith's state as celibate widow may indicate changing mores in some Hellenistic Jewish communities and may be a precursor for early Christian promotion of celibacy in contradistinction to the prevailing ethos in both Judaism and Greek culture.[42]

Precursor or not, certainly the early Christian community focused on Judith's sexual restraint and lauded her sexual choices. She was held up as an example for widows as they were urged not to remarry. In the Vulgate, Jerome does more than simply translate 16:22; he includes the comment that "chastity was joined to her virtue" in her refusal of all matrimonial proposals.[43] Jerome strongly preferred the unmarried life for men and women, embraced it himself, and advocated it for others. For example, in his letter to Salvina (a wealthy Roman woman, recently widowed), he advises: "Let those who feed on flesh serve the flesh, whose bodies boil with desire, who are tied to their husbands and who set their hearts on having offspring. Let those whose wombs are burdened cram their stomachs with flesh. But you have buried every indulgence in your husband's tomb."[44] These final verses of Judith also emphasize the husband's tomb: Judith's chastity began with Manasseh's death and burial (16:22); it continued as she grew old in "her husband's house," and when she dies, she is also buried in his tomb (16:23). His next of kin

42. Gera, *Judith*, 473.

43. Cited in Moore, *Judith*, 259.

44. Cited in ibid.

Jdt 16:21-25

21 After this they all returned home to
their own inheritances. Judith went to
Bethulia, and remained on her estate.
For the rest of her life she was hon-
ored throughout the whole country.
22 Many desired to marry her, but she
gave herself to no man all the days of
her life after her husband Manasseh
died and was gathered to his people.
23 She became more and more fa-
mous, and grew old in her husband's
house, reaching the age of one hun-
dred five. She set her maid free. She
died in Bethulia, and they buried her
in the cave of her husband Manasseh;
24 and the house of Israel mourned her
for seven days. Before she died she
distributed her property to all those
who were next of kin to her husband
Manasseh, and to her own nearest
kindred. 25 No one ever again spread
terror among the Israelites during the
lifetime of Judith, or for a long time
after her death.

inherit some of her wealth (16:24). After dying and making her a widow, as recounted in chapter 9, Manasseh is completely absent from the body of the narrative. At the end, he returns, and the text attaches his name to every stage of the rest of Judith's life.

Judith's lifelong widowhood has been a site for feminist debate about her legacy. Amy-Jill Levine argues that Judith's subversion of gender roles must, in the end, be contained. Her movement back toward gender compliance begins with her surrender of all of Holofernes's goods to God. According to Levine, such an offering expiates the sins of her appropriation of the role of priest and her rather unorthodox ritual sacrifice of the enemy general.[45] Judith's decision to remain a widow in her husband's house until the day of her death completes her redomestication.[46] She is, in a sense, buried in her husband's house long before she is buried in her husband's tomb. Thus, the danger of her gender-bending, the danger of her beauty, and the danger of her sword-wielding hand is contained and neutralized.

Other feminist interpreters view Judith's refusal of all marriage proposals more positively. By refusing to marry, she is refusing domestication and maintaining her independence. Ora Brison, while acknowledging Levine's reading, also understands her celibacy as an indication of her spiritual role as intermediary and facilitator between the human com-

45. Levine, "Sacrifice and Salvation," 221.

46. Ibid.

munity and the divine.[47] Furthermore, her refusal to marry is a refusal to have children; yet, curiously, the text never even mentions this childlessness. Childlessness is lamented by some biblical women (Rachel in Gen 30:1; Hannah in 1 Sam 10–11); yet, in the book of Judith, it is unremarked and presumably unremarkable. Judith ends her story unattached and unburdened by husband or child, free and independent until the end.

According to Deuteronomy, God's favor is demonstrated through descendants, wealth, and long life. Judith's extensive and illustrious line ends with her; however, she reaps the other gifts of divine regard. The text records her death at 105 (16:23), a rare note for a biblical woman. Before she dies, she divides her property between her husband Manasseh's family and her own; she also frees her slave (16:23). The verbal sequencing makes the timing of the manumission unclear: first, Judith lives until the age of 105; then she sets her slave free; then she dies, is buried, and mourned; but, before she dies, she distributes her property (16:23-24). When, exactly, did the slave go free? She could have been released upon Judith's death at 105; she may have been freed right before Judith died, as a part of the redistribution of Judith's other property. In either case, Judith does not follow the biblical mandate to release Israelite slaves after six years of service (Deut 15:12). Perhaps Judith's slave is not an Israelite. In a third scenario, Judith could have freed the slave much earlier. The juxtaposition in the text of her manumission and Judith's death, however, makes this situation unlikely.

The occasion of her manumission raises questions about age. Often depicted as much older than Judith, this relative age is impossible were she freed at or near Judith's death. The slave must be Judith's age or younger. More important, the occasion of the manumission raises ethical questions. Were the slave freed at the time of Judith's death, then Judith's act is neither generous nor kind.[48] The slave still has lived decades in servitude (perhaps her whole life, although we have no information about when and how she became a slave). Even if younger than Judith, she is at the time of manumission old and subject to all of the physical

47. Ora Brison, "Judith: A Pious Widow Turned *Femme Fatale*, or More?," in *A Feminist Companion to Tobit and Judith*, 196.

48. Jennifer Glancy, "Judith the Slaveholder," in *A Feminist Companion to Tobit and Judith*, 208. Commentators who understand Judith's freeing her slave as reflecting positively on Judith's character include André LaCocque, *The Feminine Unconventional: Four Subversive Figures in Israel's Tradition* (Eugene, OR: Wipf and Stock, 1990), 46; Moore, *Judith*, 260.

infirmities that come with advanced age (even thirty years younger than Judith means that her age is seventy-five years). How would an elderly ex-slave support herself, especially since Judith makes no explicit provision for her continued care?

The reality and the rhetoric of slavery must enter into our assessment of Judith's feminist legacy. The book assumes a slave owner's perspective,[49] even as it positions Judith as a new Moses, liberating her people from the threat of slavery. This dynamic is particularly resonant in the American context, a country founded in a brutal contradiction: the violence of chattel slavery and the ideals of political liberty. Judith's slave (as did thousands of African American slaves) even helps her mistress overcome the threats to Judith's own freedom, with no acknowledgment or recompense. She also risks her welfare and even her life, equally with Judith. How does it feel to be a slave after you help your owner do something that brings that owner fame and fortune? How can you return to the same forced service, as if nothing has changed for you while everything has changed for her? Judith's slave never speaks, so her readers have no window into her thoughts about her situation.

We can draw on the information we know about another slave, taken on a dangerous mission that brought fame and fortune to the owner but only continued obscurity and servitude to the slave. Judith's slave reminds us of York, the man owned by William Clark, partner of Meriwether Lewis. York accompanied Clark on the expedition of the Corps of Discovery (1804–1806). He did suffer from his unequal position and from the racism of the white explorers (there is evidence to suggest that he was, at least occasionally, the butt of cruel jokes), but he also was a full, participating member of the band. He was equally responsible for its success. As historian Thomas Slaughter notes, "However constraining York's status was on the expedition, it was also liberating by comparison with his past life."[50] Upon their return, York chafed at returning to his former state of servitude: he wanted to be with his wife (another slave, not owned by Clark) and requested his freedom. Clark denied the request. Their relationship deteriorated, and Clark even considered selling him to a plantation in the Deep South as retribution for his post-expedition behavior, behavior Clark called "insolent and sulky."[51] What happened

49. Glancy, "Judith the Slaveholder," 201.

50. Thomas P. Slaughter, *Exploring Lewis and Clark: Reflections on Men and Wilderness* (New York: Knopf, 2003), 118.

51. Letter from William Clark to his brother Jonathan Clark, as quoted in ibid., 125.

to York is a mystery; he becomes another human being whose story slips from history because his life was not deemed worthy of accurately recording. Judith's ownership of other human beings, particularly her treatment of the anonymous woman who helped her save Israel, may prove to be an even more intractable problem than questions raised over her use of seduction, deception, and murder.

In the end, when asked to assess Judith, we can only say, "It's complicated." Like all great men and great women, whether in legend or history, she is multidimensional. The tensions and contradictions cannot be resolved. There is power in this multidimensionality and resistance to resolution.

Judith's power is such that her one tremendous deed held other enemies at bay, not just during her lifetime but even after her death. The last verse in Judith functions as a kind of "happily ever after" coda: "And no one ever again spread terror among the Israelites during the lifetime of Judith, or for a long time after her death" (16:25). Despite the text's attempt to contain Judith, even Levine notes that such incorporation into acceptable gender roles is not complete. Judith's "otherness" continues to intrude. Judith has retreated from the public sphere, but her story has not. It continues on, long after her death, through "public memory and public discourse."[52] As story, it remains—she remains—uncontained and uncontrolled. Such is the power of a strong, beautiful, courageous, intrepid, and independent woman—someone who can put on a tiara and wield a sword all in equal measure.

52. Levine, "Sacrifice and Salvation," 223.

Conclusion

At a particularly tumultuous time in her career and personal life, Martha Graham read the book of Judith. Recently married to fellow dancer Erick Hawkins, the two had a passionate but "tormented" love affair.[1] In 1949, Louise Kain, a member of the Louisville Orchestra Board, conceived of a dance concerto featuring Martha Graham. Her idea of a solo dancer taking the place of a solo instrument was met with enthusiasm. Graham collaborated with composer William Schuman and the Louisville Orchestra commissioned the piece.[2] *Judith*—a solo ballet in five acts—premiered to great acclaim on January 4 and 5, 1950. According to some accounts, Graham's performance saved the Louisville Orchestra from financial ruin.[3] Following this success, Graham's dance company embarked on a European tour. Soon, however, she seriously injured her knee and was compelled to cancel the remainder of the tour. In the resulting tensions and conflicts with Hawkins, who was her dance partner on the tour, their marriage fell apart. He left her in London;

1. Mark Franco, *Martha Graham in Love and War: The Life in the Work* (New York: Oxford University Press, 2012), 9. The two began working together in 1938 and married in July 1948.

2. Jeanne Marie Belfy, "'Judith' and the Louisville Orchestra: The Rest of the Story," *College Music Symposium* 31 (1991): 43. Charles Hyman and William Sherman designed the set (although it was later resigned by Isamu Noguchi). Jean Rosenthal was the lighting director.

3. This is a widely repeated assertion, which is challenged in Belfy, "'Judith' and the Louisville Orchestra," 44–48.

she, devastated, retreated to Santa Fe. While rehabilitating both knee and heart, she returned to *Judith*. In the figure of Judith, she found an expression of despair and rage, an expression of courage and the will to fight back. She emerged from her injury to perform the twenty-five-minute piece again, this time in New York City on December 29, 1950. For Graham, according to friend and collaborator Pearl Lang, "Martha had to make that dance so she could cut off Erick's head!"[4]

Whereas Judith felt no personal animosity toward Holofernes but acted out of national pride and preservation, her singular act of beheading the general has reverberated with women for centuries. It has become an expression of proto-feminist and feminist rage against men both individually and collectively. It would be a mistake, however, to reduce either the source text or other artistic renditions of Judith to any single interpretive frame. Even Graham, whose life and work were so intertwined, was also exploring contemporary politics in her solo ballet. In the post-Holocaust world, Judith represents the Jewish will to fight against oppressors and resist annihilation. In 1962, Graham danced a version of *Judith* again (this time called *Legends of Judith*) in Israel, a clear expression of triumphant Zionism.[5] The personal and political are both explored through the figure of Judith.

Layers of interpretation continue to build as Margaret Atwood picks up Martha Graham's *Judith* and places her in a very unlikely place: at the center of a mid-level arts college. Atwood's MaddAddam trilogy is a dystopia that depicts a not-so-distant future where large transnational corporations, which develop products ostensibly for human health and wellness, control society. Commodification and corporate greed are the prevailing ethos; cultural collapse and ecological disaster are on the horizon. Several main characters end up at Martha Graham Academy, an educational institution geared toward those who could not make it into the coveted science schools run by the Corporations. The school had been founded in better times as a humanities academy with an emphasis on the performing arts. In a world where only scientific knowledge matters (and even then, only when it can be turned into profitable products),

4. As quoted in Stuart Hodes, *Part Real, Part Dream: Dancing with Martha Graham* (Concord ePress, 2011).

5. Nicole Tilford, "Judith and Her Interpreters," in *Women's Bible Commentary*, ed. Carol A. Newsom, Sharon H. Ringe, and Jacqueline E. Lapsley, 3rd ed. (Louisville: Westminster John Knox, 2012), 393; Margarita Stocker, *Judith: Sexual Warrior; Women and Power in Western Culture* (New Haven: Yale University Press, 1998), 199.

however, the school now lacks reputation, money, and enthusiasm. Its classes are small, its physical plant falling apart. At the center of the campus is a statue of Martha Graham herself, in her acclaimed role of Judith.

> Martha Graham Academy was named after some gory old dance goddess of the twentieth century who'd apparently mowed quite a swath in her day. There was a gruesome statue of her in front of the administration building, in her role—said the bronze plaque—as Judith, cutting off the head of a guy in a historical robe outfit called Holofernes. Retro feminist shit, was the general student opinion. Every once in a while the statue got its tits decorated or steel wool glued onto its pubic region—Jimmy himself had done some of this glueing [*sic*]—and so comatose was the management that the ornaments often stayed up there for months before they were noticed. Parents were always objecting to this statue—poor role model, they'd say, too aggressive, too bloodthirsty, blah, blah—whereupon the students would rally to its defense. Old Martha was their mascot, they'd say, the scowl, the dripping head and all. She represented life, or art, or something. Hands off Martha. Leave her alone.[6]

Judith and Graham slide in and out of identification as the statue becomes a site of commentary on women, art, and power in Atwood's trilogy.

Although rejecting the designation herself, Graham is a feminist figure in the world of dance, breaking boundaries and creating new ways of seeing women, their bodies, and their movements. She is a woman who lived fiercely on her own terms. A school named in her honor would embody this freedom of expression and courage to break new ground. Atwood's world, however, is complexly postfeminist. There appears to be no gender discrimination in terms of the opportunities in the Corporations. Both male and female scientists are honored and have access to great wealth and power. At the same time, child pornography is rampant, sex clubs legal and lucrative, and many of the Corporations prey on women's insecurities about aging and body image to increase their profit margins.

Graham's statue both attracts and repels the students who have come to her school, reflecting their society's ambivalent attitudes about female power. The vandalizing of her statue, targeting her breasts and pubic

6. Margaret Atwood, *Oryx and Crake* (New York: Random House, 2003), 186. Martha Graham as Judith makes another appearance in Atwood's *The Year of the Flood* (New York: Doubleday, 2013), 287.

region, highlights the rampant sexism and misogyny of the students. Juvenile puerile behavior, to be sure, but puerile behavior with a particularly sharp point. Martha Graham, Judith, Martha Graham as Judith—these are not the kind of women who are respected; these are the type of women who are sexually denigrated and humiliated. Female power is sexualized and thus degraded. Even though women have equal access to the most prestigious, powerful, and lucrative jobs in Atwood's society, a world where Graham's Academy languishes is not truly a world of equal opportunities. Rather, MaddAddam's world has lost the transformative and subversive power of art; it has no respect for the female body and—as the earth hurtles toward ecological disaster—no respect for other animal and plant bodies as well. There is still a need for a Judith, someone with the courage and the wisdom to cut off the head of Holofernes and every other toxic example of destructive masculinity wedded to military, political, and theological power. Atwood's world (and, by implication, our own) is still in need of that "retro feminist shit."

By a Woman's Hand: Judith as Feminist Activist

In the spring term of 2018, we team-taught an undergraduate Introduction to Women's and Gender Studies course. Both of us, Melissa, whose PhD is in religious studies, and Linda, whose PhD is in rhetoric and composition, quickly realized we were privileged to be teaching the course during a remarkable time. The rise of #MeToo, the February 2018 Parkland school shooting, and the burgeoning awareness of gender issues through cultural and social media made the concerns of women and children, as well as gender issues more generally, especially relevant to our traditional college students. Throughout the term it became clear our students were hungry to *do* something: they wanted to make a difference too. So in the last few weeks of the term we abandoned our initial plan to wrap up the class with a chapter on "Religion and Spirituality" from our textbook, Susan Shaw and Janet Lee's *Women's Voices/Feminist Visions*, and instead replaced it with another chapter, "Activism, Change, and Feminist Futures," which calls for concrete actions that embody feminist integrity. Shaw and Lee define integrity as "a moral positioning about the distinction between right and wrong, and . . . a consistent stance on this morality such that we act out what we believe and attempt to live our ideals." A feminist integrity, then, considers moral positionings in regard to feminist principles of equality, justice, dignity, and inclusivity.[7]

What we didn't consider during the term but do now for future iterations of the course is that the story of Judith ably illustrates important intersections of women, religion, spirituality, *and* feminist activism. We argue that Judith not only provides an excellent starting point for a discussion of women and religion but also is an excellent example of feminist activism and integrity. With her head, heart, and hands working in concert, Judith uses the powers at her disposal to effectively ensure security and peace for the Israelites throughout her long life and "for a long time after her death" (Jdt 16:25). We contend with Shaw and Lee that a feminist integrity is one that chooses courses of action grounded in feminist ideals, but we would add that a feminist integrity also requires the use of one's privilege to enact change. And how that privilege is enacted can be measured by the ideal of a feminist integrity. In looking to the ancient past, Judith offers a way toward understanding a feminist future.

Judith's Privilege as Arbiter of Activism

Activism almost always arises from those who are placed at a distinct disadvantage by the status quo, while those who possess cultural currency and the attendant power and privilege that come with it seldom desire change. Judith, however, illustrates not only how intersectionalities of gender, race, class, etc. often make for shifting positions of privilege and power within the status quo but also how varying kinds of privilege can transfer across shifting power relations. Threatened with utter destruction of her people or their complete subservience to Nebuchadnezzar, Judith uses her privileges, both earned and unearned, within her community and outside of it, not only for herself and the greater good of her people, the Israelites, but for all of humanity in her resistance to oppression. In doing so, she thinks and acts with a feminist integrity that moves toward a collective responsibility for peace, dignity, equality, inclusivity, and justice.

As a woman, Judith's privilege is clear. Some of her privilege is earned: her devotion to God, her wisdom, and her "true heart" (Jdt 8:28) are particularly valued within her community, making it such that "no one spoke ill of her" (Jdt 8:8). But other unearned privileges, such as her wealth and especially her great beauty, offer her prestige not only within her own community but outside of it

7. Susan M. Shaw and Janet Lee, *Women's Voices, Feminist Visions: Classic and Contemporary Readings* (New York: McGraw-Hill, 2007), 708–10.

too. Judith's husband provided amply for her, both in life and upon his death, leaving her an enviable estate that included a house, "gold and silver, men and women slaves, livestock, and fields" (Jdt 8:7). She retains and even elevates her privilege throughout her widowhood not only by managing her estate but especially by following the social customs and expectations for a widow: "she set up a tent for herself on the roof of her house. She . . . dressed in widow's clothing. She fasted all the days of her widowhood" (Jdt 8:4-6). Her gender conformity, piety, and resultant wisdom are beyond reproach and earn her privilege within her own community, ultimately granting her the blessings of the city's elders to leave the city and carry out her secret plan to save the Israelites from Nebuchadnezzar's oppressive regime.

While Judith uses one kind of earned privilege as a revered widow to get out of her home camp, she uses her unearned privilege of female beauty to get into Holofernes's camp, and her earned privilege of wisdom helps keep her there safely. Judith carefully prepares herself for her mission by doing all she can to "[make] herself very beautiful, to entice the eyes of all the men who might see her" (Jdt 10:3-4). When Judith and her maid enter the valley where Holofernes's army is stationed, they are quickly apprehended. Despite her lack of social status in this context, Judith's words and striking beauty quickly bestow privilege on her and are so persuasive that "a hundred men" escort her to Holofernes's tent, where everyone "marveled at the beauty of her face" (Jdt 10:14-23). Before, during, and after executing her plan, Judith maintains her devotion to God, where she is steadfast about her strong hands, deceptive words, and beguiling looks being but God's tools in the service of liberating the oppressed from the power of the wicked.

In this way, Judith engages in a kind of "cooperative nonconformity,"[8] working to change the status quo by operating within the constraints her privileges afford her. It is Holofernes, after all, whose own power bestows privilege on Judith by noting, "You are not only beautiful in appearance, but wise in speech. If you do as you have said, your God shall be my God" (Jdt 11:23). While Judith undoubtedly uses her beauty to her advantage, Holofernes is hardly at her mercy. Much has been made of Judith's seduction of Holofernes, but a modern feminist perspective would point out that it is Holofernes who commands she be brought to his tent and served food and wine. He intends to seduce her, "For it would be a disgrace if we let such a woman go without

8. Bernie Siegel as quoted in Shaw and Lee, *Women's Voices, Feminist Visions*, 711.

having intercourse with her. If we do not seduce her, she will laugh at us" (Jdt 12:12). By following social norms of passivity and obedience during Holofernes's seduction of her (and his choice to drink too much), Judith is able to act as an agent for change in upsetting the status quo.

Judith's Feminist Integrity: Change You Can Believe In

Judith promises change, and the change she brings about, we argue, exemplifies feminist integrity. By her hand, her god will deliver Israel (8:32-33). There is an integrity to her bold claims because her actions are consistent with her beliefs. Judith equates direct action with true humility. Judith's humility, grounded in her scrupulous performance of right religious rites, affords her power in her community. But for Judith, humility is not passive. Often we associate women with humble, passive activities like prayer and the "wringing of hands" and men with brave, aggressive military actions carrying out the will of god acting as "his hands." Much is written on the binaries in Judith. Yet as Judith states several times, she defeats Holofernes by her own hand. She does not invert the binary; she nullifies it. Literally, on either side of the battle, male leaders are sitting and waiting, "wringing their hands": Holofernes and his men feast and wait until the Hebrews' water runs out, while the leaders of Bethulia pray for god to deliver them.

Judith decries their inaction. Clearly, to do nothing lacks integrity. She accuses them of putting their god to a test, passively waiting for god's deliverance (8:13). Instead, she counsels that while they wait on god's deliverance, they should call on him to help them. They must continue with their acts of devotion (8:17-27). Then she boldly claims that god will deliver them by her hand, by her actions (8:33). Much is also made of right ritual actions in Judith. As long as they do not sin, they prosper, but when they depart from their god's ways, they will be defeated in battle (5:17-18). They are not defeated, indicating they have done what is right. Judith teaches that an activist cannot just wring one's hands in prayer.

For Judith, it is right and consistent to use her privilege to enact change on behalf of human dignity and worth. She represents the status quo for wealthy, pious widows, but as an activist, she converts her privilege into a plan that she alone carries out—"by her own hand." Even her companion stands outside the tent during the decapitation. Through her humility she walks hand in hand with her god into enemy territory to act out what she believes, thereby embodying a feminist activist who lives out her ideals to save the Hebrews' diverse form of spirituality. She does not arrogantly manipulate her god; rather, her complicated and brilliant plan is born out of a heart whose "disposition is right" (8:29). She nullifies the link between humility and passivity and replaces it with humility as right action. Judith advocates a doctrine of direct action.

Contrary to many scholarly interpretations of Judith, we maintain her integrity is not ambiguous. Sure, she uses deception with her words, seduces with her good looks, and murders with her own hands, but within the strictures of her situation, we maintain her integrity is intact. She is acting with consistency within a particular moral code that distinguishes right and wrong, placing the values of dignity, justice, equality, and inclusivity for all above all else. While we certainly would not advocate that deception, seduction, and murder are necessary means to an end for our modern students, we would point out the importance of asking what other means to action there are beyond the power and privilege one is given within particular social structures.

Much is made of Judith's devotion throughout the text, and we would argue that her willingness to risk the privileges she has earned is a further extension of the very same devotion, not an ambiguous act of duplicity. Acting with a feminist integrity requires one to integrate their ideas of equality, justice, dignity, and inclusivity with their actions, but a warrior for change must be willing to do more—to use, to risk, or even to relinquish one's privilege to end the oppression of others. No ambiguity here. The personal is political: Judith's bedroom politics involve using the cultural privilege afforded to women, and she knows this from the very beginning of her plot. She prepares for battle by putting on the armor of women: "She . . . anointed herself with precious ointment. She combed her hair. She put sandals on her feet, and put on her anklets, bracelets, rings, earrings, and all her other jewelry" (10:3-4). Crucially, though, she does all of this not for selfish gains, but in the service of the greater good. What else can be used but the power at one's disposal? We are trying to teach students to use the tools they have at hand to effect change, and as Judith illustrates, the enemy can fall at our own hand.

Melissa Stewart and
Linda Learman

That is, if we can regard Judith's character as "feminist." In the end, we return to the questions raised in the introduction. In the end, we again ask, "What shall we do with Judith?"[9] Throughout this commentary, we

9. Pamela J. Milne, "What Shall We Do With Judith? A Feminist Assessment of a Biblical 'Heroine,'" in *A Feminist Companion to Tobit and Judith*, ed. Athalya Brenner-Idan and Helen Efthimiadis-Keith, FCB 20, 2nd ser. (London: Bloomsbury T&T Clark, 2015).

have explored the poles of the feminist debate. For example, we have looked at perspectives like the one of Alice Ogden Bellis, who argues, "The stories of Ruth, Esther, Susanna, and Judith convey the most liberating messages for women of any of the stories of women in the first testament";[10] even more, Judith in particular "is perhaps the strongest Hebrew hero in all of biblical literature."[11] Others, like Betsy Merideth, who compares Judith to Delilah (Jdg 16), caution that even stories that applaud women can contain deeply troubling antiwoman messages. For Merideth, "The message [of Judith] could not be more clear: women's beauty and sexuality are dangerous to men because women use their attractiveness to deceive, harm and kill men."[12] Judith is undeniably a very strong, independent figure who is positively portrayed in her text. But does this mean that there are feminist aspects to her character and to the book that bears her name? Or is the antifeminist message of the book even more insidious because it is clothed in such an attractive figure? The text is open to diametrically opposed interpretations because the meaning of the text does not adhere only in the words on the page; the meaning of the text is also shaped by the context of the reader. The text itself is complex and multifaceted, and these different facets connect with different readers at different times in different ways.[13]

Adding to and sometimes coming into conflict with feminist readings, we have also brought masculinity studies and queer theory into conversation with both Judith and her interpretation. Men and their masculinity dominate (almost exclusively) the first seven chapters of Judith and play pivotal roles in the final nine chapters as well. Any reading, even a feminist reading, is incomplete without adequate attention to these male characters and masculine ideologies. Queer theory, in turn, has helped us destabilize these ideologies of both masculinity and femininity, challenging the very notion that gender and sex cohere. Gender is more fluid, less stable and coherent, more open to play than many feminist readings of Judith allow.

10. Alice Ogden Bellis, *Helpmates, Harlots, and Heroes: Women's Stories in the Hebrew Bible*, 2nd ed. (Louisville: Westminster John Knox, 2007), 189.

11. Ibid., 198.

12. Betsy Merideth, "Desire and Danger: The Drama of Betrayal in Judges and Judith," in *Anti-Covenant: Counter-Reading Women's Lives in the Hebrew Bible*, ed. Mieke Bal (Sheffield: Almond, 1989), 76.

13. For a recent concise summary of the various feminist perspectives on Judith, see Yael Shemesh, "The Stories of Women in a Man's World: The Books of Ruth, Esther, and Judith in Feminist Interpretation," in *Feminist Interpretation of the Hebrew Bible in Retrospect*, vol. 1, ed. Susanne Scholz (Sheffield: Sheffield Phoenix, 2013), 262–67.

Finally, our commentary reconsiders Judith's slave. With the notable exception of the scholarship of Jennifer Glancy, readings of Judith have lacked critical reflection on the institution of slavery that the text assumes.[14] No matter how laudable Judith is, no matter how positively we regard her from a feminist perspective (if, indeed, we do), true gender equality is not possible in economic systems of exploitation. No matter the interpretive lens, scholars have been reticent to critique Judith for her ownership of another woman. Perhaps readers are also dazzled by her beauty, or distracted by her charm, or too focused on her singular act of assassination, or blinded by their own class privilege. Slavery is inimical to a feminist vision, and feminist analysis cannot ignore this woman or remain silent about the class and economic structures that shape the story.

Martha Graham's creation of her solo work *Judith* "exposes a contradictory dynamic" between art as the product of deep emotion and art as built on textual research. Rather than a conventional blueprint of her choreography, Graham's written script of *Judith* is a "plethora of quotations and scholarly footnotes . . . fragments of literary exegesis in which all traces of story disappear."[15] The dance *Judith* is overwritten by the exegetical Judith; after Graham stopped performing her solo, she was never able to re-create it.[16] The work of commentary illuminates and the work of commentary obscures. It is our hope that this commentary manages to maintain both the art and emotion of Judith alongside the critique and the context. After all is said and done, Judith remains a fascinating figure who dances just beyond our reach.

14. Jennifer Glancy, "Judith the Slaveholder," in *A Feminist Companion to Tobit and Judith*.

15. Franco, *Martha Graham in Love and War*, 10.

16. Ibid.

Works Cited

Adams, Carol J. *The Sexual Politics of Meat: A Feminist-Vegetarian Critical Theory.* New York: Continuum, 2015.

Aguilar, Grace. *The Women of Israel.* England, 1845; New York: D. Appleton, 1872.

Anderson, Janice Capel, and Stephen D. Moore, eds. *Mark and Method: New Approaches in Biblical Studies.* 2nd ed. Minneapolis: Fortress, 2008.

Aquino, María Pilar, and María José Rosado-Nunes, eds. *Feminist Intercultural Theology: Latina Explorations for a Just World.* Studies in Latino/a Catholicism. Maryknoll, NY: Orbis Books, 2007.

Aquino, María Pilar, Daisy L. Machado, and Jeanette Rodríguez, eds. *A Reader in Latina Feminist Theology.* Austin: University of Texas Press, 2002.

Astell, Mary. *Some Reflections upon Marriage.* New York: Source Book Press, 1970. Reprint of the 1730 edition; earliest ed. 1700.

Atwood, Margaret. *Oryx and Crake.* New York: Random House, 2003.

———. *The Year of the Flood.* New York: Doubleday, 2013.

Bach, Alice, ed. *Women in the Hebrew Bible: A Reader.* New York: Routledge, 1999.

Bal, Mieke. "Head Hunting: 'Judith' on the Cutting Edge of Knowledge." In *A Feminist Companion to Esther, Judith and Susanna*, edited by Athalya Brenner, 253–85. FCB 7. Sheffield: Sheffield Academic, 1995.

———. *Lethal Love: Feminist Literary Readings of Biblical Love Stories.* Bloomington: Indiana University Press, 1987.

———. *Narratology: Introduction to the Theory of Narrative.* Toronto: University of Toronto Press, 1985.

Barucq, André. *Judith, Esther.* 2nd ed. Paris: Cerf, 1959.

Baskin, Judith R. "Women and Post-Biblical Commentary." In *The Torah: A Women's Commentary*, edited by Tamara Cohn Eskenazi and Andrea L. Weiss, xlix–lv. New York: URJ Press and Women of Reform Judaism, The Federation of Temple Sisterhoods, 2008.

Beavis, Mary Ann, Irmtraud Fischer, Mercedes Navarro Puerto, and Adriana Valerio, eds. The Bible and Women: An Encyclopaedia of Exegesis and Cultural History. https://www.bibleandwomen.org.

Belfy, Jeanne Marie. "'Judith' and the Louisville Orchestra: The Rest of the Story." *College Music Symposium* 31 (1991): 36–48.

Bellis, Alice Ogden. *Helpmates, Harlots, and Heroes: Women's Stories in the Hebrew Bible*. 2nd ed. Louisville: Westminster John Knox, 2007.

Benedetti, Laura. "Reconstructing Artemisia: Twentieth-Century Images of a Woman Artist." *Comparative Literature* 51 (1999): 43–61.

Benjamin, Mara H. "Tracing the Contours of a Half Century of Jewish Feminist Theology." *JFSR* 36 (2020): 11–31.

Benshoff, Harry M. *Monsters in the Closet: Homosexuality and the Horror Film*. Manchester: Manchester University Press, 1997.

Bird, Phyllis A. *Missing Persons and Mistaken Identities: Women and Gender in Ancient Israel*. Minneapolis: Fortress, 1997.

Bissell, Edwin Cone. *The Book of Judith*. The Apocrypha of the Old Testament. New York: Scribner's Sons, 1886.

Boccaccini, Gabriele. "Tigranes the Great as 'Nebuchadnezzar' in the Book of Judith." In *A Pious Seductress: Studies in the Book of Judith*, edited by Géza G. Xeravits, 55–69. Berlin: de Gruyter, 2012.

Børresen, Kari Elisabeth, and Adriana Valerio, eds. *The High Middle Ages*. The Bible and Women: An Encyclopaedia of Exegesis and Cultural History. Atlanta: SBL Press, 2015.

Branch, Robin Gallaher, and Pierre Jordaan. "The Significance of Secondary Characters in Susanna, Judith and the Additions to Esther in the Septuagint." *Acta Patristica et Byzantina* 20 (2009): 389–416.

Branch, Robin Gallaher. "Judith: A Remarkable Heroine, Parts 1 and 2." *Bible History Daily*. https://www.biblicalarchaeology.org/daily/people-cultures-in-the-bible/people-in-the-bible/judith-a-remarkable-heroine/; https://www.biblicalarchaeology.org/daily/people-cultures-in-the-bible/people-in-the-bible/judith-a-remarkable-heroine-part-2/. First published 2012; updated August 12, 2016.

———. "Joakim, Uzziah, and Bagoas: A Literary Analysis of Selected Secondary Characters in the Book of Judith." *OTE* 25 (2012): 57–83.

Brettler, Marc Zvi. "The Canonization of the Bible." In *The Jewish Study Bible*, edited by Adele Berlin and Marc Zvi Brettler, 2153–58. 2nd ed. Oxford: Oxford University Press, 2014.

Brison, Ora. "Judith: A Pious Widow Turned *Femme Fatale*, or More?" In *A Feminist Companion to Tobit and Judith*, edited by Athalya Brenner-Idan with Helen Efthimiadis-Keith, 175–99. FCB 20, 2nd ser. London: Bloomsbury T&T Clark, 2015.

Brooten, Bernadette J. *Love Between Women: Early Christian Responses to Female Homoeroticism*. Chicago: University of Chicago Press, 1996.

Burke, Sean D. *Queering the Ethiopian Eunuch: Strategies of Ambiguity in Acts*. Minneapolis: Fortress, 2013.

Butler, Judith. *Gender Trouble: Feminism and the Subversion of Identity*. New York: Routledge, 1990.

Camp, Claudia. *Wisdom and the Feminine in the Book of Proverbs*. Sheffield: Sheffield Academic, 1981.

Cannon, Katie G. "The Emergence of Black Feminist Consciousness." In *Feminist Interpretation of the Bible*, edited by Letty M. Russell, 30–40. Philadelphia: Westminster, 1985.

Caponigro, Mark Stephen. "Judith, Holding the Tale of Herodotus." In *"No One Spoke Ill of Her": Essays on Judith*, edited by James C. VanderKam, 47–59. EJL 2. Atlanta: Scholars Press, 1992.

Carr, David M. *Holy Resilience: The Bible's Traumatic Origins*. New Haven: Yale University Press, 2014.

Carter, Warren. *The Gospel of Matthew in Its Roman Imperial Context*. London: T&T Clark, 2005.

———. *The Roman Empire and the New Testament: An Essential Guide*. Nashville, TN: Abingdon, 2006.

Castelli, Elizabeth. "*Les Belles Infidèles*/Fidelity or Feminism? The Meanings of Feminist Biblical Translation." In *Searching the Scriptures: A Feminist Introduction*, vol. 1, edited by Elisabeth Schüssler Fiorenza with the assistance of Shelly Matthews, 189–204. New York: Crossroad, 1993.

Chapman, Cynthia R. *The Gendered Language of Warfare in the Israelite-Assyrian Encounter*. Winona Lake, IN: Eisenbrauns, 2004.

Christiansen, Ellen Juhl. "Judith: Defender of Israel—Preserver of the Temple." In *A Pious Seductress: Studies in the Book of Judith*, edited by Géza G. Xeravits, 70–84. Berlin: de Gruyter, 2012.

Ciletti, Elena. "Judith Imagery as Catholic Orthodoxy in Counter-Reformation Italy." In *The Sword of Judith: Judith Studies across the Disciplines*, edited by Kevin R. Brine, Elena Ciletti, and Henrike Lähnemann, 345–68. Cambridge: Open Book, 2010.

Ciletti, Elena, and Henrike Lähnemann. "Judith in the Christian Tradition." In *The Sword of Judith: Judith Studies across the Disciplines*, edited by Kevin R. Brine, Elena Ciletti, and Henrike Lähnemann, 41–65. Cambridge: Open Book, 2010.

Claassens, L. Juliana, and Carolyn J. Sharp, eds. *Feminist Frameworks and the Bible: Power, Ambiguity, and Intersectionality*. LHBOTS 630. London: Bloomsbury T&T Clark, 2017.

Claassens, L. Juliana, and Irmtraud Fischer, eds. *Prophecy and Gender in the Hebrew Bible*. The Bible and Women: An Encyclopaedia of Exegesis and Cultural History. Atlanta: SBL Press, 2021.

Clines, David J. A. *Interested Parties: The Ideology of Writers and Readers of the Hebrew Bible*. Sheffield: Sheffield Academic, 1995.

Clover, Carol J. *Men, Women, and Chain Saws: Gender and the Horror Film*. Princeton: Princeton University Press, 1993.

Consolino, Franca Ela, and Judith Herrin, eds. *The Early Middle Ages*. The Bible and Women: An Encyclopaedia of Exegesis and Cultural History. Atlanta: SBL Press, 2020.

Conway, Colleen. *Behold the Man: Jesus and Greco-Roman Masculinity*. Oxford: Oxford University Press, 2008.

———. *Sex and Slaughter in the Tent of Jael: A Cultural History of a Biblical Story*. Oxford: Oxford University Press, 2017.

Craven, Toni. "Artistry and Faith in the Book of Judith." *Semeia* 8 (1977): 75–101.

———. *Artistry and Faith in the Book of Judith*. Chico, CA: Scholars Press, 1983.

Crawford, Sidnie White. "Esther Not Judith: Why One Made It and the Other Didn't." *BR* 18 (2002): 22–31, 45.

———. "In the Steps of Jael and Deborah: Judith as Heroine." In *"No One Spoke Ill of Her": Essays on Judith*, edited by James C. VanderKam, 5–16. EJL 2. Atlanta: Scholars Press, 1992.

Creangă, Ovidiu. "Introduction." In *Hebrew Masculinities Anew*, edited by Ovidiu Creangă, 1–16. Sheffield: Sheffield Phoenix, 2019.

D'Angelo, Mary Rose. "Women Partners in the New Testament." *JFSR* 6 (1990): 65–86.

Daly, Mary. *Beyond God the Father: A Philosophy of Women's Liberation*. Boston: Beacon, 1985.

Dinkler, Michal Beth. *Literary Theory and the New Testament*. AYBRL. New Haven: Yale University Press, 2019.

DiPalma, Brian Charles. "Scribal Masculinity and the Court Tales of Daniel." In *Hebrew Masculinities Anew*, edited by Ovidiu Creangă, 229–48. Sheffield: Sheffield Phoenix, 2019.

Dolce, Rita. *"Losing One's Head" in the Ancient Near East: Interpretation and Meaning of Decapitation*. New York: Routledge, 2018.

Dube, Musa W., ed. *Postcolonial Feminist Interpretation of the Bible*. St. Louis: Chalice, 2000.

Duran, Nicole. "Having Men for Dinner: Deadly Banquets and Biblical Women." *BTB* 35 (2005): 117–24.

Eagleton, Terry. *Ideology: An Introduction*. London: Verso, 2007.

———. *Literary Theory: An Introduction*. 3rd ed. Minneapolis: University of Minnesota Press, 2008.

Efthimiadis-Keith, Helen. *The Enemy Is Within: A Jungian Psychoanalytic Approach to the Book of Judith*. Leiden: Brill, 2004.

———. "Judith, Feminist Ethics, and Feminist Interpretation." In *A Feminist Companion to Tobit and Judith*, edited by Athalya Brenner-Idan with Helen Efthimiadis-Keith, 141–63. FCB 20, 2nd ser. London: Bloomsbury T&T Clark, 2015.

Elder, Linda Bennett. "Judith's *Sophia* and *Synesis*: Educated Jewish Women in the Late Second Temple Period." In *Biblical and Humane: A Festschrift for*

John F. Priest, edited by Linda Bennett Elder, David L. Barr, and Elizabeth Struthers Malbon, 53–69. Atlanta: Scholars Press, 1996.

Elliott-Smith, Darren. *Queer Horror Film and Television: Sexuality and Masculinity at the Margins*. London: I. B. Tauris, 2016.

Enslin, Morton S., and Solomon Zeitlin. *The Book of Judith*. Leiden: Brill, 1972.

Eskenazi, Tamara Cohn, and Andrea L. Weiss, eds. *The Torah: A Women's Commentary*. New York: URJ Press and Women of Reform Judaism, The Federation of Temple Sisterhoods, 2008.

Exum, J. Cheryl. "Second Thoughts about Secondary Characters: Women in Exodus 1.8–2.10." In *A Feminist Companion to Exodus to Deuteronomy*, edited by Athalya Brenner, 75–97. FCB 6. Sheffield: Sheffield Academic, 1994.

Exum, J. Cheryl, and David J. A. Clines, eds. *The New Literary Criticism and the Hebrew Bible*. Valley Forge, PA: Trinity Press International, 1993.

Falk, Marcia. "Toward a Feminist Jewish Reconstruction of Monotheism." *Tikkun* 4 (July–August 1989): 53–56.

Fehling, Detlev. *Herodotus and His "Sources": Citation, Invention, and Narrative Art*. Arc Classical and Medieval Texts, Papers and Monographs 21. Leeds: Francis Carrus, 1989.

———. "The Art of Herodotus on the Margins of the World." In *Travel Fact and Travel Fiction: Studies on Fiction, Literary Traditions, Scholarly Discovery and Observation in Travel Writing*, edited by Zweder von Martels, 1–15. Brill Studies in Intellectual History 53. Leiden: Brill, 1994.

Feinstein, Eve Levavi. "Bathing in the Hebrew Bible." Bible Odyssey. https://www.bibleodyssey.org/en/people/related-articles/bathing-in-the-hebrew-bible.

Fell, Margaret. *Women's Speaking Justified, Proved and Allowed by the Scriptures*. London, 1667.

Feminist Biblical Interpretation: A Compendium of Critical Commentary on the Books of the Bible and Related Literature. Translated by Lisa E. Dahill, Everett R. Kalin, Nancy Lukens, Linda M. Maloney, Barbara Rumscheidt, Martin Rumscheidt, and Tina Steiner. Edited by Luise Schottroff and Marie-Theres Wacker. Grand Rapids: Eerdmans, 2012.

Fewell, Danna Nolan, and David M. Gunn. *Gender, Power, and Promise: The Subject of the Bible's First Story*. Nashville: Abingdon, 1993.

Fischer, Irmtraud, and Mercedes Navarro Puerto, with Andrea Taschl-Erber, eds. *Torah*. The Bible and Women: An Encyclopaedia of Exegesis and Cultural History. Atlanta: Society of Biblical Literature, 2011.

Franco, Mark. *Martha Graham in Love and War: The Life in the Work*. New York: Oxford University Press, 2012.

Freud, Sigmund. "The Taboo of Virginity." In *The Standard Edition of the Complete Psychological Works of Sigmund Freud*, edited by James Strachey, 191–208. London: Hogarth Press, 1957.

Frymer-Kensky, Tikva. *Reading the Women of the Bible*. New York: Schocken Books, 2002.

Garrard, Mary D. *Artemisia Gentileschi: The Image of the Female Hero in Italian Baroque Art*. Princeton: Princeton University Press, 1989.

Gehman, Henry Snyder, ed. *The New Westminster Dictionary of the Bible*. Philadelphia: Westminster, 1970.

Gera, Deborah Levine. "The Jewish Textual Traditions." In *The Sword of Judith: Judith Studies across the Disciplines*, edited by Kevin R. Brine, Elena Ciletti, and Henrike Lähnemann, 23–39. Cambridge: Open Book, 2010.

———. *Judith*. CEJL. Berlin: de Gruyter, 2014.

———. "Shorter Medieval Hebrew Tales of Judith." In *The Sword of Judith: Judith Studies across the Disciplines*, edited by Kevin R. Brine, Elena Ciletti, and Henrike Lähnemann, 81–95. Cambridge: Open Book, 2010.

Getty-Sullivan, Mary Ann. *Women in the New Testament*. Collegeville, MN: Liturgical Press, 2001.

Glancy, Jennifer A. "Judith the Slaveholder." In *A Feminist Companion to Tobit and Judith*, edited by Athalya Brenner-Idan with Helen Efthimiadis-Keith, 200–211. FCB 20, 2nd ser. London: Bloomsbury T&T Clark, 2015.

Gonzalez, Michelle A. "Latina Feminist Theology: Past, Present, and Future." *JFSR* 25 (2009): 150–55.

Good, Deirdre J. "Reading Strategies for Biblical Passages on Same-Sex Relations." *Theology and Sexuality* 7 (1997): 70–82.

Graybill, Rhiannon. *Are We Not Men? Unstable Masculinity in the Hebrew Prophets*. New York: Oxford University Press, 2016.

———. "Day of the Woman: Judges 4–5 as Slasher and Rape Revenge Narrative." *Journal of Religion and Popular Culture* 30 (2018): 193–205.

Grimké, Sarah. *Letters on the Equality of the Sexes and the Condition of Woman*. Boston: Isaac Knapp, 1838.

Guest, Deryn. *Beyond Feminist Biblical Studies*. Sheffield: Sheffield Phoenix, 2012.

———. *When Deborah Met Jael: Lesbian Biblical Hermeneutics*. London: SCM, 2005.

Habel, Norman C., and Peter Trudinger. *Exploring Ecological Hermeneutics*. SBLSymS 46. Atlanta: SBL 2008.

Halberstam, Judith. *Skin Shows: Gothic Horror and the Technology of Monsters*. Durham: Duke University Press, 1995.

Hartog, François. *The Mirror of Herodotus: The Representation of the Other in the Writing of History*. Berkeley: University of California Press, 1988.

Hearon, Holly E., and Philip Ruge-Jones, eds. *The Bible in Ancient and Modern Media: Story and Performance*. Eugene, OR: Cascade Books, 2009.

Hens-Piazza, Gina. *The New Historicism*. GBS, Old Testament Series. Minneapolis: Fortress, 2002.

Herodotus. *The History*. Translated by David Grene. Chicago: University of Chicago Press, 1987.

Herodotus and His "Sources": Citation, Invention, and Narrative Art. Arca Classical and Medieval Texts, Papers and Monographs 21. Leeds: Francis Carrus, 1989.

Hezser, Catherine. *Jewish Slavery in Antiquity*. Oxford: Oxford University Press, 2006.

Hodes, Stuart. *Part Real, Part Dream: Dancing with Martha Graham*. Concord ePress, 2011.

Hoffman, Lawrence S. "A Response to Marcia Falk." *Tikkun* 4 (July–August 1989): 56–57.

Hopkins, Denise Dombkowski. "Judith." In *Women's Bible Commentary*, edited by Carol A. Newsom, Sharon H. Ringe, and Jacqueline E. Lapsley, 383–90. 3rd ed. Louisville: Westminster John Knox, 2012.

Hornsby, Teresa, and Ken Stone, eds. *Bible Trouble: Queer Readings at the Boundaries of Biblical Scholarship*. Atlanta: SBL, 2011.

Howe, Timothy, and Lee L. Brice, eds. *Brill's Companion to Insurgency and Terrorism in the Ancient Mediterranean*. Leiden: Brill, 2016.

Ilan, Tal, Lorena Miralles-Maciá, and Ronit Nikolsky, eds. *Rabbinic Literature*. The Bible and Women: An Encyclopaedia of Exegesis and Cultural History. Atlanta: SBL Press, 2022.

Isasi-Díaz, Ada María. *Mujerista Theology: A Theology for the Twenty-First Century*. Maryknoll, NY: Orbis Books, 1996.

Jackson, Richard, Eamon Murphy, and Scott Poynting. "Introduction." In *Contemporary State Terrorism: Theory and Practice*, edited by Richard Jackson, Eamon Murphy, and Scott Poynting, 1–11. New York: Routledge, 2010.

Janes, Regina. *Losing Our Heads: Beheadings in Literature and Culture*. New York: New York University Press, 2005.

Jobling, David. *The Sense of Biblical Narrative: Three Structural Analyses in the Old Testament*. JSOTSup 7. Sheffield: Sheffield University, 1978.

Jobling, David, and Tina Pippin, eds. *Semeia* 59: *Ideological Criticism of Biblical Texts*. Atlanta: Scholars Press, 1992.

Johnson, Elizabeth A. "God." In *Dictionary of Feminist Theologies*, edited by Letty M. Russell and J. Shannon Clarkson, 128–30. Louisville: Westminster John Knox, 1996.

———. *She Who Is: The Mystery of God in Feminist Theological Discourse*. New York: Crossroad, 1992.

Junior, Nyasha. *An Introduction to Womanist Biblical Interpretation*. Louisville: Westminster John Knox, 2015.

———. "Womanist Biblical Interpretation." In *Engaging the Bible in a Gendered World: An Introduction to Feminist Biblical Interpretation in Honor of Katharine Doob Sakenfeld*, edited by Linda Day and Carolyn Pressler, 37–46. Louisville Westminster John Knox, 2006.

Kaufman, Michael. "The Seven P's of Men's Violence." In *Men's Lives*, edited by Michael S. Kimmel and Michael A. Messner, 542–47. 9th ed. Boston: Pearson, 2013.

Kessler, Gwynn. "Teaching Rape, Slavery, and Genocide in Bible and Culture." In *Rape Culture and Religious Studies: Critical and Pedagogical Engagements*, edited by Rhiannon Graybill, Meredith Minister, and Beatrice Lawrence, 55–72. Lanham, MD: Lexington Books, 2019.

Kitzberger, Ingrid Rosa, ed. *Autobiographical Biblical Interpretation: Between Text and Self*. Leiden: Deo, 2002.

Koosed, Jennifer L. *Reading the Bible as a Feminist*. Brill Research Perspectives. Leiden: Brill, 2017.

———. "Moses, Feminism, and the Male Subject." In *The Bible and Feminism: Remapping the Field*, edited by Yvonne Sherwood, 223–39. New York: Oxford University Press, 2018.

Kraemer, Ross Shepard, and Mary Rose D'Angelo, eds. *Women and Christian Origins*. New York: Oxford University Press, 1999.

LaCocque, André. *The Feminine Unconventional: Four Subversive Figures in Israel's Tradition*. Eugene, OR: Wipf and Stock, 1990.

LaCugna, Catherine Mowry. *God for Us: The Trinity and Christian Life*. San Francisco: HarperCollins, 1991.

Lang, Judith. "The Lord Who Crushes Wars: A Study of Judith 9:7; 16:2 and Exodus 15:3." In *A Pious Seductress: Studies in the Book of Judith*, edited by Géza G. Xeravits, 179–87. Berlin: de Gruyter, 2012.

Lerner, Gerda. "One Thousand Years of Feminist Bible Criticism." Chap. 7 (pp. 138–66) in *Creation of Feminist Consciousness: From the Middle Ages to Eighteen-Seventy*. New York: Oxford University Press, 1993.

Levine, Amy-Jill. "A Jewess, More and/or Less." In *Judaism Since Gender*, edited by Miriam Peskowitz and Laura Levitt, 149–57. New York: Routledge, 1996.

———. "The New Testament and Anti-Judaism." In *The Misunderstood Jew: The Church and the Scandal of the Jewish Jesus*, 87–117. San Francisco: HarperSanFrancisco, 2006.

———. "Sacrifice and Salvation: Otherness and Domestication in the Book of Judith." In *A Feminist Companion to Esther, Judith and Susanna*, edited by Athalya Brenner, 208–23. FCB 7. Sheffield: Sheffield Academic, 1995.

Llewellyn, Kathleen M. "The Example of Judith in Early Modern French Literature." In *The Sword of Judith: Judith Studies across the Disciplines*, edited by Kevin R. Brine, Elena Ciletti, and Henrike Lähnemann, 213–25. Cambridge: Open Book, 2010.

Lorde, Audre. "The Master's Tools Will Never Dismantle the Master's House." In *Sister Outsider: Essays and Speeches*, 110–14. Berkeley: Crossing Press, 1984, 2007.

Lostracco, Joseph, and George Wilkerson. *Analyzing Short Stories*. 7th rev. ed. Dubuque, IA: KendallHunt, 2008.

Luther, Martin. *Luther's Works*. Vol. 35: *Word and Sacrament I*. Edited by E. Theodore Bachmann. Minneapolis: Fortress, 1960.

Maier, Christl M., and Nuria Calduch-Benages, eds. *The Writings and Later Wisdom Books*. The Bible and Women: An Encyclopaedia of Exegesis and Cultural History. Atlanta: SBL Press, 2014.

Maier, Cristl M., and Carolyn J. Sharp. *Prophecy and Power: Jeremiah in Feminist and Postcolonial Perspective.* London: Bloomsbury, 2013.

Marchal, Joseph A. "Queer Studies and Critical Masculinity Studies in Feminist Biblical Studies." In *Feminist Biblical Studies in the Twentieth Century: Scholarship and Movement*, edited by Elisabeth Schüssler Fiorenza, 261–80. The Bible and Women: An Encyclopaedia of Exegesis and Cultural History. Atlanta: SBL Press, 2014.

McFague, Sallie. *Models of God: Theology for an Ecological, Nuclear Age.* Philadelphia: Fortress, 1987.

McKinlay, Judith E. *Reframing Her: Biblical Women in Postcolonial Focus.* Sheffield: Sheffield Phoenix, 2004.

McKnight, Edgar V., and Elizabeth Struthers Malbon, eds. *The New Literary Criticism and the New Testament.* Valley Forge, PA: Trinity Press International, 1994.

Merideth, Betsy. "Desire and Danger: The Drama of Betrayal in Judges and Judith." In *Anti-Covenant: Counter-Reading Women's Lives in the Hebrew Bible*, edited by Mieke Bal, 63–78. Sheffield: Almond, 1989.

Meyers, Carol. *Discovering Eve: Ancient Israelite Women in Context.* New York: Oxford University Press, 1991.

Meyers, Carol, Toni Craven, and Ross Shepard Kraemer, eds. *Women in Scripture.* Grand Rapids: Eerdmans, 2001.

Mikalson, John D. *Herodotus and Religion in the Persian Wars*. Chapel Hill: University of North Carolina Press, 2003.

Miller, Chanel. *Know My Name: A Memoir*. New York: Random House, 2019.

Miller, Geoffrey D. "A Femme Fatale of Whom 'No One Spoke Ill': Judith's Moral Muddle and Her Personification of Yahweh." *JSOT* 39 (2014): 223–45.

Milne, Pamela J. "A Self-Response: What Would I Do with Judith Now?" In *A Feminist Companion to Tobit and Judith*, edited by Athalya Brenner-Idan with Helen Efthimiadis-Keith, 137–40. FCB 20, 2nd ser. London: Bloomsbury T&T Clark, 2015.

———. "What Shall We Do with Judith? A Feminist Assessment of a Biblical 'Heroine.'" In *A Feminist Companion to Tobit and Judith*, edited by Athalya Brenner-Idan with Helen Efthimiadis-Keith, 117–36. FCB 20, 2nd ser. London: Bloomsbury T&T Clark, 2015.

Montague, George T. *The Books of Esther and Judith.* New York: Paulist Press, 1973.

Montley, Patricia. "Judith in the Fine Arts: The Appeal of the Archetypal Androgyne." *Anima* 4 (1978): 37–42.

Moore, Carey A. *Judith.* AB 40. Garden City, NY: Doubleday, 1985.

Moore, Stephen D., and Janice Capel Anderson. "Taking It Like a Man: Masculinity in 4 Maccabees." *JBL* 117 (1998): 249–73.

Moore, Stephen D. *The Bible in Theory: Critical and Postcritical Essays.* Atlanta: SBL, 2010.

———. *Poststructuralism and the New Testament: Derrida and Foucault at the Foot of the Cross.* Minneapolis: Fortress, 1994.

Munro, Ealasaid. "Feminism: A Fourth Wave?" *Political Insight* (September 2013). https://journals.sagepub.com/doi/pdf/10.1111/2041-9066.12021.

Narito, Z. C. "The Book of Judith." In *Women of Courage: Asian Women Reading the Bible*, edited by Oo Chung Lee, Man Ja Choi, Sun Ai Lee-Park, Elli Kim, Mirza Rodriguez, and Debra Goodsir, 53–62. Seoul: SaDange, 1992.

Navarro Puerto, Mercedes, and Marinella Perroni, eds.; Amy-Jill Levine, English ed. *Gospels: Narrative and History*. The Bible and Women: An Encyclopaedia of Exegesis and Cultural History. Atlanta: SBL Press, 2015.

Newman, Barbara. *Sister of Wisdom: St. Hildegard's Theology of the Feminine.* Berkeley: University of California Press, 1987.

Niditch, Susan. "Eroticism and Death in the Tale of Jael." In *Gender and Difference in Ancient Israel*, edited by Peggy L. Day, 43–57. Minneapolis: Fortress, 1989.

———. *"My Brother Esau Is a Hairy Man": Hair and Identity in Ancient Israel.* Oxford: Oxford University Press, 2008.

———. *A Prelude to Biblical Folklore: Underdogs and Tricksters*. Champaign: University of Illinois, 2000.

Nowell, Irene. *Women in the Old Testament.* Collegeville, MN: Liturgical Press, 1997.

Penchansky, David. "Deconstruction." In *The Oxford Encyclopedia of Biblical Interpretation*, edited by Steven McKenzie, 196–205. New York: Oxford University Press, 2013.

Pippin, Tina, ed. *Ideological Criticism of Biblical Texts: Semeia* 59 (1992).

de Pizan, Christine. *A Medieval Woman's Mirror of Honor: The Treasury of the City of Ladies*. Edited by Madeleine Pelner Cosman. New York: Persea Books, 1989.

Plaskow, Judith. "Anti-Judaism in Feminist Christian Interpretation." In *Searching the Scriptures: A Feminist Introduction*, vol. 1, edited by Elisabeth Schüssler Fiorenza with the assistance of Shelly Matthews, 117–29. New York: Crossroad, 1993.

Pollock, Griselda. "Feminist Dilemmas with the Art/Life Problem." In *The Artemisia Files: Artemisia Gentileschi for Feminists and Other Thinking People*, edited by Mieke Bal, 169–206. Chicago: University of Chicago Press, 2005.

Propp, Vladimir. *Morphology of the Folktale.* Austin: University of Texas Press, 1968.

Prouser, Ora Horn. "The Truth about Women and Lying." *JSOT* 61 (1994): 15–28.

Pui-lan, Kwok. *Postcolonial Imagination and Feminist Theology.* Louisville: Westminster John Knox, 2005.

Rampton, Martha. "Four Waves of Feminism." October 25, 2015. https://www.pacificu.edu/magazine/four-waves-feminism.

Reeder, Caryn A. "Gender, War, and Josephus." *Journal for the Study of Judaism in the Persian, Hellenistic and Roman Period* 46 (2015): 65–85.

Reis, Pamela Tamarkin. "Uncovering Jael and Sisera: A New Reading." *SJOT* 19 (2005): 24–47.

Ress, Mary Judith. *Ecofeminism in Latin America*. Women from the Margins. Maryknoll, NY: Orbis Books, 2006.

Ringe, Sharon H. "When Women Interpret the Bible." In *Women's Bible Commentary*, edited by Carol A. Newsom, Sharon H. Ringe, and Jacqueline E. Lapsley. 3rd ed. Louisville: Westminster John Knox, 2012.

Roitman, Adolfo D. "Achior in the Book of Judith: His Role and Significance." In *"No One Spoke Ill of Her": Essays on Judith*, edited by James C. VanderKam, 31–45. EJL 2. Atlanta: Scholars Press, 1992.

Rosellini, Michèle, and Suzanne Saïd. "Women's Customs among the 'Savages' in Herodotus." In *Herodotus*, vol. 2: *Herodotus and the World*, edited Rosaria Vignolo Munson, 213–44. Oxford: Oxford University Press, 2013.

Ruether, Rosemary Radford. *Sexism and God-Talk: Toward a Feminist Theology.* Boston: Beacon, 1993.

Rutledge, David. *Reading Marginally: Feminism, Deconstruction and the Bible.* BibInt 21. Leiden: Brill, 1996.

Sakenfeld, Katharine Doob. *Just Wives? Stories of Power and Survival in the Old Testament and Today.* Louisville: Westminster John Knox, 2003.

Schmitz, Barbara. "Holofernes's Canopy in the Septuagint." In *The Sword of Judith: Judith Studies across the Disciplines*, edited by Kevin R. Brine, Elena Ciletti, and Henrike Lähnemann, 71–80. Cambridge: Open Book Publishers, 2010.

Schneiders, Sandra M. *The Revelatory Text: Interpreting the New Testament as Sacred Scripture.* Rev. ed. Collegeville, MN: Liturgical Press, 1999.

Scholz, Susanne, ed. *Feminist Interpretation of the Hebrew Bible in Retrospect.* Recent Research in Biblical Studies 7, 8, 9. Sheffield: Sheffield Phoenix, 2013, 2014, 2016.

———. "From the 'Woman's Bible' to the 'Women's Bible,' The History of Feminist Approaches to the Hebrew Bible." In *Introducing the Women's Hebrew Bible*, 12–32. IFT 13. New York: T&T Clark, 2007.

———. "Judges." In *Women's Bible Commentary*, edited by Carol A. Newsom, Sharon H. Ringe, and Jacqueline E. Lapsley, 113–27. 3rd ed. Louisville: Westminster John Knox, 2012.

Schottroff, Luise. *Lydia's Impatient Sisters: A Feminist Social History of Early Christianity.* Translated by Barbara and Martin Rumscheidt. Louisville: Westminster John Knox, 1995.

Schottroff, Luise, and Marie-Theres Wacker, eds. *Feminist Biblical Interpretation: A Compendium of Critical Commentary on the Books of the Bible and Related Literature*, translated by Lisa E. Dahill, Everett R. Kalin, Nancy Lukens, Linda M. Maloney, Barbara Rumscheidt, Martin Rumscheidt, and Tina Steiner. Grand Rapids: Eerdmans, 2012.

Schuller, Eileen, and Marie-Theres Wacker, eds. *Early Jewish Writings.* The Bible and Women: An Encyclopaedia of Exegesis and Cultural History. Atlanta: SBL Press, 2017.

Schüssler Fiorenza, Elisabeth, ed. *Feminist Biblical Studies in the Twentieth Century: Scholarship and Movement.* The Bible and Women: An Encyclopaedia of Exegesis and Cultural History. Atlanta: SBL Press, 2014.

———. *In Memory of Her: A Feminist Theological Reconstruction of Christian Origins.* New York: Crossroad, 1994.

———. *Jesus: Miriam's Child, Sophia's Prophet; Critical Issues in Feminist Christology.* New York: Continuum, 1994.

———. *The Power of the Word: Scripture and the Rhetoric of Empire.* Minneapolis: Fortress, 2007.

———. *Wisdom Ways: Introducing Feminist Biblical Interpretation.* Maryknoll, NY: Orbis Books, 2001.

Schutte, P. J. W. "When *They*, *We*, and the Passive Become *I*—Introducing Autobiographical Biblical Criticism," *HTS Teologiese Studies / Theological Studies* 61 (2005): 401–16.

Shaw, Susan M., and Janet Lee. *Women's Voices, Feminist Visions: Classic and Contemporary Readings.* New York: McGraw-Hill, 2007.

Shemesh, Yael. "The Stories of Women in a Man's World: The Books of Ruth, Esther, and Judith in Feminist Interpretation." In *Feminist Interpretation of the Hebrew Bible in Retrospect*, edited by Susanne Scholz, vol. 1, 248–67. Sheffield: Sheffield Phoenix, 2013.

Sherwood, Yvonne. *A Biblical Text and Its Afterlives: The Survival of Jonah in Western Culture.* Cambridge: Cambridge University Press, 2000.

———. "Introduction." In *The Bible and Feminism: Remapping the Field.* New York: Oxford University Press, 2017.

Slaughter, Thomas P. *Exploring Lewis and Clark: Reflections on Men and Wilderness.* New York: Knopf, 2003.

Smit, Peter-Ben. *Masculinity and the Bible: Survey, Models and Perspectives.* Brill Research Perspectives. Leiden: Brill, 2017.

Smith, Susan L. "Woman on Top." In *Women and Gender in Medieval Europe: An Encyclopedia*, edited by Margaret Schaus, 844–45. London: Taylor & Francis, 2006.

Sohn-Kronthaler, Michaela, and Ruth Albrecht, eds. *Faith and Feminism in Nineteenth-Century Religious Communities.* The Bible and Women: An Encyclopaedia of Exegesis and Cultural History. Atlanta: SBL Press, 2019.

Sojourner Truth. "Ain't I a Woman?" Modern History Sourcebook. https://sourcebooks.fordham.edu/mod/sojtruth-woman.asp.

Stanton, Elizabeth Cady. *The Woman's Bible.* Part 2. Seattle: Coalition Task Force on Women and Religion, 1974.

Steinberg, Naomi. "Social Death as Gendered Genocide: The Fate of Women and Children." *BibInt* 26 (2018): 23–42.

Stocker, Margarita. *Judith: Sexual Warrior; Women and Power in Western Culture.* New Haven: Yale University Press, 1998.

Stone, Ken. "Affect and Animality in 2 Samuel 12." In *Reading with Feeling: Affect Theory and the Bible*, edited by Fiona C. Black and Jennifer L. Koosed, 13–36. Atlanta: SBL Press, 2019.

———. "Gender Criticism: The Un-Manning of Abimelech." In *Judges and Method: New Approaches in Biblical Studies*, edited by Gale A. Yee, 183–201. Minneapolis: Fortress, 2007.

Taitz, Emily, Sondra Henry, and Cheryl Tallan, eds. *JPS Guide to Jewish Women 600 B.C.E.–1900 C.E.* Philadelphia: JPS, 2003.

Tamber-Rosenau, Caryn. *Women in Drag: Gender and Performance in the Hebrew Bible and Early Jewish Literature*. Biblical Intersections 16. Piscataway, NJ: Gorgias Press, 2018.

Taylor, Marion Ann, and Agnes Choi, eds. *Handbook of Women Biblical Interpreters: A Historical and Biographical Guide*. Grand Rapids: Baker Academic, 2012.

Thomas, Rosalind. "Ethnicity, Genealogy, and Hellenism." In *Herodotus*, vol. 2: *Herodotus and the World*, edited by Rosaria Vignolo Munson, 339–59. Oxford: Oxford University Press, 2013.

Thurston, Bonnie. *Women in the New Testament: Questions and Commentary*. Companions to the New Testament. New York: Crossroad, 1998.

Tilford, Nicole. "Judith and Her Interpreters." In *Women's Bible Commentary*, edited by Carol A. Newsom, Sharon H. Ringe, and Jacqueline E. Lapsley, 391–95. 3rd ed. Louisville: Westminster John Knox, 2012.

Tolbert, Mary Ann. "Social, Sociological, and Anthropological Methods." In *Searching the Scriptures: A Feminist Introduction*, vol. 1, edited by Elisabeth Schüssler Fiorenza with the assistance of Shelly Matthews, 255–71. New York: Crossroad, 1993.

Trible, Phyllis. *God and the Rhetoric of Sexuality*. OBT. Philadelphia: Fortress, 1978.

van Henten, Jan Willem. "Judith as a Female Moses: Judith 7–13 in the Light of Exodus 17, Numbers 20 and Deuteronomy 33:8-11." In *Reflections on Theology and Gender*, edited by Fokkelien van Dijk-Hemmes and Athalya Brenner, 33–48. Leuven: Peeters, 1994.

———. "Judith as Alternative Leader: A Rereading of Judith 7–13." In *A Feminist Companion to Esther, Judith and Susanna*, edited by Athalya Brenner, 224–52. FCB 7. Sheffield: Sheffield Academic, 1995.

van Wolde, Ellen. "Sentiments as Culturally Construed Emotions: Anger and Love in the Hebrew Bible." *BibInt* 16 (2008): 1–24.

———. "Yaʿel in Judges 4." *ZAW* 107 (1995): 240–46.

Vander Stichele, Caroline, and Todd Penner, eds. *Her Master's Tools? Feminist and Postcolonial Engagements of Historical-Critical Discourse*. Atlanta: SBL 2005.

von Bingen, Hildegard, *De Operatione Dei*, 1.4.100; PL 197:885bc, as cited in Lerner, *Feminist Consciousness*.

Walcott, Derek. *Omeros*. New York: Farrar, Straus and Giroux, 1990.

Walker, Alice. *In Search of Our Mothers' Gardens: Womanist Prose*. New York: Harcourt Brace Jovanovich, 1967, 1983.

Washington, Harold C. "Violence and the Construction of Gender in the Hebrew Bible: A New Historicist Approach." *BibInt* 5 (1997): 324–63.

Weems, Renita J. *Battered Love: Marriage, Sex, and Violence in the Hebrew Prophets*. OBT. Minneapolis: Fortress, 1995.

———. *Just a Sister Away: A Womanist Vision of Women's Relationships in the Bible*. San Diego: Lura Media, 1988.

Weingarten, Susan. "Food, Sex, and Redemption in *Megillat Yehudit* (the 'Scroll of Judith')." In *The Sword of Judith: Judith Studies across the Disciplines*, edited by Kevin R. Brine, Elena Ciletti, and Henrike Lähnemann, 97–125. Cambridge: Open Book, 2010.

West, Delno C., and August Kling. *The Libro de las Profecías of Christopher Columbus*. Gainesville: University of Florida Press, 1991.

Wetter, Anne-Mareike. *"On Her Account": Reconfiguring Israel in Ruth, Esther, and Judith*. London: T&T Clark, 2015.

Wills, Lawrence M. *The Jewish Novel in the Ancient World*. Ithaca: Cornell University Press, 1995.

Wojciechowski, Michael. "Moral Teaching of the Book of Judith." In *A Pious Seductress: Studies in the Book of Judith*, edited by Géza G. Xeravits, 85–96. Berlin: de Gruyter, 2012.

Xeravits, Géza G. "The Supplication of Judith (Judith 9:2-14)." In *A Pious Seductress: Studies in the Book of Judith*, edited by Géza G. Xeravits, 161–78. Berlin: de Gruyter, 2012.

Yee, Gale. " 'I Have Perfumed My Bed with Myrrh': The Foreign Woman (*'iššа zārâ*) in Proverbs 1–9." *JSOT* (1989): 53–68.

———. ed. *Judges and Method: New Approaches in Biblical Studies*. Minneapolis: Fortress, 1995.

Zakovitch, Yair. "Sisseras Tod." *ZAW* 93 (1981): 364–74.

Index of Scripture References and Other Ancient Writings

Wisdom of Solomon

Index of Authors and Subjects

Authors

Jennifer L. Koosed is professor of religious studies at Albright College in Reading, Pennsylvania. She is the author of several books, including *(Per) mutations of Qohelet: Reading the Body in the Book* (Continuum, 2006), *Gleaning Ruth: A Biblical Heroine and Her Afterlives* (University of South Carolina, 2011), and *Reading the Bible as a Feminist* (Brill, 2017). She is also the editor of several works, including *The Bible and Posthumanism* (SBL Press, 2014) and *Reading with Feeling: Affect Theory and the Bible* (with Fiona C. Black; SBL Press, 2019).

Robert Paul Seesengood is associate dean for first year and general studies and professor of religious studies at Albright College in Reading, Pennsylvania. He received his ThM (New Testament) from Princeton Theological Seminary and his PhD (History of Ancient Christianity) from Drew University. He is a frequent lecturer, an editor, and an author of several essays and monographs, including *Philemon* (Bloomsbury, 2017), *Paul: A Brief History* (Wiley-Blackwell, 2010), and, with Jennifer L. Koosed, *Jesse's Lineage: The Legendary Lives of David, Jesus and Jesse James* (T&T Clark, 2013).

Volume Editor

Amy-Jill Levine is university professor of New Testament and Jewish Studies, Carpenter Professor of New Testament Studies, and professor of Jewish Studies at Vanderbilt Divinity School and College of Arts and Science; she is also affiliated professor, Centre for the Study of Jewish-Christian Relations, Cambridge, United Kingdom. Her recent publications include *The Misunderstood Jew: The Church and the Scandal of the Jewish Jesus* (HarperSanFrancisco, 2006) and *Short Stories by Jesus: The Enigmatic Parables of a Controversial Rabbi* (HarperOne, 2014). Dr. Levine is also coeditor of The Jewish Annotated New Testament (Oxford University Press, 2011).

Series Editor

Barbara E. Reid, general editor of the Wisdom Commentary series, is a Dominican Sister of Grand Rapids, Michigan. She is the president of Catholic Theological Union and the first woman to hold the position. She has been a member of the CTU faculty since 1988 and also served as vice president and academic dean from 2009 to 2018. She holds a PhD in biblical studies from The Catholic University of America and was also president of the Catholic Biblical Association in 2014–2015. Her most recent publications are *Luke 1–9* and *Luke 10–24* co-authored with Shelly Matthews (WCS 43A, 43B; Liturgical Press, 2021), *Wisdom's Feast: An Invitation to Feminist Interpretation of the Scriptures* (Eerdmans, 2016), and *Abiding Word: Sunday Reflections on Year A, B, C* (3 vols.; Liturgical Press, 2011, 2012, 2013).